Contents

Foreword

Ronald M. Nowak

Conservation is controversial. That's not just a play on words. Saving for future use rather than immediate consumption can be a dilemma. Wildlife conservation is a particular challenge. It's easy to argue for maintaining quantity or quality of air, water, soil, minerals, and forests that benefit our health or economy. The value of wildlife is less definitive and much more restrictive. The preservation of endangered species is an even more difficult proposition. Since total protection is usually required, we have no sport, food, furs, or other useful products to show for the effort. Almost by definition an endangered species is one too far gone to be of any direct economic value or to play much of a role in maintaining a widespread ecosystem. Saving an endangered big predator is exceptionally demanding. Not only is the animal devoid of material benefit, it is potentially destructive, even dangerous to human welfare. The ultimate conservation challenge, and hence the most controversial, is bringing a big predator back to an area from which it had been eliminated by people. Cat Urbigkit's *Yellowstone Wolves* covers one such action — the reintroduction of the wolf to Yellowstone.

When I was employed by the US Fish and Wildlife Service (FWS) Office of Endangered Species in 1973, I knew battles lay ahead. I fully anticipated that helping animals in decline, especially the wolves and other large carnivores in which I specialized, would bring me up against hunters, trappers, wildlife traders, stockmen, land developers, and others with commercial and political avocation. I was right, though I must add that during my career in wildlife regulation, I met and came to like and respect many people in such fields. My intent was never to interfere with their interests, despite what sometimes has been written about me, but only to uphold the purposes of the Endangered Species Act (ESA). What I never expected when I took on that charge, however, was that my biggest enemy would be my own agency.

In 1953, science fiction author Ray Bradbury published the novel *Fahrenheit 451*, depicting a future in which the function of firemen is not to extinguish fires, but instead to dash about starting them — specifically to burn books intolerable to the government. During my time with the endangered species program, I saw the role of its personnel drift more and more in the same direction as Ray Bradbury's firemen. Rather than properly identify and protect species and populations in peril, as mandated by the Act, these agency personnel have been required to do everything possible to delay, dilute, and avoid such classification and regulation.

The Office of Endangered Species was established during the surge of environmental enthusiasm that swept the nation in the 1960s. With passage of the Endangered Species Act of 1973, the office was greatly expanded. The Act called for an intensive program to properly classify all threatened wildlife and plants of the world, to do all within the power of the US government to protect such species and populations, and to institute efforts for their recovery. A team of biologists, mostly young and fresh from academia, was hired to develop what were formally designated the United States Lists of Endangered and Threatened Wildlife and Plants. But as these people compiled the necessary data for classification and published pursuant regulatory measures in the *Federal Register*, the established bureaucracy reacted. Unable and unwilling to carry out the required protections and recovery efforts set forth by the Act, FWS, backed by its political and commercial clientele, decided simply to stop listing. Within a couple years of the Act's passage came the first attempt to destroy the Office of Endangered Species' listing branch. Aided by outside conservation groups and sympathetic congressmen, the office survived.

But bureaucracy is relentless, knowing its goal is not product but process, and knowing also that the expenses resulting from its delays and convolutions are borne not by itself but by the public. One

$\mathcal{Y}$ELLOWSTONE $\mathcal{W}$OLVES

A Chronicle of the Animal, the People, and the Politics

*Zoology is not yet a static science
and the days of discovery are not yet over.*

Willy Ley, *Dawn of Zoology*

To Jim

YELLOWSTONE WOLVES

A Chronicle of

the Animal, the People, and the Politics

by

Cat Urbigkit

Foreword by

Ronald M. Nowak

The McDonald & Woodward Publishing Company

Blacksburg, Virginia

The McDonald & Woodward Publishing Company
Blacksburg, Virginia, and Granville, Ohio
www.mwpubco.com

YELLOWSTONE WOLVES
A Chronicle of the Animal, the People, and the Politics

Copyright © 2008 by Cat Urbigkit
Foreword © 2008 by Ronald M. Nowak

All rights reserved
First printing October 2008
Printed in Canada
By Friesens, Altona, Manitoba

10 9 8 7 6 5 4 3 2 1
17 16 15 14 13 12 11 10 09 08

Library of Congress Cataloging-in-Publication Data

Urbigkit, Cat.
 Yellowstone wolves : a chronicle of the animal, the people, and the poli-
tics / by Cat Urbigkit ; with a foreword by Ronald M. Nowak.
  p. cm.
 Includes bibliographical references and index.
 ISBN 978-0-939923-70-0 (pbk. : alk. paper)
 1. Wolves—Yellowstone National Park. 2. Endangered species—
Yellowstone National Park. 3. Wildlife management—Yellowstone National
Park. I. Title.
 QL737.C22U73 2008
 333.95'9773097875—dc22

                                                        2008032257

by one the listing biologists were fired, transferred, or cowed into submission. In October, 1987, after a decade of internal struggle, repeated schemes to destroy the listing branch, on-and-off listing moratoria, and whistleblowing and countermeasures, the entire Office of Endangered Species was abolished. The effort to bring United States regulations into line with the extent and diversity of the world's declining fauna and flora was over. A nominal endangered species program would continue through a scattering of successor units, but the goal would now be to find any means possible to reduce and even overturn the legal classification of deserving species.

My two formal positions while in FWS were mammalogist for the Office of Endangered Species and, after its destruction, listing biologist for foreign species. In this regard it is instructive to compare US listing activities with those of the foremost international organization involved in endangered species classification, the World Conservation Union (IUCN). Late in 1987, the FWS and IUCN listings of mammals were closely comparable, each containing just over 400 species and subspecies. Since abolishment of the Office of Endangered Species, however, there has been a net gain of only 35 mammals on the US List of Endangered and Threatened Wildlife (43 added but 8 delisted). During the same period, the IUCN has added a net of approximately1,750 mammals to its list in categories corresponding to those of the US list.

My last substantive effort with FWS was a proposal to have the US adopt the IUCN list for purposes of species found outside of the United States. I reasoned that whereas I was the sole FWS listing biologist for foreign species, the IUCN relies on over one hundred permanent specialist groups that draw on 8,000 authorities from all around the world. They would be in a far better position than I, or anyone in FWS, to provide the "best available data," as required by the Act, for listing. My proposal got nowhere. Since I retired late in 1997, FWS has technically listed a few South American caimans because of their "similarity of appearance" to endangered caimans, and has listed four foreign species of mammals, for which I already had handled the proposed regulations and all necessary research and review.

Otherwise, since 1997, FWS has initiated the proposal and listing of only two fully foreign species, the beluga sturgeon and the Tibetan antelope, and even those measures stemmed from petitions that were external to the agency.

When challenged for its miniscule listing output since 1987, FWS complains of insufficient funds. And yet FWS always seems able to spend huge sums to combat legal measures to force it to list deserving species, and, especially, to undertake extremely complex and controversial measures to DElist and reduce protection of species such as the alligator, brown pelican, bald eagle, and grizzly bear. The agency has been particularly vehement in pursuit of deregulation of the wolf. In the early 1980s, FWS tried to reduce protection of the wolf in Minnesota and open the species to public hunting and trapping, but failed to meet the ESA's requirement that such measures could be undertaken only if beneficial and the sole means of controlling excessive wolf populations.

Proponents warned that if wolf protection was not moderated, there would be widespread illegal killing that would further jeopardize the species. I was ordered to prepare the regulation. I refused and subsequently testified against FWS through a lengthy process of court trial and appeal. Ultimately, FWS was defeated and the wolf retained protection. The result was continued expansion of the species, but without the drastic repercussions forecast by those who wanted the Minnesota populations delisted. Viable wolf populations were restored, not only in much of Minnesota but, for the first time in decades, in Michigan and Wisconsin. Measures were drafted to have me thrown out of the agency then and there but were overruled by the FWS director, who did not want to create a "martyr." Of course, any hope for my own advancement ended, and I eventually was subject to harassment that culminated in having me followed about by parties, with whom I had a discordant history, in an apparent effort to provoke a possibly violent confrontation that could indeed have been used as grounds to have me fired. After I finally did leave, in disgust but voluntarily, FWS proceeded to delist the wolf populations of Minnesota, Michigan, and Wisconsin.

If it is surprising that such behavior permeates a federal agency, it may be even more startling to learn the degree of antagonism within scientific circles, particularly in the field of taxonomy. When most of us become interested in wildlife conservation, the last thing we imagine is widespread disagreement as to the identity of our favorite species. And yet taxonomy regularly plays a critical role in whether an animal or plant is carefully protected as an endangered species or ignored. Scientists, even specialists in the same field, often battle for decades as to whether a particular population is identifiably distinct from other species, whether it is a full species or just a subspecies or race, and if it is merely a hybrid or pathological variant. These disputes sometimes become weapons that have little to do with the original scientific discourse. One taxonomist may use recognition or rejection of a species as a means of riling or belittling a rival. A particular clique, in control of a prestigious professional journal, may refuse to accept a paper submitted by an outsider and hence prevent that person's work from ever being publicly available.

Such contention may become quite exacerbated, even entwined with matters of sexual discrimination. In the 1980s, a young woman biologist discovered a population of unusual silvery rice rats on a remote Florida island and named it as a distinct but endangered species. Just before it was formally placed on the FWS list, a group of prominent male taxonomists, whose own expedition had failed to find the animal, claimed it was merely a part of another species and had the listing stopped. Many years and expensive litigation would go by before the woman prevailed and had the animal listed as endangered. In another case, a male taxonomist, apparently angered by a young woman's charges of sexual harassment, struck back by not recognizing, in the new edition of a book he contributed to, an endangered species championed by the woman's supervisor.

Taxonomic questions are common and often are seized upon by nonscientific groups with their own interests. Indeed, these situations developed in the classification and/or management of the majority of native US species that I worked on during my career. Such examples include kangaroo rats in California, beach mice in Florida, shrews in

Virginia, pronghorn antelope in Arizona, and black bears in Louisiana. Typically, a conservation organization may wish to see the animal population and/or its habitat protected, while another group believes that exploitation of the involved population or habitat would be adversely affected by having it classified as an endangered population or taxon. Each party may be able to find a taxonomist willing to testify on its behalf. Another kind of case involves the potentially illegal killing of an animal, which one side claims is the member of a species already designated as endangered, while the other side argues it is not.

The vagaries and variances of endangered species conservation now are brought together in Cat's book. She has taken the above and much more and shown us the unimaginable interplay of biology, politics, factionalism, economics, and emotion that may revolve about the recognition, management, and political manipulation of an endangered species. She accomplishes this not merely as an observant reporter, though she fills that function well, but as one intimately involved in the events of which she writes. Remarkably, she tells the story from the perspective of both a conservationist devoted to saving an endangered wolf and as a rural resident whose livelihood may be jeopardized by the wolf.

Cat's book may provide the most lucid and revealing account available of the consequences of taxonomy on conservation. She shows how a practice, usually restricted to museums, laboratories, and technical journals, came to dominate the fate of western wolves. But in a sense, she continues a longstanding debate. For many decades taxonomy has had a key role in our approach to wolves, perhaps more so than in any other mammal. Domestic dogs are descended from wolves, or at least from the same line that gave rise to each. Dogs are the most variable of all mammals, and this condition was inherited directly from wolves, which maintain a remarkable range of characters that may be used in seeking taxonomic distinction. And yet wolves are among the most mobile of terrestrial mammals. They quickly move and spread and interact with others, thereby tending to erase distinctions that may develop locally. Therefore, if distinguishing characters are maintained between populations, it is likely that they represent true taxonomic distinction resulting from earlier divergence of phylogenetic lineage.

Most zoologists recognize only two full species of living wolves, the gray (*Canis lupus*) and the red (*Canis rufus*). The gray wolf is by far the more wide-ranging of the two; found almost throughout all of North America and Eurasia, it sometimes has been divided into dozens of subspecies or geographic races. However, my own taxonomic assessment of North American wolves, based mainly on cranial morphometrics, distinguished only five subspecies of the gray wolf, together with the separate red wolf in the southeastern part of the continent. All six kinds have kindled the taxonomic battles that have engulfed wolves in recent years.

The original Yellowstone wolf population, sometimes designated *Canis lupus irremotus,* is or was part of a wide-ranging subspecies, which I referred to *Canis lupus nubilus,* of mid-sized wolves throughout much of the western and central parts of North America. A key argument in Cat's book is that this subspecies is distinct from *Canis lupus occidentalis,* the subspecies that is found to the north in western Canada and most of Alaska. *C. l. nubilus* presumably also is represented by the population in Minnesota and on Isle Royale. There it is the subject of further taxonomic issues, some zoologists claiming it is actually part of another species allied with the red wolf and/or has been intensively hybridized with coyotes. I also assigned the population of the southeast Alaskan panhandle to *nubilus*. When conservation groups petitioned to have that population protected through the ESA, FWS tried to avoid the listing by citing my work as evidence that it was not a distinctive subspecies. In so doing, FWS ignored the Act's requirement that distinct population segments, as well as subspecies, must be listed.

The other three North American subspecies of gray wolf that I recognized are *Canis lupus lycaon, Canis lupus baileyi,* and *Canis lupus arctos. Canis lupus lycaon* is the small timber wolf of southeastern Ontario and southern Quebec. It is currently the center of a vigorous taxonomic dispute, with different authorities regarding it as a subspecies of gray wolf, as a full species that also includes the red wolf, as a hybrid wolf-x-coyote, or as a hybrid gray wolf-x-red wolf. The Mexican wolf (*Canis lupus baileyi*) is also a question mark. While there is rare agreement among taxonomists, using both morphometric and genetic methodology, that it originally was a distinctive subspecies, there is less certainty regarding the existing populations. Some authorities believe that certain of the lineages have been intermixed with other gray wolf lines or domestic dogs. There also is argument that the reintroductions of this subspecies are being carried out within the range of another subspecies. Even *Canis lupus arctos,* the wolf of the far northern arctic islands, has not escaped taxonomic disagreement, there being claims — I think they are ludicrous — that it has undergone widespread hybridization with sled dogs.

But by far the most controversial and longest running taxonomic battle involves the red wolf, which once occurred all along the East Coast and ranged westward to central Oklahoma and Texas. In the past it has sometimes been treated as a subspecies of the gray wolf, as a subspecies of the coyote, or as a distinct species. My own work, developed over forty years, suggests that it is a full species that hybridized, about a century ago, with the coyote in the western part of its range and, thousands of years ago, with the gray wolf in the northeast. A largely non-hybrid population survived until recently on the Texas and Louisiana coast and some individuals from there were taken into captivity.

Recently, a prestigious team of authorities from the West Coast of the US, using new genetic and DNA methodologies, has claimed that the red wolf is an artifact that was created when colonists along the East Coast disrupted the habitat and allowed the gray wolf and coyote to hybridize there. This team, however, has never been able to explain why there are no fossil or historical records of gray wolves or coyotes in that region at any time from the end of the Pleistocene, about 10,000 years ago, to the late twentieth century. Meanwhile, a separate Canadian team, using the same methodologies, found the red wolf — and the eastern timber wolf — to be a distinctive species that is closely related to the coyote, *Canis latrans,* and that originated about a million years ago.

Notwithstanding the arguments, all involved taxonomists agree that the red wolf is critically endangered. In its original form, it now survives only in captivity and as an introduced population on the coast of North Carolina. The survival of the introduction and conservation effort has been jeopardized by political interests, which have embraced claims that the entire species is nothing more than a modern hybrid.

The Old World mirrors North America in both wolf distribution and taxonomic controversy. Recently, Indian DNA specialists published evidence that *Canis lupus pallipes,* the relatively small and vanishing wolf found from Israel to India, also is a separate species. They also suggested that still another species of wolf exists in the Himalayan region. I already had found *pallipes* to have the closest affinity to *rufus* of any other kind of wolf. Still smaller kinds of wolves inhabit the Arabian Peninsula and northern Egypt. Both are clearly threatened, but there are questions as to whether the former, *Canis lupus arabs,* is a pure wolf, and if the latter, *Canis lupus lupaster,* is actually a large jackal. Another small wolf, *Canis lupus hodophilax,* once inhabited most of Japan but was killed off a century ago and few specimens survive. Was it really a gray wolf subspecies, a completely separate species, a form of feral domestic dog, or a representative of an entirely different genus, the dhole (*Cuon*)? No one knows for sure.

Wolves and domestic dogs readily hybridize when brought together in captivity. Fortunately, hybrids do not seem to persist in the wild and reportedly have a different breeding season, so that their young are born in the autumn and thus do not survive through the winter. In Italy, a population of a few hundred individuals of the wolf subspecies *Canis lupus italicus* has persisted for centuries amidst intensive human activity and millions of dogs. I recently examined a large collection of specimens from Italy and found the wolf population to have maintained its natural characters. Genetic studies have confirmed a lack of introgression. I also have assessed hundreds of wolf specimens collected in the western US in the early 1900s, when the last wolves of that region were being relentlessly pursued by an intensive federal extermination program. There is absolutely no evidence of introgression of dog genes, hence giving hope that a wild wolf population can maintain its taxonomic integrity even when greatly reduced in numbers, fragmented, and enveloped by much larger numbers of dogs.

Such is the scientific and emotional imbroglio on which Cat develops her story. She believes a remnant population of the original wolves of the western US survived in the Yellowstone area. She suggests it was a natural part of the ecosystem, with a relatively benign influence on both wildlife and human interests. The grand plan to move wolves from Canada — from another subspecies — to Yellowstone in the 1990s was not a true reintroduction but the introduction of a non-native and aggressive life form that would genetically swamp the surviving native wolves.

Introductions, as opposed to reintroductions, can be, and usually are, devastating to natural ecosystems. Alien house cats, foxes, and mongooses have destroyed or endangered entire species of native birds and small mammals in Australia and on many Pacific and Caribbean islands. Feral pigs in North America and goats in Eurasia have wiped out the vegetative cover and forage needed by indigenous wildlife. Red foxes brought from Europe have replaced or crossed with original subspecies throughout the conterminous United States, probably restricting pure populations of the latter to the highest mountain ranges of the West.

In contrast, reintroductions, if properly researched and implemented, should restore natural ecosystems. Among large mammals, such endeavors have been done mostly with game species, depleted by hunting and returned for the same purpose. Deer, translocated to many parts of the US, are usually welcomed by sportsmen but not farmers or gardeners. Intensive efforts to restore large carnivores were almost unknown prior to the recent red and gray wolf programs. In the 1960s, however, many black bears were captured in Minnesota and quietly released in Arkansas and Louisiana, apparently without consideration of the presence of tiny but viable groups of the original populations. About 3,000 bears now inhabit the Ozarks, seemingly in harmony with their environment and most human interests.

The project, thankfully, was less successful in lowland Louisiana. The introduced bears were placed adjacent to a unique subspecies

holding out in the eastern swamps of the state. I investigated this subspecies in the 1980s and prepared a report urging its formal listing.
True to form, FWS tried to avoid protection, claiming alternately that
the native bear either was too common or already extinct. It required
a petition and then litigation from outside conservationists to finally
achieve listing.

The proposed introduction of gray wolves from Canada into the
Yellowstone area was a scheme involving an unusual alliance. Hard
line conservation groups pushed for wolves, lots of wolves, in
Yellowstone and adjacent country as quickly as possible and at any
cost. Bureaucrats went along with this pressure, Cat subtly implies,
not because they cared about restoring wolves or what kind of wolves
they would be. They only wanted to take advantage of a regulatory
quirk that would allow an introduced wolf population to be declared
"experimental," and thus be free from the usual protections offered
by an official endangered classification. By the 1990s, the Canadian
wolf subspecies *occidentalis* had expanded naturally into western
Montana and seemed headed for the Yellowstone. Since all wolves in
the lower forty-eight states were on the List of Endangered and Threatened Wildlife, the invading wolves would carry their classification
with them. So, if they began to prey on livestock or otherwise jeopardized human interests, counter action would be difficult. If, however,
the government moved first and introduced an experimental wolf population, control measures, usually killing the offending animals, could
be undertaken routinely.

Oddly, Cat put together an opposing alliance, albeit a much
weaker one, of preservationists favoring the maintenance of the original Yellowstone wolf population along with local livestock and political interests wishing to avoid the introduction of big Canadian
wolves. Each group cited scientific authorities to support its own position as to whether a native wolf population survived and whether it
was a subspecies distinct from that of Canada. The pro-introduction
side prevailed through a long political and legal struggle, thus en-
abling the most successful and widespread introduction of a large
predator ever carried out. The project actually had been pioneered by

the somewhat smaller-scale red wolf introduction program in North Carolina. I believe both involved placing one subspecies into an area where another had lived. In the case of the red wolf, there was no doubt that the original subspecies had vanished long ago.

For the Yellowstone wolf, the issue was indeed questionable. Although I provided some of the evidence for the possible survival of the native population, I was not convinced. The collection of one or two specimens resembling the original subspecies is not conclusive. By definition, a subspecies is not consistently distinguishable. Also, a captive colony, descended from wolves collected just north of Yellowstone early in the twentieth century, still exists and there have been reports of escapes and surreptitious introductions.

Moreover, there is the question of whether a viable wolf population could have maintained itself for decades without definitively revealing its presence. Wolves, unlike mountain lions and certain other predators, are notoriously overt to those familiar with their habits. They move in open country, follow regular routes, travel in groups, leave abundant tracks and other sign, and make lots of noise. They also substantially affect the big game populations on which they prey and, sooner or later, tend to come into frequent conflict with livestock activity and other human interests.

Cat provides the best available compilation of reports showing that wolves occurred in the Yellowstone region from the 1920s, when they supposedly had been extirpated, until the 1990s, when the introduction of Canadian wolves occurred. She has not necessarily demonstrated that those occurrences represent the continuous presence of an original breeding population. Had such a population existed, why did it not become more obvious? Wolves are rapid breeders, capable of doubling their numbers annually. Indeed, the wolves introduced to Yellowstone in the 1990s quickly expanded numerically and geographically, and as Cat so assiduously documents, became all too obvious to local shepherds and ranchers.

Why didn't any surviving native population show up to such an extent? Cat suggests that the original race may have had different behavioral characteristics or that it assumed certain survival adaptations, such as reported for remnant wolf populations in Europe. Perhaps it was more secretive, less vocal, and more solitary. Would it also have become less fecund? Actually, a wolf population distributed mainly in pairs would be expected to produce far more young than a population composed of large packs, in which reproduction tends to be restricted to one or two dominant females.

It also should not be thought that the large northern wolves, even if characterized by different racial behavior, are by nature any less subject to human control measures. It sometimes is forgotten that these northern wolves were themselves once pushed to the edge of extinction. At the same time the southern wolves were being exterminated early in the twentieth century, a massive poisoning campaign had forced the northern subspecies far back into Canada and even greatly reduced its numbers on the ranges of the barren ground caribou. Depression, war, and changing economics may have allowed a large-scale recovery of these northern wolves from the 1930s to the 1950s. By the 1970s, wolves had again reached the US border and soon after were pushing south through Montana. Would they have kept going and occupied Yellowstone anyway? Cat suggests that there was a very serious fear that they would, and that such concern was the real basis of the introduction.

So, was the highly touted, and admittedly spectacular, return of the Yellowstone wolf simply another expression of government underhandedness? Of the firemen running wild? I have met many wolf biologists and managers in FWS and other federal and state agencies. By and large they are among the finest people I know, thoroughly dedicated to conservation and research and entirely different from the office-bound bureaucrats who ignored their legal responsibilities and persecuted those of us who would not. And yet even a conscientious administrator or scientist may have an outlook restricted by focus on a specific and immediate objective. What may seem to the advantage of a particular animal population at a particular time may not be in keeping with the original intent of the ESA, which places foremost priority on long-term maintenance of natural ecosystems. Cat has shown us a scenario in which the possibly well meaning were misled.

While we may question her evidence and conclusions, she has demonstrated the complexity and anguish of wolf conservation and provided a unique perspective on a fascinating story.

Preface

In 1992, an elk hunter shot a black wolf, one of a pack of five, as the animals ran through the Teton Wilderness south of Yellowstone National Park (YNP). The hunter said it was like shooting a dinosaur — a member of a species long thought to be extinct from the region. The timing of the event made it of national significance.

When the black wolf was shot, the US Fish and Wildlife Service (FWS) — the federal agency charged with managing the recovery of endangered species — was in the process of finalizing plans to reintroduce gray wolves, *Canis lupus*, into Yellowstone park, an area the agency claimed had not heard the howls of wolves for more than sixty years. FWS immediately launched a publicity blitz to head off the obvious conclusion that there was at least one pack of wolves inhabiting the Yellowstone area and that reintroducing wolves was, therefore, unnecessary.

Federal biologists with FWS claimed that the four animals that were with the wolf when it was killed were, amazingly, coyotes. The agency did not acknowledge the numerous reports that had accumulated over the years that multiple wolves had been sighted in the Teton Wilderness, wolves that had been seen by federal and state resource agency employees. The agency also did not say that the legality of the reintroduction proposal hinged on there being no wolves in the area.

For nearly a decade before the black wolf was shot, however, a Wyoming couple — namely my husband Jim and me — had been collecting reports of wolf sightings in western Wyoming. The wolves were already there and, although elusive, they had left diverse physical evidence of their presence. The wolves left carcasses of elk they had fed on near the Green River Lakes entrance to the Bridger Wilderness of the Wind River Mountain Range, which we photographed.

They left piles of dung on Straight Creek in the Wyoming Range Mountains, which we collected. They left tracks in the foothills of the mule deer winter range near Half Moon Lake, from which we made plaster casts. They left hair on a branch in an overhang used to wait out a winter storm, which we gathered. And, our howls were returned from wild wolves in the Mount Leidy Highlands and Johnson Ridge.

Local residents of the mountain country — men who grazed cattle on high during the summer months, outfitted and hunted in the fall, and cut wood in the spring — would see the wolves, their kills, and their sign, and send us back on the trail of the elusive predator. The evidence we collected led us to know that the wolves were remnant populations of the native wolf — the supposedly extirpated subspecies *Canis lupus irremotus*.

The wolf biologists who were pushing the reintroduction were based in offices in Helena, Montana, hundreds of miles away from Yellowstone. The reintroduction would be the biggest experimental relocation of a large carnivore population ever undertaken in the history of wildlife management and the basis of a huge fundraising opportunity for national environmental interests.

FWS pushed the concept of wolf reintroduction into Yellowstone strongly and developed support for the project from across the nation. Returning wolves to Yellowstone, the nation's first national park, would, according to FWS, be a grand gesture that would correct an injustice done to nature many years prior. FWS claimed that the subspecies of wolf native to Yellowstone had been extirpated early in the twentieth century through predator control efforts, so wolves belonging to a different subspecies, *Canis lupus occidentalis,* would be brought from Canada and released into the park. The Canadian wolves were breathtaking to behold — the largest subspecies of wolf in the world and the most numerous.

As support for the FWS wolf relocation proposal grew and as evidence of the wolves already present in the Yellowstone area was ignored or dismissed, Jim and I came to feel that no one was willing to fight to save the native wolf. To us, it was apparent that they were facing deliberate extinction — so we took steps to prevent it. We fought their extinction all the way to the federal Tenth Circuit Court of Appeals.

When Secretary of the Interior Bruce Babbitt finally signed the official decision to release Canadian wolves into Yellowstone and central Idaho, we filed a lawsuit challenging the legality of the action. Having little money and unable to find an attorney willing to take the case, we studied the law and presented the case ourselves. Two other lawsuits, spearheaded by environmental and agricultural groups, took much the same position as ours and were heard at the same time. The release of Canadian wolves was conducted while the lawsuit was being argued in the courtroom in Casper, Wyoming. The litigation dragged on for years.

On December 12, 1997, five years after the black wolf was killed in the Teton Wilderness, Federal Judge William Downes ruled that the reintroduction of wolves was illegal because wolves already existed in the area. By that time, however, the reintroduction effort was already underway and some 160 Canadian wolves were present in the Yellowstone area. Soon a higher court overruled Judge Downes's decision, declaring that the Canadian wolves could stay and that the protection of a subspecies, the basis of our litigation, was not mandated by the Endangered Species Act (ESA).

This judicial reversal was a tragedy. Rather than a victory for wildlife, we viewed it with heartbreak — an action that would cause the extinction of populations of a truly distinct animal, our native wolf.

After spending more than ten years fighting to save our native Wyoming wolves, we called it quits. A federal appeals court had ruled against us and the released Canadian wolves were quickly expanding their population and spreading beyond Yellowstone throughout all of western Wyoming.

During our political and legal battle over wolves, we had invested every spare dollar, every spare hour, in the effort to save the native wolf. Jim had worked as an oilfield roughneck, earning good money and commonly working five days on, away from home, and five days off. I had worked as a waitress and an organizer for non-profits that were not involved with the reintroduction of wolves. And we added a new member to our family, our son Cass. What we had not done was save any money or develop any careers.

So, with the court decisions behind us, we turned our attention elsewhere and became caretakers of a small old ranch in Sublette County, hundreds of miles from Yellowstone and the epicenter of the wolf issue.

To make and keep the ranch productive, it had to have livestock. First we tried running a few head of young cows owned by the land-owner, but I never accepted the idea of trying to out-wrestle an animal weighing ten times as much as I did. Jim suggested I would like sheep, so with encouragement from the late Bill Thoman and his wonderful family, we soon had thirty small, helpless orphan lambs to look deep into my eyes and make me fall in love. I was a goner. We bottle-fed those babies, which grew into productive gentle ewes and eventually became great-grandmother ewes.

Our love of animals made becoming shepherds natural for us and was imminently more relaxing than the years we had spent in a very public debate. We settled into our new lives, with Jim working for a construction company and me becoming a reporter, raising sheep and our young son.

We were through with the wolf battle, but little did we know that the wolves were not quite through with us.

Acknowledgments

Many individuals and organizations helped with the research and litigation involved with our effort to save the native wolf popula-tions of the Yellowstone area and with the preparation of the manu-script for *Yellowstone Wolves*.

Field work, aerial surveys, and legal expenses were funded in part by contributions from Dave Flitner, Arlene Hanson, Don Strube, Rod Matthews, Paul VonGontard, Rendezvous Ranch, Quarter Circle Five Ranch, 7L Livestock Company, Sublette County People for the USA, and the Fremont County Audubon Chapter. Early on in the process of gathering information for use in this book, the Wyoming Outdoor Council helped to fund a survey of Wyoming outfitters and guides to learn of their wolf reports. Special thanks go to Leigh Henning for his encouragement and arguments, to Larry Bourret for putting up a good fight with a wild sense of humor, and to Steve Lechner for helping Jim and me navigate the morass of the federal court system.

Barbara Oakleaf and the Fremont County Library in Lander were of invaluable assistance in obtaining scientific literature on interlibrary loan for my use. Bruce Hampton also shared information about sources. Appreciation goes to Larry Roop and Ron Nowak for the expertise they shared with me and for directing me to the A. Starker Leopold correspondence. Thanks go to Al Boss, George Gruell, and Reid Jackson for speaking out.

The Wyoming Historical Society provided funding to assist in writing *Yellowstone Wolves* through its Loma Homsher Award in 2005. Laurie Latta and Ann Chambers Noble reviewed an early draft of the manuscript and provided comments that made it better than it otherwise would have been.

Thanks go to Chad Baldwin and Linda Fantin for telling our side of the story and to Janet Montgomery and the *Sublette Examiner* chicks for letting me do my thing.

Chapter 1

Divergent Evolution

The gray wolf, *Canis lupus*, has been around for a long time. The species appears to have evolved in Asia and to have spread into North America several hundred thousand years ago. Like so many members of the dog family, Canidae, wolves are intelligent, versatile, adaptable, and resilient. Among all living mammals, other than human beings, *Homo sapiens*, only lions, *Panthera leo*, ever achieved more widespread natural distribution than did the gray wolf.

⌒

Wolf remains dating back to about 1,000 years ago have been discovered in Lamar Cave in Yellowstone National Park (YNP) (figures 1–3; Table 1). The remains consist of two toe bones.[1] A Russian proverb says that a wolf is kept fed by its feet.[2] It somehow seems appropriate that bones from that part of a wolf's body were found by investigators who were searching for clues to the life of the past.

Wolf remains have been discovered in other archaeological and paleontological sites throughout the Northern Rocky Mountains of the US. Kenneth Cannon of the National Park Service's Midwest Archeological Center in Lincoln, Nebraska, conducted a review of evidence of the prehistoric presence of wolves in the northern Rockies, with the Yellowstone region his area of focus. He found that at least fourteen sites have produced remains of gray wolves, with the oldest of these dating back more than 15,000 years.[3] The gray wolf has long been a resident of the northern Rockies.

Taxonomist E. A. Goldman (Table 2) published an article in 1937 that established a framework for modern North American wolf taxonomy. Goldman described the wolf that occurred in the northwestern Wyoming area and regions to the north and west as the Northern

Figure 1. Place names mentioned in text: National and tri-state region.

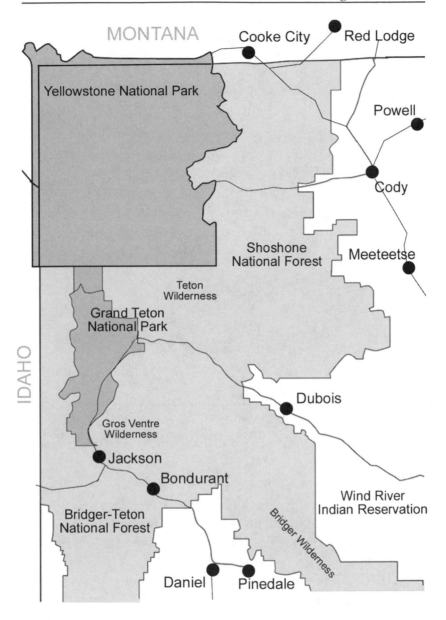

Figure 2. Place names: Northwestern Wyoming region.

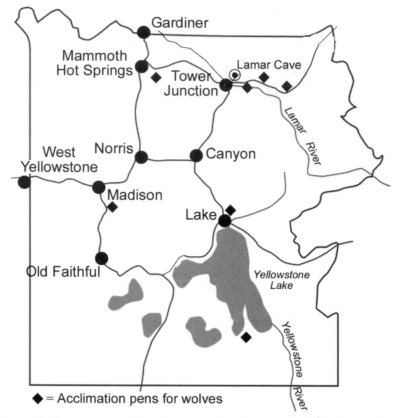

◆ = Acclimation pens for wolves

Figure 3. Place names and location of acclimation pens for Canadian wolves: Yellowstone National Park.

Rocky Mountain Wolf, *Canis lupus irremotus*. Goldman's early work recognized that the wolf in this region was different from those that occurred in surrounding areas. This work established the subspecific distinctiveness of *Canis lupus irremotus*.[4]

In 1944, Goldman, along with colleague Stanley P. Young, published a 600-page tome on North American wolf taxonomy that included the results of yet more extensive research and provided more detailed information than Goldman's earlier work.[5] In this volume, Young and Goldman described *irremotus*, along with twenty-two other subspecies of wolf that historically ranged throughout the continent.

Table 1. Abbreviations Used in Text

ADC	Animal Damage Control, later renamed Wildlife Services
AP	Associated Press
BLM	Bureau of Land Management
DEIS	Draft Environmental Impact Statement
DW	Defenders of Wildlife
EDF	Environmental Defense Fund
EIS	Environmental Impact Statement
ESA	Endangered Species Act
FEIS	Final Environmental Impact Statement
FOIA	Freedom of Information Act
FWS	US Fish and Wildlife Service
GYC	Greater Yellowstone Coalition
NAS	National Audubon Society
NEPA	National Environmental Policy Act
NPCA	National Parks and Conservation Association
NPS	National Park Service
NWF	National Wildlife Federation
US	United States
USDA	US Department of Agriculture
USDI	US Department of the Interior
USDJ	US Department of Justice
USFS	US Forest Service and its successor, the USDA Forest Service
USGS	US Geological Survey
WGF	Wyoming Game and Fish Department
WRP	Northern Rocky Mountain Wolf Recovery Plan
YNP	Yellowstone National Park

Table 2. People Whose Names Appear Repeatedly in *Yellowstone Wolves*.

Bruce Babbitt	Secretary, US Department of Interior (1993–2001)
Ed Bangs	EIS coordinator, US Fish and Wildlife Service
Norman Bishop	Research interpreter, Yellowstone National Park
Al Boss	Wildlife biologist, Bridger-Teton National Forest
Wayne G. Brewster	Field supervisor, Endangered Species Program, US Fish and Wildlife Service, then research chief, Yellowstone National Park
Glen F. Cole	Research biologist, Yellowstone National Park
William Downes	Judge, US District Court of Wyoming
Frank Dunkle	Director, US Fish and Wildlife Service (1986–1989)
Steven R. Fain	Forensics specialist, US Fish and Wildlife Service
David D. Freudenthal	United States Attorney, then Wyoming Governor
Steven H. Fritts	Wolf Recovery Coordinator, US Fish and Wildlife Service
E. A. Goldman	Senior Biologist, US Fish and Wildlife Serivce
George Gruell	Wildlife biologist, Bridger-Teton National Forest
Mike Jimenez	Wyoming wolf biologist, US Fish and Wildlife Service
Jerry Kysar	Elk hunter who shot wolf in Teton Wilderness
Manual Lujan, Jr.	Secretary, US Department of Interior (1989–1993)
William Penn Mott, Jr.	Director, National Park Service (1985–1989)
Ronald M. Nowak	Taxonomist, US Fish and Wildlife Service
John Turner	Director, US Fish & Wildlife Service (1989–1993)
James R. Urbigkit	Cat Urbigkit's husband
John D. Varley	Chief of research, Yellowstone National Park
John L. Weaver	Wolf researcher
Stanley P. Young	Senior Biologist, US Fish and Wildlife Serivce

While modern taxonomists recognize considerably fewer subspecies of the North American gray wolf, Goldman's descriptions of *irremotus* and the Canadian subspecies *occidentalis* are still relevant today. That animals native to and from these two areas — the Northern Rocky Mountains of the US and western Canada, respectively — represented two different subspecies was the focus of the debate during the 1990s over wolf recovery in the Yellowstone area.

Goldman described *irremotus*, the Northern Rocky Mountain wolf, as a light-colored subspecies of medium to large size. In contrast, *occidentalis*, the Canadian wolf, was described as the largest of the North American wolves, with a large and massive skull. *Irremotus* differed from *occidentalis* in its "decidedly smaller size."[6]

Wolf taxonomist Ronald M. Nowak has suggested that movements of the late Pleistocene ice sheets may have had substantial effects on the distribution and composition of gray wolf populations that occurred historically throughout North America. He theorized that a wolf population, isolated in Alaska by late Pleistocene glaciation, spread eastward following withdrawal of the ice sheet and gave rise to the present day wolf type found in Alaska and western Canada.

Nowak proposed that other gray wolf populations in what is now the US may have been isolated by the Pleistocene glaciers and these populations might have expanded their ranges northward as the ice receded. The population of the central US could have repopulated the western Great Lakes region, as well as the mountains and plains area of the West. Wolves that occurred south of the ice in what is now the eastern US might have given rise to the wolves found historically in that region and eastern Canada. A fourth group would have survived in Mexico, giving rise to the Mexican wolf, and a fifth group, the Arctic wolf, would have survived in extreme northeastern North America.[7] Nowak noted that the most distinct differences between wolves that occupied the western part of the continent historically occurred along a line that, from the Pacific Ocean eastward to about the Great Lakes, closely corresponded to the Canada-US border. Those wolves that were north of this line were distinctly larger than those to the south of it.

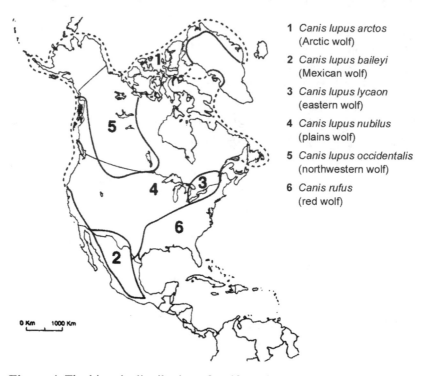

1 *Canis lupus arctos*
   (Arctic wolf)

2 *Canis lupus baileyi*
   (Mexican wolf)

3 *Canis lupus lycaon*
   (eastern wolf)

4 *Canis lupus nubilus*
   (plains wolf)

5 *Canis lupus occidentalis*
   (northwestern wolf)

6 *Canis rufus*
   (red wolf)

Figure 4. The historic distribution of wolf species and subspecies in North America. (After Nowak, 2003)

This model, if true, indicates that the differences seen today in wolves across North America are not just minor differences, but are the result of thousands of years of divergent evolution. Each of the five groups of wolves managed to survive the last Pleistocene glaciation in isolated pockets, and each managed to adapt to changing local conditions over long periods of time. It is this existing diversity and evolutionary potential which humans, through their various management practices and other influences, either effectively conserve or eradicate. During the 1990s, Yellowstone's native wolf, *Canis lupus irremotus*, became the subject of a brilliant battle to both protect and eradicate.

Nowak's 1994 revision of the taxonomy of North American wolves recognized two species (Figure 4) — *Canis lupus,* the gray wolf, and *Canis rufus,* the red wolf. Within *Canis lupus,* he recognized a mere five subspecies. Nowak placed *irremotus* into a southern group of wolves (*Canis lupus nubilus*), made up of smaller subspecies, and placed *occidentalis* into a northern group (*Canis lupus occidentalis*), which contains the generally larger subspecies.[8] Nowak noted that wolf subspecies situated east to west appeared more closely related to each other, while the southern wolves had little affinity to their neighbors to the north.

In short, according to Nowak, Yellowstone's native wolves were similar to Minnesota's wolves, but different than their Canadian neighbors. Yet it was the western Canadian wolf that the US Fish and Wildlife Service (FWS) placed into YNP. The battle in Wyoming over the wolf recovery experiment would eventually focus on this point of fact — that the native Yellowstone wolves were different than the Canadian wolves.

Chapter 2

Shark of the Plains

Modern day pundits have written the history of the war to eradicate wolves in the West many times over (Table 3). These histories are based on the idea that early settlers sought to eradicate the wolf because of the species' reputation as an evil animal. The theory maintained that settlers had grown up hearing stories such as Little Red Riding Hood and based their actions on some long-held cultural fear of, and hatred for, the wolf. While this may have been the case in some areas of the US, the historic record indicates that it was not the case in the northern Rockies. The accounts of the first white trappers and explorers to become familiar with the wolf in the Rocky Mountain West tells a different story. References to wolves during this time indicates that attitudes toward wolves may have gradually undergone a transition from annoyance, to fear and hatred, and eventually, to respect.

Mountain men such as Joe Meeks, Jim Bridger, and Osborne Russell spent time in and around Yellowstone in the early 1800s. Trappers worked the Rocky Mountains in the 1820s through the 1830s, harvesting beaver for the fashion trade. Wolves were of little or no economic value. Journals of these early explorers make little mention of wolves other than to state their presence or abundance.

During these years of exploration and trapping, mountain men, traders, and Indians met near present-day Daniel, Wyoming, for the annual Green River Rendezvous. These gatherings offered an opportunity to socialize, hear news, resupply, and swap goods. "They drank together, they sang, they laughed, they whooped; they tried to outbrag and outlie each other in stories of their adventures and achievements."[1]

Tragedy struck at the 1833 Green River Rendezvous. A white wolf, believed to be rabid, attacked several men and horses in Captain

Table 3. A Chronology of the History of Yellowstone Wolves

1820s	Beginning of the fur trade era
1840s	Emigration era begins
1860s	Homestead Act — western settlement increases
1870s	Professional wolf hunters killing wolves in Yellowstone
1872	Yellowstone becomes first US National Park
1875	Wyoming Territorial Legislature authorizes bounty on wolves
1881	Wolves nearly exterminated in Yellowstone
1883	Hunting in Yellowstone National Park becomes illegal
1886	United States Cavalry in charge of managing Yellowstone
1890	Wyoming becomes a state
1896	Wolves cause one million dollars worth of damage in Wyoming
1900s	Wolf bounties increase repeatedly in Wyoming
1914	Congress calls for elimination of predators from public lands
1915	US Biological Survey initiates predator control in Wyoming
1916	US government creates National Park Service, initiates wolf control
1926	Only few wolves remain in western states
1935	National Park Service begins protecting predators
1943	Wolf killed on Wind River Indian Reservation in Wyoming
1950s	Government predator campaign continues
1960s	Predator poisons dropped from airplanes in western Wyoming
1960s	Reports of wolves escalate in Yellowstone
1967	Ranger captures video footage of wolf in Yellowstone
1970s	Reports indicate small population of wolves in Wyoming
1971	First Northern Rocky Mountain wolf interagency meeting
1972	Use of poisons on public lands prohibited
1973	Endangered Species Act enacted, Northern Rocky Mountain subspecies of wolf placed on list of endangered species
1977	Wolves reclassified to delete subspecies listing, while entire species protected as endangered
1978	John L. Weaver publishes *The Wolves of Yellowstone*
1980s	Wolf reports in Yellowstone drop, while push for reintroduction increases

(continued on next page)

Table 3. A Chronology . . . , continued

1980s	Wolf reports continue from areas outside of Yellowstone park in Wyoming
1982	Endangered Species Act amended to include provision for release of "experimental populations"
1986	Bridger-Teton National Forest biologist reports small, scattered wolf population
1987	Wolf recovery plan officially calls for wolf reintroduction program
1988	Wolf hit and killed by motor vehicle north of Yellowstone park
1990	Congress appoints "Wolf Management Committee"
1991	Wolf Management Committee recommends experimental wolf reintroduction program
1991	First lawsuits against reintroduction dismissed as premature
1992	Environmental impact statement process on wolf reintroduction begins
1992	Filmmaker Ray Paunovich captures Yellowstone wolf on film
1992	Elk hunter Jerry Kysar shoots a wolf in the Teton Wilderness
1993	Draft environmental impact statement released
1994	US Fish and Wildlife Service ordered by a federal court to release wolf sighting information
1994	Final rule on reintroduction issued, prompting lawsuits
1995	First Canadian wolves placed in pens in Yellowstone, others are released in Idaho
1996	Oral arguments in wolf lawsuits are held
1997	Several naturally occurring wolves confirmed in western Wyoming
1997	Federal court issues decision that wolf reintroduction is illegal, appeals filed
1998	Another naturally occurring wolf killed in western Wyoming
1999	Reintroduced wolf population grows, while appeals court considers case
2000	Tenth Circuit Court of Appeals decides reintroduced populations can stay
2000	As wolf population grows, so do problems with livestock predation

(continued on next page)

Table 3. A Chronology . . . , continued

2003	Wyoming Legislature plans for state management of wolves
2003	State wildlife officials complain of wolf-related problems with elk
2003	Federal officials reject Wyoming's wolf plan
2004	Yellowstone wolves are confirmed as far south as Colorado and Utah
2004	Federal officials with wolves accused of trespassing on private land
2004	Wyoming files lawsuit over federal rejection of state's wolf plan
2005	Federal court rejects Wyoming's lawsuit, appeal filed
2005	Reports of wolves behaving aggressively toward humans increase
2007	Wyoming revises its wolf plan, gains federal support for state management of wolves
2008	Northern Rockies wolves removed from federal protection late in winter, then again receive protection in summer

Benjamin L. E. Fontenelle's camp before it escaped into the night. Several nights later, the wolf struck again at a camp four miles away, biting three men in the face while they slept and attacking the party's largest bull. The bull and most of the men died. The wolf was later shot. Events such as this fatal attack on humans were rare occurrences.[2]

Brigadier General Hiram Martin Chittenden viewed the wolf as a source of extreme annoyance. "Such was the wolf, an animal of little value to man, yet one that he had to take account of because of its troublesome habits."[3] Wolves would sneak into camp at night, kill tethered livestock, and steal articles while the occupants slept. Chittenden noted "They were thus always a source of extreme annoyance."[4]

Trapper Osborne Russell would have agreed. After carefully caching a supply of meat by burying it deep in a snow drift, topping it with stones, and burning gunpowder on it as a deterrent, he returned to it the next morning to find that "The wolves had dug it up and taken the best of it notwithstanding our precautions."[5]

George Ruxton, who traveled through the Rockies in the 1840s, complained that wolves would come into camp and chew up saddle leather, ropes, and buffalo hides.[6]

Biologist Durward Allen described these early encounters in a book that became a classic for studies of wolves. "Yet knowledgeable travelers had no fear of wolves and usually did not waste ammunition shooting them. The animals lurked about waiting to share the spoils of a hunt, and at worst they were a nuisance."[7]

Searches of numerous historic documents revealed no accounts of wolves having been killed in the Yellowstone area during the heyday of the beaver fur trade.

Russell described his experience with a wolf in 1835 near Ray's Lake, southwest of present day YNP. "About an hour before day I was awakened by the howling of wolves who had formed a complete circle within 30 paces of me and my horse at the flashing of my pistol however they soon dispersed."[8] Yet he also wrote, "They are not ferocious towards man and will run at sight of him."[9] Chittenden agreed, stating, "The animal was rarely, if ever, known to attack man, even when impelled by extreme hunger."[10]

Perhaps Russell even felt some sympathy for the wolf, as suggested in his description of an incident that happened in 1836 when, upon catching the scent of his dinner, a wolf, "fearing to approach nearer he sits upon a rock and bewails his calamities in piteous moans which are re-echoed among the Mountains."[11]

Early settlers and visitors in the late 1860s through the early 1870s, in describing the howl of a wolf, did not describe the blood-curdling howls of an evil beast, but instead used words such as "mournful," "dismal," "plaintive," and "doleful."[12] These words are all associated with sadness, so regardless of whether these men actually held any compassion for the animal, perhaps they at least felt some slight empathy. Ruxton most certainly did. After a large gray wolf had followed him for several days of travel in which "I had him twenty times a day within reach of my rifle, but he became such an old friend that I never dreamed of molesting him." Later, while spending a cold miserable night in a storm near Pikes Peak, Colorado, Ruxton noted, "Our old friend the wolf, however, was still a companion, and sat all night within sight of the fire, howling piteously from cold and hunger."[13]

Ruxton also described an interesting incident that occurred while he was camping in a heavy snowstorm on a tributary of the Platte River. "In the middle of the night I was awakened by the excessive cold, and turning towards the fire, which was burning bright and cheerfully, what was my astonishment to see a large gray wolf sitting quietly before it, his eyes closed, and his head nodding in sheer drowsiness! Although I had frequently seen wolves evince their disregard to fires, by coming within a few feet of them to seize upon any scraps of meat which might be left exposed, I had never seen or heard of one approaching so close as to warm his body, and for that purpose alone. However, I looked at him for some moments without disturbing the beast, and closed my eyes and went to sleep, leaving him to the quiet enjoyment of the blaze."[14] These words are not descriptive of an animal the mountain men feared or hated.

By 1838, beaver were getting scarce in the Rockies and the price of beaver pelts had declined due to the change in fashions — from beaver hats to silk hats. Trapper Jim Bridger noted wolf presence in the Yellowstone area in his explorations in 1849. By the 1850s, the beaver population had been decimated in the Rocky Mountain West and attention had turned to wolves and bison. In 1860, Bridger guided Captain W. F. Raynolds's exploratory expedition of the Yellowstone country, with Raynolds's ensuing report noting that the area had an "immense number of wolves."[15]

Wolves were easily taken by lacing bison carcasses with strychnine poison. In 1897, George Bird Grinnell wrote, "Often while this is being done, the wolfer would be surrounded by a circle of ten or a dozen or more wolves, waiting patiently for him to complete his operations and go away, so that their meal might begin. In those days wolves had no fear of man. They were seldom shot at, and knew of the gun chiefly as an implement to call them to a feast."[16]

Wolf biologist Stanley Young summarized similar events, such as that of John Townsend. "I have often been surprised at the perseverance and tenacity with which these animals will sometimes follow the hunter for a whole day, to feed upon the carcass he may leave behind him. When an animal is killed, they seem to mark the operation, and stand still at a most respectful distance with drooping tail and ears, as though perfectly indifferent to the matter in progress. Thus will they stand until the same is butchered, the meat placed upon the saddle, and the hunter is mounted and on his way; then, if he glances behind him, he will see the wily forager stealthily crawling and prowling along towards the smoking remains and pouncing upon it, and tearing it with tooth and nail, immediately he gets out of reach."[17]

Horace Greeley commented on wolves after his 1859 trip across the country. "It is very common for these wolves to follow at night a man traveling the road on a mule, not making any belligerent demonstration, but waiting for whatever may turn up."[18]

Historians Paul Schullery and Lee Whittlesey provided an exhaustive summary of encounters with wolves in the Yellowstone area that were recorded in journals dating from the 1800s.[19] They reported that on April 19, 1863, in the Gallatin Valley, north of present day YNP, guide James Stuart was serenaded by a pack of wolves one night while on guard duty. On September 16, 1869, a party of explorers heard a wolf howl while camped near Calfee Creek. In August, 1870, in the Lamar drainage of what would become YNP, A. B. Henderson, a prospector, reported that not long after setting up camp, it was attacked by a pack of wolves. This event was never fully explained and much debate has been generated about whether it actually occurred.[20]

In 1871, Truman Everts, after becoming separated from the other members of the Washburn party, reported hearing wolf howls on several occasions in the Yellowstone area.[21] Several parties of travelers, including C. C. Clawson, R. W. Raymond, and Henry Bird Calfee, reported wolves in the Yellowstone area in 1871. In 1872, Harry Norton's party, while in the northern part of what that year became the country's first national park, saw two wolves that ran away at their approach.

The West was changing. The early fur trappers and explorers had told of the richness and diversity of nature to be found to the West. By 1845, at least 5,000 emigrants had followed the Oregon

Trail, crossing the Rocky Mountains at South Pass, Wyoming, to settle the Willamette Valley of Oregon, the Garden of Eden with its free virgin land. In 1847, Brigham Young, the new leader of the Mormon Church, began settlement of the Salt Lake Basin, and organized a huge migration to the new Zion. In 1849, the gold rush to California began.

Freighters became "wolfers" — professional wolf hunters — during the winter, when travel was restricted due to the season. Thousands of dollars worth of wolf hides, at only fifty cents a hide, were shipped from the Upper Missouri during the 1860s, the large volume made possible by the use of strychnine. In 1862, Congress passed the Homestead Act which furthered the cause and increased the rate of western settlement. The "long drives" of cattle began in 1866, and a year later Horace Greeley urged Easterners to "Go west, young man."

This great westward movement may have led to the era of fear and hatred of the wolf. While early explorers and trappers in the uninhabited Rockies had been adventuresome, self-reliant outdoorsmen who had no real reason to fear or hate the wolf, later emigrants encountered an entirely different reality. The emigrants, who faced a 2,000 mile trek from the Missouri River to the Pacific Coast, would leave the Missouri River early in May. One history book described the travelers. "More often than not, men made the decision to make the crossing. Wives either went with their husbands or faced being left behind. Four out of five men on the overland trail had picked up stakes and moved before, some of them several times. Most had little cash, but they needed only strong legs, a few staples, and a willingness to tighten the belt when game was scarce. The majority of people traveled in family groups, including in-laws, grandchildren, aunts, and uncles."[22]

The first leg of the journey, following the North Platte River to Fort Kearney in what is today south-central Nebraska, was fairly pleasant and normally completed by late May. But the second leg, which led across the Great American Desert and Wyoming Territory, was hell for the emigrants. There was no wood for campfires and the blazing summer sun burned the grass. Indian wars sometimes raged. Hurrying to beat the snowfall, travelers rushed on to South Pass in southwestern Wyoming, a barren land that had cold, frosty nights even in mid-July. By this point on the trail, the emigrants were exhausted, yet months of travel were ahead of them even to get as far as Fort Hall, Idaho, before winter set in.

Wyoming was the land of desolation to these travelers. After months of hardship on the trail, and miles more to go, wolves proved to be one physical manifestation of everything that had gone wrong, or that could go wrong, on the trail. They were always there, in view, watching and waiting for the next misfortune to befall the travelers. The wolves were the evil demons waiting to confound or end the emigrants' dreams.

General Chittenden observed, "The wolf was the most ignoble of the inhabitants of the plains. It personified cowardice, beggary, craftiness, deceit, mercilessness, and all the group of evil qualities that are comprised in the term wolfishness. It was the shark of the plains, and it followed the caravans for whatever it might find along the route, such as the refuse of camps, or the remains of buffalo and other game slain by the hunters. It delighted to disinter the bodies of persons who died on the way, and only the most thorough protection could save the graves of the dead from this desecration.

"In the night it filled the air with its unearthly and hideous howlings, and gave an impression of power out of all proportion to what it really possessed."[23]

Stanley Young wrote: "During the earlier days of western settlement, the eating of dead humans by wolves seems to have occurred whenever bodies were available. During the outbreak of cholera among the traveling emigrants in the years 1849–1851, accounts of the epidemic state that more than 500 fresh graves on the south side of the Platte between the Missouri and Fort Laramie were visible along the trail. Brigham Young admonished the migrating Mormons to avoid this part of the road while traveling west for fear of the epidemic. Narratives of the Mormon trek stated: Scarcely a grave had not been robbed of its contents by wolves, and the bones of its occupants lay bleaching on the prairie. At the same time those who perished on the trail while trekking to try their fortunes at gold digging in California were reported disinterred by wolves."[24]

Many emigrants heading west would first experience the hardships of travel; then the trauma of sickness and eventual death of fellow travelers, friends, or beloved family members; and then the need to bury these loved ones in hastily dug graves along the trail. Once that was done, they would then have to witness the "shark of the plains" quickly excavate the graves and consume the remains. The wolf indeed personified hardship and death, and it was evil.

By the middle of the nineteenth century, numerous scouting parties had explored the Yellowstone area and its wonders had been reported back to the public. Travelers in the park increased. Trappers, tourists, hunters, and those out to make a living from the sale of wildlife skins headed into Yellowstone. In 1871, an eastern tannery discovered that buffalo hides made quality leather, and the hunting of bison increased. In the 1870s, there was a mass slaughter of wildlife in and around the park. The market value of an elk skin ranged from three to eight dollars. In 1875, it was reported that over two thousand elk were slaughtered in the vicinity of Mammoth Hot Springs alone. Just the skins were taken, leaving the antlers and carcasses on the ground to rot. The area's designation as a national park did nothing to protect the wildlife — poaching abounded, with no law enforcement evident. By 1877, bison hunting began to decline, and by 1884 only a few hundred bison remained.

In the 1870s, wolfers were using poisoned baits in the park. Wolf skins could be sold for four to six dollars each, to say nothing of the amount of money to be made by collecting government bounties, and many wolves could be taken by poisoning the carcasses of other animals which the wolves would eat. A few journals mentioned the presence of wolves in Yellowstone park, according to Schullery and Whittlesey. One night in August, 1873, a wolf kept watch over the camp of geologist Theodore Comstock near Steamboat Point, and in October, 1876, Gustavos Doane reported hearing a wolf pack howling near Stevenson Lake.

Yellowstone Superintendent P. W. Norris wrote that wolves had at one time been numerous in the park, but by 1881 most, but not all, had been exterminated. He attributed this to the use of strychnine-laced bait. Interestingly, Norris also reported that the park harbored not only wolves and coyotes, but also a third dark-colored species that fell between the two in size.[25]

In 1883, hunting became illegal in Yellowstone park. In an attempt to stem the widespread poaching, the US Cavalry took over management of the park in 1886. A few wolves were reported in the park in 1886 and 1894. A pack of three wolves was seen in 1899 near Slough Creek, and single wolves were also reported three times that year in the same area. In 1901, tracks were reported on two occasions in the park, and in 1902, a pack of six wolves, a pair, and several single animals were reported. Only reports of pairs or singles were reported in the park from 1904–1911.[26]

As bison were eliminated and western rangelands were stocked with herds of cattle, wolves began to change their prey base. Stanley Young wrote:

"The wolf was thus brought into direct competition with the livestock producer, and provoked continued warfare. Every known means such as guards, guns, traps, poisons, bounties, wolf-proof enclosures, were sooner or later employed to obtain relief from wolf depredations. Although disease might decimate his flocks and herds, or drought or severe winters might result in starvation or extreme cold losses, none of these factors seemed to arouse such outstanding resentment and determination of the stockman-farmer to adopt every means of elimination, as when the wolves killed on the open prairie or mountain range, or maimed and mutilated his range cattle and entered corrals to prey upon domestic stock. The cowman of the Old West wrought special vengeance on the wolf.

"Combating the wolf was not, however, a matter of mere revenge. Losses caused by this animal were often the chief factor in determining whether a season's range operations were to produce a profit, or the reverse, to the individual stockman, particularly the small producer."[27]

Chapter 3

Last of the Lobos

While the cavalry attempted to protect wildlife in Yellowstone, war had been declared on wolves throughout the West because of their depredations on livestock. In 1875, the Wyoming Territorial Legislature authorized a fifty-cent bounty to be paid on wolves, then increased it to one dollar in 1879 and to $1.50 in 1884. The 1875 and 1879 laws were entitled acts "for the protection of sheep," and wolves were the only predators bountied. Only later were the laws expanded to address losses caused by other predators.

Wyoming became a state in 1890, and by 1893, the bounty was up to eight dollars per wolf. Ranchers and stock associations offered rewards of up to one thousand dollars for the killing of individual renegade wolves which were responsible for the loss of thousands of dollars worth of livestock.

In 1883, Montana enacted legislation offering a bounty of one dollar per wolf. During the next three years, 10,261 wolf bounties were paid in that state. The law was repealed in 1888, but reenacted at two dollars per wolf in 1891, then increased to three dollars per wolf in 1895. From 1889 through 1906, at least 17,000 wolves were killed for state bounties that ranged from two to ten dollars in Montana.[1]

By 1896, it was estimated that wolves were causing almost a million dollars worth of damage to the Wyoming livestock industry each year. Wyoming's US Senator Thomas B. Kendrick testified before a congressional committee that wolves had sometimes destroyed as much as fifty percent of the year's calf crop.

From 1895 to 1907, 24,113 wolves were bountied by the State of Wyoming for three to five dollars per pelt. Bounties on these wolves also could be collected from stock organizations and local governments, with payments ranging from a few dollars to fifty dollars per wolf (Table 4).[2]

While wolves were taking their toll on local livestock, ranchers and trappers were fighting back. In October, 1902, wolves killed three head of cattle on the McBride Ranch near Jackson Hole. McBride,

Table 4. Wolf Bounty Records for Wyoming, 1895–1918[1]

Year	Number of Wolves Bountied	Bounty $/Wolf
1895	1,699	3.00
1896	3,458	3.00
1897	897	4.00 (Adults)
		0.75 (Pups)
1898	3,384	4.00
1899/1900	4,908	3.00
1901/1902	4,480	3.00
1903/1904	2,256	5.00
1905/1906	3,214	3.00
1907[a]	447	3.00
1908	2,928	5.00
1909/1910	3,419	5.00
1911/1912[a]	313	5.00
1913/1914	1,559	5.00
1915	100	5.00
1916	113	7.50 (Adult males)
		12.00 (Adult females)
		5.00 (Pups)
1917/1918	71	15.00 (Adults)
	241	10.00 (Pups)

[1] This table includes only those bounties paid by the State of Wyoming. Local associations and governments, and private individuals, often offered their own bounties.

[a] This decrease reflects the fact that the wolf bounties were halted for a period of time, then reinstated.

with the help of his dog, managed to track down and kill six wolves while they were at their bedding site.[3]

When the Wyoming Legislature lowered the wolf bounty from five to three dollars early in 1905, the citizenry was outraged, as is evident by the following report from a 1905 issue of the *Pinedale Roundup*, a newspaper in Sublette County, Wyoming.

"Sights now witnessed on the range are such as to take all the heart away from the sturdy ranchman who has worked for the upbuilding of this country. The damnable terrorists of the timber — the wolves — are sweeping down on the range and playing havoc with the cattle. Riders coming in every day tell of the damage being done. Animals have been found hamstrung, and with portions of the carcass eaten away, while others have been found in a crippled form, but had managed to get away from the beasts.

"The shame should be pointed in the face of every member of our late legislature who opposed the bounty appropriation or had any part in the reduction of the bounty on predatory wild animals. A little hamstringing of some of them one year from next fall might prove compulsively that the voice of the people must be respected."[4]

The depredations continued. The Wyoming Legislature appealed to the US Congress for assistance, which came, but not until several years later. The stockmen continued on their own. The killing of wolves was always news, and these events often made the local newspapers. In May, 1905, near Pinedale, trapper N. Galloway killed four wolves — two adults and two pups. In November of that year, a nearly white wolf was killed by Buck Elmore near Duck Creek Flats, just outside present-day Pinedale.

Problems with wolves were reported in 1906 from Jackson Hole to Pinedale. The killing had started with the appearance of the wolves in the lower country in mid-January of that year. The *Pinedale Roundup* reported: "Ranchers are using up good horse flesh every day in riding after them but to no avail. Nearly a score of cattle have been reported killed by the varmints which sweep down at night. The sight is heartrending to the rancher who must ride among his cattle and note the work of destruction. Many that were not killed have been badly bitten, chunks being taken out, leaving them badly crippled."[5]

Locals formed bounty associations in an attempt to provide some relief. It seemed the wolf population was increasing (Figure 5). Charles Budd, who ranched near Big Piney, had yearling calves and four colts killed in his pasture in a six-week period centering around March of 1905. In one area near Pinedale, twenty-two head of cattle were killed between January and April. These were significant numbers for individual ranchers to lose, and they fought back.

In 1906, a bounty of twenty dollars per adult male wolf was offered by Pinedale area ranchers, but the bounty on female wolves was higher, at forty dollars for a female with pups, while the pups themselves were worth ten dollars each.[6] Charley, Will, and Frank Alexander killed three wolves out of a pack of eight in February, and also had killed four wolves the previous fall.[7] In April it was reported that six adult wolves and four pups had been killed.[8] A week later, federal trapper Vernon Bailey was reported to have destroyed four

Figure 5. A wolf pup on the hood of a car in front of the Bridger-Teton National Forest office. (Photo courtesy Wyoming State Archives, Department of State Parks and Cultural Resources)

Figure 6. Federal trapper Vernon Bailey located this female wolf with her nine whelps in front of a den near Big Piney, Wyoming, in 1907. (Photo courtesy Wyoming State Archives, Department of State Parks and Cultural Resources)

wolf dens and taken thirty-five pups from the area (Figure 6). Because he was employed by the government, these kills were not subject to bounty payments.[9] Bailey reported:

"The wolves breed mainly below the edge of the forest reserves or on the reserves only where partly open foothill country is included. In talking with hunters, trappers, ranchmen, and forest rangers who have been much in the northern mountains in winter I have not found one who ever saw wolf tracks in the mountains during the breeding season or knew of a wolf den above the foothills.

"In the upper Green River Valley of Wyoming between the Salt River and Wind River mountains, wolves were apparently just as numerous in March, 1906, as on a previous trip that I made through the valley thirteen years before. Fresh tracks were seen on the snow almost every day, usually of wolves in pairs, but in one case a band of nine. Between March 24 and April 21, 1906, four dens containing 32 wolf pups, were found, with 2 old wolves at each den: and evidently there were two or three other dens in the valley. Forty old wolves, or approximately one to a township, would seem a fair estimate of the number in this valley, while, as far as could be learned, the number that had been killed over the same area during the previous fall, winter, and spring was but 16.

"Along the east base of the Wind River Mountains, from Miners Delight to Union, at least 19 wolves were killed during the year of 1905, and 5 pups were taken from one den near Lander on May 1, 1906.

"In Fremont County, including most of the Wind River and Sweet Water valleys and a large part of the Green River Valley, bounties were paid on 69 wolves in 1905 and on 45 wolves from January 1 to May 1 in 1906. Reports from different sections of Wyoming show that in 1893 wolves were common in the Green River Valley, on the head of LaBarge Creek."[10]

Historians have often discounted the importance of the impact of losing a few head of livestock. The late Eva Hayes of Lander, Wyoming, grew up in the Split Rock area of central Wyoming in the early 1900s. She described to the author how wolves had come onto the ranch one night and killed the family's turkeys. The family had invested all of their life savings in these turkeys, and the wolves had effectively cleaned out the family's entire assets in one night. The family was heartbroken, angry, and destitute.

By 1908, Wyoming was again paying a five-dollar bounty on wolves, and from 1908 to 1910, the state paid over six thousand bounties (Figure 7). A 1911 report on the legislative bounty appropriation noted "The last appropriation (1909) made under this act was $60,000, but it was all spent on bounties long before the meeting of the next legislature, when another appropriation might be made."[11]

But in 1911, Governor Joseph M. Carey, believing the bounty program was not working, vetoed the legislation. The citizens felt this was unjust. "The stopping of bounty payments was a mistake of the present administration and a poor economy plan for the man who owns a ranch and a small bunch of cattle has as much right to protection

Figure 7. Tom Dodge with a wolf he shot in March, 1908. The wolf was 7.5 feet in length from the tip of its nose to the tip of its tail. (Photo courtesy Wyoming State Archives, Department of State Parks and Cultural Resources)

from predatory animals, as the citizen of any town has in having police protection."[12] Governor Carey again vetoed a bounty bill in 1913, but he subsequently reversed his position before the end of the legislative session.

From 1905 to 1916, the State of Montana conducted a mange research program which consisted of paying $15 for each wolf delivered alive to them, which was then infected with mange, and released back into the wild. The program was intended to control wolf populations, but failed. By 1912, the bounty for an adult wolf in Montana had reached a high of fifteen dollars, and 1,233 wolves were bountied by the state that year.[13]

The number of wolves seen together in Yellowstone increased during the years 1912–1914, and historians generally agree that the wolf population was on the increase. In 1912, packs of three to four wolves were reported in the park on three occasions, and in 1913, a pack of nine animals was reported.

By late April, 1912, fifteen wolves had been killed in the Pinedale area alone. Denning activities netted nine pups from a den at New Fork Canyon, and six pups from a den at Soda Lake.[14]

In 1914, the US Congress passed legislation calling for the elimination of predators from all public lands, including national parks. Yellowstone park records for 1914 include a report of a single wolf and of packs consisting of from three to eleven members. The US Cavalry killed seven wolves in the park that year, and on December 31, Captain F. T. Arnold of the 12th Cavalry wrote to the Secretary of the Interior that wolves "are present in considerable numbers and are destroying much game."

The US Biological Survey took over predator control efforts in Wyoming in 1915. Wolves were reportedly abundant in Yellowstone at the time and doing much damage to wildlife in the park. Hundreds of wolves were killed in the following years (Table 5).

Wolves were causing problems in more areas than just Yellowstone. In 1914, ranchers in the Jackson area began combining their herds of cattle on summer range because of the recent depredations by wolves (Table 6). Wolves were believed to have been on

Table 5. Wolves Killed in Wyoming by the US Biological Survey, 1919–1926

Year	Number
1919	88
1920	26
1921	104
1922	116
1923	52
1924	14
1925	1
1926	12

Table 6. Wolves Taken in the Jackson Hole Region, 1918–1920

Year	Adults	Pups
1918	1	6
1919	-	15[a]
1920	2	8

[a] Four of these pups were taken alive from a den near Mount Leidy by William Dunn. One of these was raised by Jackson Hole tailor Fred Vincent, alongside his coyote, and was reported as still being in captivity in 1921. The three other pups were sent to the Soldiers' and Sailors' Home in Dayton, Ohio.

the increase in northwestern Wyoming during the years from 1912 to 1925.[15] Ranchers formed "wolf bounty associations" in the Jackson Hole and Pinedale areas in 1914, assessing a per-head fee on live-stock to raise the money to hire wolf hunters and pay bounties to alleviate their wolf depredations. Bounties offered by these groups were as high as twenty dollars for a wolf pup, and fifty to sixty dollars for an adult wolf. Some of these organizations eventually evolved into the present day livestock associations.[16]

In 1915, Vernon Bailey found evidence of wolf presence in numerous areas of the park, and he noted a scarcity of elk calves while the wolf scats he observed were made up entirely of elk hair.[17] Others reported wolf packs in the park on ten occasions in 1915, with pack sizes ranging from three to eleven animals — one pack of three, one of nine, one of eight to ten, and seven not specifying a number. Single wolves were reported on four occasions.

YNP records indicate that in June, 1915, a Mr. Frazier killed two half-grown wolf pups and captured alive two more male pups which he kept chained up at the Buffalo Ranch at Lamar for some time before they were eventually shipped alive, on November 16, 1915, to the National Zoological Park in Washington, DC. Other wolf mortalities that year included a female trapped near Rose Creek and both a black male and black female killed near Slough Creek, all taken in the month of October.

That same year, in the Jackson area south of YNP, forty wolves were killed in a matter of a few weeks, mainly by denning.[18] Wolf packs that escaped persecution were known to inhabit the Turpin Creek, Spread Creek, and Zenith areas.[19] By early April, 1916, another seventeen pups had been taken from dens in the Upper Gros Ventre region near Jackson Hole.[20]

In 1916, the National Park Service (NPS) was created and management of YNP was transferred from the cavalry to this new agency. During the thirty years that Yellowstone was managed by the US Cavalry, only twelve wolves were reportedly killed in the park, with an additional two wolves being captured and removed alive (Table 7). But Congress had stated its intent to eradicate predators and NPS actively participated in wolf eradication efforts. In its first ten years, the

Table 7. Wolves Taken in Yellowstone National Park, 1914–1926

Year	Number	Adult	Pup	Unknown	Alive
1914	7	7	-	-	-
1915	7	3	4	-	2
1916	10	4	6	-	-
1917	2	2	-	-	-
1918	36	-	-	36[a]	-
1919	6	2	-	4	-
1920	28	13	15	-	-
1921	24	13	11	-	-
1922	26	16	10	-	10
1923	8	3	5	-	5
1924	0	-	-	-	-
1925	0	-	-	-	-
1926	2	0	2	-	-
Total	156	63	53	40	17

[a] Many of these are believed to be pups killed at den sites, as 19 were killed in April, 7 in May, and 4 in June of that year.

agency either killed or removed alive over one hundred wolves from Yellowstone.

Two special rangers employed to exterminate predators in Yellowstone killed from ten to twelve wolves, many of these being pups found in dens, in 1916. Additional evidence of wolf presence in the park included four reports of wolf pairs, three reports of three or four wolves being seen together, ten reports of wolves that did not specify how many animals were seen, and several reports of lone wolves.

In 1916, 311 wolves were taken on national forest lands in Wyoming, which was estimated to be about one percent of the state's wolf population.[21]

In the early 1900s, wolf roundups would occasionally be held in the western states. Whole communities would turn out to watch the roundups, and people would travel from around the state to attend. Riders would mount horses and attempt to drive wild animals out of a vast area into a series of corrals. These roundups rarely resulted in anything but wild horses being corralled, but served as great opportunities for people to socialize and to hold rodeos, dances, dinners, and other events. One such gathering, the Farlow Wolf Roundup, was held in Fremont County in 1917. No wolves were taken.[22]

Records for 1917 indicate that wolves were not numerous in Yellowstone park, but two were killed in the park that year and another ten pups were taken from dens in the Jackson area by a lion hunter named Elgins. The next year a pack of up to sixteen wolves was reported to inhabit the Specimen Ridge area of the park.[23]

Newspapers of the times reflected public sentiment about wolves and their impacts on game animals in YNP. In 1922, after a pack of wolves killed and partially consumed five elk calves, park ranger Harry Anderson killed three members of the pack. According to the *Livingston Enterprise,* "The others escaped, but the park ranger has vowed to avenge the death of the tiny elk and is determined to clean out all wolves in Wonderland."[24]

Of the wolves taken from the park in 1922, it was noted that ten pups were captured alive in April, but what happened to these pups is not known (figures 8 and 9). Two large wolves, one gray and one black, were killed in October in the Pelican and Raven creeks area of the park. Of the eight wolves taken in the park in 1923, five of these were pups that were brought out alive for display at Mammoth. Another four wolves were killed in the Jackson region in 1923.[25]

By 1924, wolf sightings were becoming rare in the park but, nonetheless, several sightings of lone animals were recorded. One report each of a pair, three animals, and a pack of twelve or thirteen near Elk Park were recorded. No wolves were killed in the park during 1924, although three were reportedly observed there in 1925. In May, 1926, a hunter captured nine pups and one adult alive in the Upper Gros Ventre region to be sent to parks and zoological gardens in the East.[26]

By 1926, only a few wolves remained in western Wyoming. The US Biological Survey and its cooperators had killed 566 wolves in the ten years prior to 1927. By 1928, the Biological Survey estimated that there were no more than five adult wolves left ranging in Wyoming outside YNP.[27]

In spite of the massive efforts to eradicate all the wolves from Yellowstone park, a few wolves had survived. In 1926, lone wolves were seen on two occasions in the park, as was a pair of wolves. Two wolf pups were trapped and killed while feeding on a bison carcass near Soda Butte in October of the same year. After 1926, wolves were so rare in the park that control of their numbers was no longer a priority. Yet, NPS continued to kill other predators in the park for another ten years, until 1935.

In 1927, wolves were rarely seen in Yellowstone, although a pair was believed to inhabit Slough Creek. Wolf sign was rarely observed the next year, and in 1929 a pair was sighted near Yellowstone Lake.

In 1928, the US Biological Survey issued a report detailing the effectiveness of its predator control campaign and called for continued efforts for the western ranges "to be entirely cleaned of predatory animals." The report stated: "Our modern civilization requires that we harmonize as nearly as possible the lives of our wild native animals with our agricultural activities. This calls for the protection and

Figure 8. Yellowstone Chief Ranger Sam Woodring holding two of ten wolf pups in front of the blacksmith's shop. (Photo courtesy National Park Service)

Figure 9. These wolf pups were captured in Yellowstone National Park in April, 1922. (Photo courtesy National Park Service)

preservation of elk, deer, antelope, moose, mountain sheep, and other valuable forms of wild life. To do this, we must eliminate certain predatory animals that prey upon those wild mammals that we consider beneficial, and on domestic stock."[28]

By 1922, wolves had been extirpated in the southern reaches of British Columbia and Alberta as a result of control programs nearly identical to those that were occurring in the western United States.[29] In the 1930s and 1940s, however, the wolf population of Alberta experienced a tremendous increase in numbers, and by the mid-1940s had expanded southward into the southern portion of the province. Mainly due to the threat of rabies, eradication efforts were re-initiated in the 1950s, and by the mid-1950s it was estimated that only about five hundred wolves remained in Alberta. The wolf population began expanding again in the 1960s and spread southward until it finally reached the border with the US late in the 1970s.[30]

Wolves were eradicated from British Columbia by 1930, but the population subsequently rebounded and low numbers extended their range into the southern part of the province by the early 1950s. A few packs and scattered individuals were reported near the Canada-US border region in the early 1950s. However, the wolf population remained low or nearly nonexistent in southern British Columbia through the mid-1970s. Control efforts have fluctuated over the years. Since the late 1970s, wolves have again extended their range, and in recent years have appeared in low numbers in the southern portion of the province.[31]

Idaho's wolf eradication history is similar to the programs already described. The first bounty law was enacted in Idaho in 1907, although wolf control had been practiced for quite some time, with wolfers using strychnine-laced bison carcasses up until about 1890. By about 1895, wolf numbers had been reduced in Idaho, but wolves remained scattered throughout the state, with populations seemingly more numerous in the southeastern portions of the state.[32] Under the federal government's predator control program, 258 wolves were killed in Idaho in 1919–1928, with 184 of these taken in 1919 and 1920.[33] It was estimated that, by 1939, a total of forty-eight wolves remained on national forest lands in Idaho.[34] Researchers have noted that reports of wolves from the 1940s to 1960 reflected little change from the 1900–1939 period.[35] Intensive predator control was maintained through the 1950s in Idaho.

Although wolf eradication efforts were widespread in the western states, a few wolves had survived in northeastern Utah, near the Wyoming border, in the 1920s and 1930s. Carlos Cornia trapped the Wheat Grass area west of Woodruff, Utah, in the winter of 1926. In January, 1927, Cornia made $150 from poisoning one wolf with a strychnine bait and shooting a female wolf, both members of a pack of five that lived in the area. Aseal Jacobsen reportedly later killed the other three members of this pack.[36]

Jay Sundberg wrote of an interesting event that happened to him as a fourteen-year-old boy while herding sheep in northeastern Utah in 1936. Upon being approached by a lone wolf, Sundberg "stopped the attack on me by throwing rocks, but he gutted a sheep before I finally drove him off." This occurred five miles north of Henefer,

Utah, which is approximately fifty miles south of the area where five wolves had been killed ten years earlier.[37]

The last lobos, the renegade wolves that were named by the physical characteristics unique to each individual, and which became the worst livestock killers of all time, prompted a change in public attitude towards the species. These wolves were wary, clever animals that seemed almost impossible to stop, regardless of the enormous efforts made to capture or kill them. These wolves gained the respect of their audiences, albeit only a grudging respect. Even the wolf hunters that in time dispatched the last of these legendary stock killers expressed some hesitancy about their work. H. P. Williams, after finally catching up to and killing the legendary Custer Wolf in 1920, stated: "I tell you I'd built up such respect for the old devil that, if he hadn't had a trap on one foot, I might not have killed him. I really think I might have let him go."[38]

The 1927 Wyoming Legislature reenacted the wolf bounty at $5 for each wolf, but lowered it to three dollars two years later. The low bounty and few wolves remaining made bounty hunting an unprofitable business. Government trapper R. B. Goodrich killed a "dandy big male wolf" in the Boulder area in 1929, "evidently an unioneer, from the battle scars he carried." News of the wolf killing made the front page of the local newspaper. "This is the first wolf caught in these parts for some time."[39] By 1939, the US Forest Service (USFS) estimated that only six wolves remained on the national forests in Wyoming.[40]

In 1943, a sheepman on the Wind River Indian Reservation killed a male wolf, later stating: "It was kind of sad to think that he was the only one that I'd ever seen and I killed him. Of course, at the time I was thinking there was nothing else I could do. But at the time he was endangering my sheep herd."[41]

In 1944, Young noted: "In many parts of the West ranchmen are still to be found who vividly recall the depredations and the costliness of these renegade wolves. It is probable that never did more intelligent wolves exist. Rarely have more dramatic hunts been planned and carried out, not greater ingenuity employed, than the efforts put forth by the hunters who trailed these wolves and finally killed them. These animals had become wise beyond all other wolves through constant experience with the devises employed for capturing them. At times they seemed possessed of uncanny intelligence in avoiding steel traps, and in detecting various poisons, despite the variety of methods used in attempting to give the drugs to them. They likewise seemed to know when a man was weaponless. With every hand turned against them, their wisdom was respected by the stockmen upon whose cattle they depredated, as well as by the wolf trappers who finally eliminated them at the cost of much time, money, and patience."[42]

The short era of the lobos produced a startling effect. With the recent memory of the monetary damage wolves could cause to livestock, these last wolves instilled in at least a few people a very different attitude. These wolves were worthy adversaries — cunning, intelligent, bold animals who could strike back in vengeance. The wolves had won respect.

Chapter 4

Those that Remained

Although the Wyoming wolf population had been decimated by the 1930s, a few wolves had managed to survive.[1] Wolf presence in Yellowstone was still being recorded, usually in the park supervisors' and district rangers' monthly and annual reports. Of the thirty-one reports recorded in the 1930s and 1940s, eight were of two or more animals, with pairs being reported in the park in 1932, 1934, 1936, 1940, and 1947. Three wolves seen together were reported in 1937, and packs of four were reported in 1934 and 1936.

These reports included several rangers' accounts of wolves killing elk in the park and numerous reports of rangers encountering wolves and their tracks. It is evident, considering the continuity of the reports, that these wolves were remnants of the formerly widespread population.

In 1930, a wolf reportedly killed two elk calves in the Tower Falls area of the park. In 1932, a pair of wolves was observed feeding on a dead elk in the park. In 1934, a pack of four wolves was observed at Tower Creek, and in 1936, four wolves were seen near Old Faithful. Several freshly killed elk carcasses were found, believed to have been killed by the wolf pack. These reports indicate that at least two packs of wolves were present during the 1930s in Yellowstone. While not a "viable" population by any means, they certainly were survivors of the predator control era.

In 1933, NPS policy was changed to protect predators system-wide, but predator control continued in Yellowstone until 1935. While predator control became prohibited in the park, poisons — coyote-getters and Compound 1080 baits — continued to be used outside the boundaries of the park until 1972. Although records of wolf presence in Wyoming during the war years of the 1940s are scarce, a few wolves were killed in the state during this time.

In 1946, federal wildlife agent Troy Terrel was reported to have said that 1927 was the year that the last wolf had been killed in Wyoming. This was not accurate, and several Wyoming ranchers were quick to point out that wolves still inhabited the state and had been sighted, as late as 1943, as far southeast of Yellowstone as Boysen Reservoir and Shoshone.[2] In fact, several wolves were killed in Wyoming in the 1940s.

In January, 1940, Wyoming Game and Fish Department (WGF) Deputy Game Warden H. B. Sanderson of Greybull shot a large male wolf on the north rim of Shell Canyon. This specimen measured sixty-four inches from the nose to the tip of the tail.[3]

On May 23, 1943, Leo Cottenoir, a sheepherder on the Wind River Indian Reservation, heard what he thought were coyotes "yipping" up a draw in the Muddy Creek area of the Owl Creek Mountains. Leo saddled a horse and rode up the ridge to investigate. He saw what "looked like an old coyote and two pups" down in the draw. As he went closer to the animals, they ran, and Leo succeeded in killing the largest animal — a wolf.

After killing the wolf, Leo said he believed that the animals he saw were actually one wolf with two full-grown coyotes, instead of the full-grown coyote with two pups as he had earlier believed. Tracks of this seventy- to eighty-pound male wolf were reported to have been seen where the animal crossed over the Owl Creeks to Muddy Creek, where it was shot.[4]

On Thanksgiving Day, 1949, federal animal control agent Charles Wilson, using a cyanide poison set, killed an old white male wolf. This occurred at a Table Mountain ranch near Lander, Wyoming. The pelt reportedly stretched almost seven feet from tip to tip.[5]

Reports of wolf occurrences in YNP in the 1950s were almost double those of the 1940s. Thirty-one total reports were recorded; twenty-five were of single animals, while two were of pairs, three were of three animals, and one was of four animals.

In 1952, a USFS employee, an old aerial bounty hunter, reported seeing three wolves feeding on a bison carcass in the park. Wolves were breeding in Yellowstone in 1956, based on one report in June of an adult with three pups that had been seen in the north-central area of the park, and another two months later by NPS employees, of an adult with two half-grown pups seen in an adjacent area.

A federal wildlife service employee reported seeing a wolf just north of the park in 1953. In 1959 and 1960, a NPS employee heard wolf howls in the Grouse Creek area of the park, and later in 1960, a federal wildlife agent recorded wolf tracks in the same area that measured 3 ½ by 4 ½ inches.

Biologist John L. Weaver wrote that Philip Norton of Cora, Wyoming, reported that he had trapped a wolf at the head of the Gros Ventre River in 1950. According to Weaver, Norton believed that two or three wolves were present in the area during 1952–1953, as indicated by sightings and tracks.

The bounty for wolves in Wyoming remained on the books at two to three dollars through the late 1950s, even though control of predators was mainly accomplished by predatory animal control districts and other government programs, employees of which were unable to collect bounties. These government predator control programs were not aimed at controlling individual problem animals, but instead were geared toward complete eradication of all predatory animals and rodents, usually through the use of Compound 1080 poison baits.

In the 1960s, poison baits were dropped from airplanes throughout western Wyoming, until the ban on this poison went into effect in 1972. One Gros Ventre area rancher, Snook Moore, described the extent of the campaign, in which rabbit carcasses laced with poison were loaded onto an airplane in Rock Springs, Wyoming, and dropped throughout western Wyoming.

Snook and his wife Evelyn had personal experience with this, as a poisoned rabbit was dropped into the barnyard of the Moore ranch, which their dog attempted to eat and was subsequently poisoned. Coyotes that had eaten the baits came down to Tosi Creek to drink and would fall dead in the water. This Tosi Creek water was the source of drinking water for the Moore Ranch.

Poisoning stations were also used. According to Snook: "They would kill a horse and use strychnine pills on it, and scatter it all around. They killed anything that would eat meat, foxes, coyotes, wolves . . . They started over there on the Gros Ventre just above Kelly and they put these poison stations clear up the Gros Ventre to Fish Creek to Fish Creek Park and back over to Pinion Ridge and clear down onto the New Fork . . . They had poison stations every so far."[6]

Wolves were seen periodically by local residents outside the park, but there were so few wolves that they were viewed more with pleasure than as a threat. Even the old timers who remembered past damages were not inclined to kill a wolf unless it caused trouble.

Snook Moore's stepfather had hunted wolves in the early 1900s for the Fish Creek Wolf Association of the Jackson Hole region, and Snook had seen a few wolves on his ranch in the Gros Ventre Mountains periodically during the second half of the twentieth century, but had never shot at one. When asked whether he was tempted to shoot the wolf he spotted out his kitchen window in 1992, he replied: "No, I didn't want to shoot it. I could have, but I didn't want to."

Moore explained that there were always a few wolves around until the government started using Compound 1080, but then, "That poison situation, they really destroyed the wolves, there is no doubt about it."

The few wolves living in Wyoming offered opportunities for rare wildlife encounters that residents enjoyed. But Snook also cautioned, "If the wolves get thick, they'll bother."

According to Moore, the public, including many ranchers, "felt pretty bad about that poison 'cause it killed so damned much stuff than what they was putting it out for . . . We raised so much hell, they made it illegal to use 1080."[7]

A 1953 Sublette County newspaper included a news account of a white wolf being spotted by Dr. J. G. Wanner of Rock Springs on Big Flat Top Mountain in the Upper Green River region.[8] The article noted:

"White wolves were not uncommon. Charlie Alexander killed a white female on Dumphrey Creek in 1903. Roy Lozier and Paul Snyder (Snyder was a professional hunter and used a hound pack) got two out of a pack of three on the Mesa in 1925. One of these was a white one.

The 'white' color was not necessarily snow-white but a very pale yellow and denoted old age.

"Since the wolves have been reported wiped out occasional singles and pairs have been seen. Presumably these came down out of the Yellowstone Park. There are many places in our mountains where these animals could exist a long time and never be seen by man."[9]

The 1960s saw an explosion of wolf reports in YNP, starting with a report of an adult wolf accompanied by three pups in 1963, and peaking with a total of seventy-two reports in 1969 alone. Of the 133 total reports for the park in the 1960s, 105 reports were of single animals, twenty-eight were of two or more animals, including fourteen reports of pairs and fourteen reports of three to five animals each.

In 1967, a seasonal ranger captured footage of a wolf in the Lamar Valley on film. Federal wildlife agents reported seeing a pair of wolves in the park in 1969, and finding wolf tracks that same year. One account describing an adult with three pups in July, 1963, coupled with the twenty-eight reports of two or more animals indicated that wolves were still breeding in Yellowstone during the 1960s. Outside the park, FWS agents confirmed that a pair of wolves lived along the Anderson Fork of the Greybull River.

The *Jackson Hole Guide*, in October, 1969, printed a photograph of a wolf that had been shot the week before in the Snake River Canyon by Larry Pastor. The paper noted, "The animal is probably the first wolf shot by a hunter in the 30 years since bounty hunters nearly wiped them out of Wyoming."[10]

Reported wolf activity in Yellowstone park expanded sharply in 1969. While this increase could have reflected a real growth of the park's wolf population, the data are too limited to permit this conclusion. A more likely explanation is that Glen Cole, supervisory research biologist in the park at the time, began the first real effort to record the occurrences of wolves in the park.

In an April 11, 1969, memo to the park superintendent, Cole wrote: "The wolf still should be considered rare in Yellowstone. This writer has spent a great deal of field time in Yellowstone during the past two years and has only two animals seen, plus one track to his credit. Sightings of a probable three different pairs of wolves (from the Lamar to the Firehole) during the present breeding season are considered encouraging. The lack of any protection for the species just outside our boundaries is, however, an uncomfortable situation."[11]

In his April, 1969, research note on wolves in YNP, Cole concluded, "The present remnant wolf population in Yellowstone may not be in excess of a dozen animals."[12]

While NPS recognized that a remnant wolf population had survived in the park through the late 1960s, it also recognized that the population was in danger of extinction. Wolves were protected within the boundaries of the park, but were not afforded any protection outside the park until 1973.

Rumors have persisted of a supposed secret release of wolves into Yellowstone late in the 1960s, and versions have been published in several manuscripts.[13] Some claim that this release explains the increase in wolf sightings in the park in 1969 through the early 1970s, although it has been noted that record keeping in the park was vastly improved at this time.[14]

Writer Alston Chase accused Glen Cole of manufacturing wolf sighting reports to demonstrate that wolves were never completely eradicated — of filling in gaps in the record from the time of the last confirmed wolf kills in the park in 1926 to the time Cole arrived in the park in the late 1960s, when the wolf reports increased — an accusation with little, if any, substance.

It is true that wolf reports did increase dramatically at this time, but it should also be noted that NPS had started to actively solicit these reports, so an increase was fairly predictable.

Several second- or third-hand accounts about this purported release have circulated. Some claim to have been told by high level NPS officials about the release, while others claim to have seen photographs of the release itself. No one has presented any evidence to support these claims, so they remain unsubstantiated. Even former Wyoming Governor Stan Hathaway told of a secret release. In 1989, Hathaway told the *Jackson Hole Guide* that Jack Anderson, who served as the YNP superintendent from 1967 to 1975, told him NPS had obtained several pairs of wolves from Alaska and secretly released them into the park. Hathaway said he saw one of the wolves on a trip into the park with Anderson. Hathaway was quoted in the *Guide* as stating that he never told the story publicly until after Anderson's death because he did not want to get Anderson in trouble.[15]

A secret release of wolves was investigated to some extent in the mid-1970s. While little can be found in writing, correspondence between two prominent wildlife scientists, Durward Allen and A. Starker Leopold, is revealing.

Leopold, apparently in response to his locating at least four sets of wolf tracks on the Yellowstone River in 1971, wrote, "Yellowstone National Park was considering trying to reintroduce wolves for many years before the 1971 observation."

Leopold went on to explain that at least two park superintendents had questioned the ranching community about the idea, and presented the proposal in speeches in states adjacent to Yellowstone. "And then the wolf showed up," he wrote.

Leopold took part in developing a plan to protect wolves that might stray out of the park, and a special meeting of the Natural Sciences Advisory Committee was held in Portland, Oregon, to formalize the plan.

"It is absolutely inconceivable to me that all this was a hoax," Leopold wrote.

Leopold offered one explanation for the rumor of a secret release. "But at that time the Craighead feud was underway, and among other statements made by Frank and John was the assertion that the Park had introduced the wolves surreptitiously. They have repeated this over and over again, and continue to do so in an apparent effort to embarrass the park. The rumor was given credence by the acknowledged early plan to try an introduction. It is going to require some pretty solid evidence to convince me otherwise. I think that remnant population was there all the time."[16]

Durward Allen responded. "Many thanks for your letter about the Yellowstone wolves. It is a confirmation of the way I sized up the situation. In short, I have been told firmly and plainly by people who would know that there has been no release of imported wolves in the park. I am certain they would not have misled me, and you are in the same position."[17]

Leopold suggested that somehow a small wolf population had survived in the mountains of Yellowstone, never coming down with the big game migrations, but staying in the high country, feeding off big game that remained in isolated pockets.[18]

YNP historian Paul Schullery noted that a dispute did exist between the Craigheads and Glen Cole, as well as with other park officials, over the Craigheads' grizzly bear studies in the park.[19] The Craigheads accused NPS of incompetence, poor-management, and flat-out illegally killing bears. NPS responded by accusing the Craigheads of being less than objective, inaccurate, and of trying to force their point of view on the agency. The Craigheads accused Cole of taking over parts of their studies, ignoring their data, and not believing the data that the Craigheads presented. It is conceivable that these ill feelings could have overflowed from the grizzly dispute to the dispute over the supposed secret wolf release, which occurred during the same period.

Contacted in 1991, Cole admitted that YNP was indeed occupied by wolves while he was there. He believed that there was "occasional evidence of pairs and pups" but, otherwise, there was no significant pack activity. Cole thought that reintroduction was appropriate because wolves had ample opportunity to make a "comeback" in the park, with poison bans, ample food, and vulnerable prey, but the population had not increased. He expressed the view that wolves were not fulfilling their ecological niche. Cole confirmed he saw wolves several times in the park while he worked as a research biologist.[20]

It is doubtful if the public will ever learn whether a secret release of wolves into Yellowstone occurred. It is evident that the reintroduction of wolves had been proposed in the late 1960s as a method to augment the existing population, so it is possible that the supposed release actually did take place. Whether it did or did not take place, and even though wolf sightings had persisted in the Yellowstone area prior to this time and after, the seed for reintroduction had been planted.

At the First Interagency Meeting for the Management of the Northern Rocky Mountain Wolf, held in YNP in 1971, FWS and NPS officials discussed wolf reintroduction.[21] At the meeting, Cole mentioned that he was concerned about the limited gene pool of Yellowstone's wolves, and wanted to strengthen it by bringing in more wolves. The overpopulation of elk in the park was a management problem, and FWS noted: "Now the park needs an unknown number of wolf packs to control these ungulates. Possibly 30 to 40 wolves in the northern Yellowstone area could be accommodated. Cole indicated that the park would accept live-trapped wolves even though they might disrupt some of the existing packs."

In 1970, wolf expert Durward Allen had written:

"I share the view of many others about transferring animals around here and there without regard for their taxonomic position. This has happened to the bison and many other species, even where there were professional people around to counsel against it . . .

"In the West, I think Yellowstone is one place where we could support a wolf population and a few animals are there already. Are they loners? Perhaps so. Maybe they came down from British Columbia or Alberta. Until we have evidence of a breeding pack in Yellowstone, I don't think the situation promises very much. If we do ever decide to put more wolves in Yellowstone, then they probably should be the nearest animals we can get, which would be those in British Columbia. We should make certain that these are the same race as the original stock in Yellowstone."[22]

Unfortunately, history would record that Allen's cautionary advice would not be followed.

Chapter 5

The 1970s and 1980s

Reports of wolves in YNP more than doubled once again from the 1960s to the 1970s (Figure 10; Table 8). Of the 336 reports on record for the 1970s, 269 were of single animals, forty-five were of pairs, eleven were of three animals, eight were of four animals, and three were of five animals. In the two-year period of 1970 and 1971, twenty-four reports of more than one animal were recorded. Two of the reports from 1970 refer to pups or juveniles.

Wolf researcher John Weaver also reviewed the YNP reports from 1968–1971. He wrote, "Based upon geographical distribution of the sightings and some pelage differences, up to 10 of these canids may have occupied separate areas in the Yellowstone region around 1970."[1]

In April, 1971, Glen Cole again explained the Yellowstone wolf situation. "Apparently the relatively few sightings that were officially reported between 1930 and 1967 led to some hesitancy in concluding that wolves were actually resident in the park. Observations by qualified persons were either buried in park files or not officially recorded."

Cole concluded that the 1969 and 1970 reports were due to one or two pairs of wolves producing young. "Considerations of coat color, group size, area, etc., indicate a minimum of 10 and possibly 15 different animals may be represented by the 1969 and 1970 observations. The subject wolf is probably *Canis lupus irremotus*. Its presence in Yellowstone can afford an opportunity to preserve this particular subspecies which is less numerous in the United States than *C. l. lycaon*, which is already classed as endangered."[2]

Well-known wolf biologist L. David Mech noted that rangers in Yellowstone had recorded the existence of a few wolves in the park, and said, "An immediate and concerted program is necessary. Logic dictates that the subspecies of wolves occurring in these areas, presumably

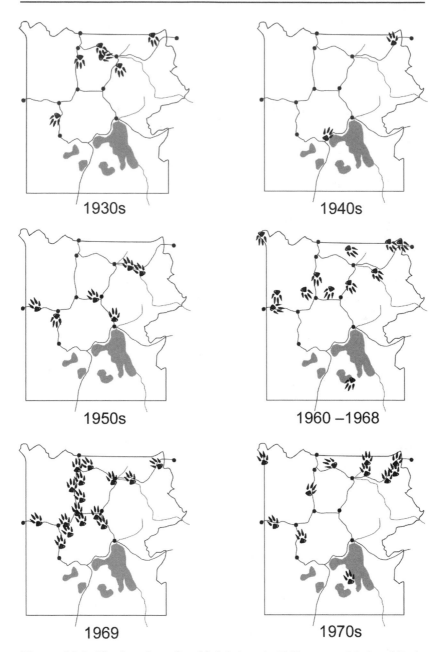

Figure 10 A. The location of wolf sightings in Yellowstone National Park: 1930s–1970s.

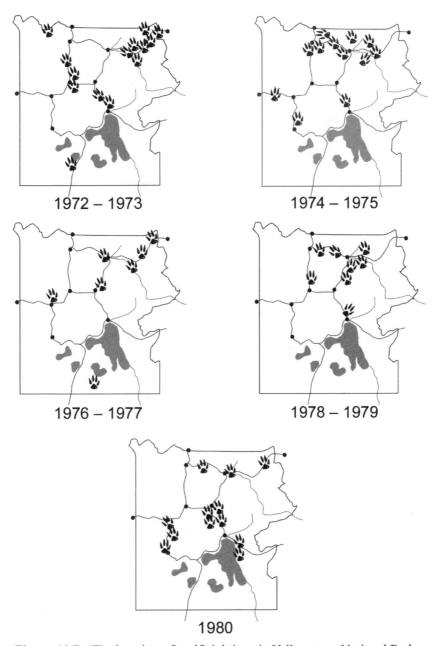

Figure 10 B. The location of wolf sightings in Yellowstone National Park: 1972–1980.

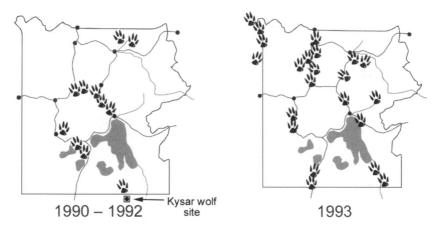

Figure 10 C. The location of wolf sightings in Yellowstone National Park: 1990–1993. Note the location of the site at which elk hunter Jerry Kysar shot and killed a wolf in 1992.

Canis lupus irremotus, formerly thought to be extinct there, should be declared an endangered animal, for there must be far fewer members of this race left than of the eastern timber wolf, which has been declared endangered."[3]

The 1971 reports indicated that the park harbored two or three resident packs, one in the Hayden Valley area and one or two in the Madison River area. During the next two years, the number of sightings of more than one wolf decreased slightly, with most of these reports consisting of pairs. Several sightings were recorded in the northeast section of the park, in the Lamar River-Slough Creek area. This is an area that has had consistent wolf activity throughout the history of the park. A Yellowstone ranger reported watching three dark-colored canids frolicking together in 1971, and in early 1972 a group of snow survival trainees watched four wolves as they traveled together in single file through the snow. Cole reported finding tracks of three wolves in 1974, a busy year in terms of reported wolf activity outside the park.

In August, 1974, a US Geological Survey (USGS) crew watched five wolves in an extremely remote area just southeast of the park

Table 8. Wolf Sightings in Yellowstone National Park, 1930s–1993

Year of Report	Total # of Reports	1	2	3	4	5	Multiple
1930s	13	7	3	1	2		
1940s	18	16	2				
1950s	31	25	2	3	1		
1960–1968	61	49	3	4	4	1	
1969	72	56	11	3	2		
1970	41	29	7	0	4	1	
1971	54	42	6	5	0	1	
1972 & 1973	82	68	12	1	1		
1974 & 1975	92	80	8	2	2		
1976 & 1977	27	20	4	2	0	1	
1978 & 1979	40	30	8	1	1		
1980s	88	76	8	4			
1990–1992	93	82	7	2	1	1	
1993	162	140	17	3	1	0	1

boundary in the Teton Wilderness, and J. C. Antweiler wrote a fascinating account of the experience.[4]

"As our helicopter topped the west shoulder of Overlook Mountain, about 9:15 A.M., and headed westward along the drainage divide between the Howell Fork of Mountain Creek and Open Creek, our pilot, Tom Rice, pointed to several animals. We thought at first they were bighorn sheep because we had seen bighorns near here previously, and the setting was typical: a small grassy area about a thousand feet above the treeline, and almost inaccessible from all directions — steep cliffs, rock-strewn slopes, narrow ridges.

"The animals were headed eastward when we first saw them, but as the helicopter approached the grassy area, which was the only landing possibility for a considerable distance, they reversed their direction and headed for the rocky cliffs. All three of us, Tom, my son

Ron, and I, excitedly realized we had encountered a small wolf pack. There were five we were sure of, but in an instant they had disappeared into the rocks."

After alighting from the helicopter, Ron and J. C. found tracks just large enough for Ron's fist to fit into, about 3 ¾ inches across. Continuing across the ridge, the Antweilers saw two of the animals about 500 feet below them. J. C. reported, "I was sure I saw an animal that I thought had long since vanished from this part of the country."

A week later, the geologists were back in the area, this time establishing a four-day base camp near Open Creek. Antweiler's report continues:

"Our party consisted of Greg Lee, John Antweiler, Ron Antweiler, and myself. After eating, we sat around our campfire talking for about an hour or two after dark. As the last flames of the campfire were replaced by smoking coals, Ron and I sought the comfort of the sleeping bags, and John and Greg said they would follow shortly. Ron and I had not yet had time to fall asleep when we were literally terrified by a low-pitched cry followed by a bark and a growl that seemed close enough to touch.

"I have seen and heard coyotes all my life in the Teton Wilderness and elsewhere but this was a different cry from any I have ever known. After exchanging gasps, all four of us decided to be very quiet. In a few minutes the cry was repeated and answered, and during the next several minutes was repeated over and over again. There were at least two animals and they were very interested in our meat sack. Cautiously, John and Greg got flashlights and crept towards the tree. The lights from a distance did not greatly deter the wolves. John and Greg were able to approach within less than a hundred feet and could see the eyes quite well as the wolves circled.

"As the boys crept closer, the animals trotted away at the edge of the timber, so John and Greg returned to the campfire. No longer sleepy, they built up the fire, and we thought the excitement was all over. I had possibly drifted into sleep, when we had a repeat performance that lasted fully an hour . . . The animals did not abandon their desires to get at the meat sack until perhaps 2:30 or 3:00 A.M."

Two months later, as Antweiler wrote about this incident, he stated, "I sincerely hope that public awareness of these animals will not lead to their destruction."

Also in 1974, a federal animal damage control agent reported that a wolf had killed three sheep on the LU Sheep Ranch near Worland, Wyoming. A year later, a wolf killed two more lambs on the same ranch. Wildlife officials confirmed that a wolf was in the area — agents saw it, heard its howls, and found its tracks.[5]

In the summer of 1974, Wes Vining of Northwest Community College in Powell, Wyoming, began an investigation of wolf presence in northwestern Wyoming outside of YNP in cooperation with several of the natural resource agencies in the area. He collected 323 canine scats, of which he believed fifty-nine could be classified as potentially wolf scat. While unwilling to conclude definitively that wolves were in the area, Vining noted that his study "strongly suggested the occurrence of two distinct species of canine co-existing on the Shoshone National Forest. One species was the coyote, *Canis latrans*, and the other being unidentified but somewhat larger."[6] Vining called for further investigation into the status of wolves in the area.

In 1978, Terry Lemke was hired by the Worland District of the Bureau of Land Management (BLM) to conduct a short-term study of wolves in the Owl Creek area by compiling information on twenty-nine reports of wolves that had been filed since 1970. Included were reports of observers seeing wolves, hearing their howls, and finding wolf tracks. Several of the reports were made by natural resource personnel working in the region. Lemke was as evasive as Vining about formally stating that wolves were present, saying instead that the reports "indicate there is a possibility of some large canid utilizing the study area."[7] Lemke recommended that further research be conducted on the status of wolves.

Federal wildlife control agents confirmed wolf presence just northwest of Yellowstone park in the Gravelly Range in both 1974 and 1975.[8] On October 14, 1974, a federal agent investigated a deer kill on Ruby Reservoir. The investigators found evidence that five or six animals with tracks measuring 4 ¼ to 4 ½ inches had chased a deer onto the mud flats and killed her. The agent reported that the evidence indicated these animals were wolves, and he had received other reports of wolves being in the area. Federal officials recommended that transect flights be made to survey for wolf presence.

On June 20, 1975, agents flew the area on a wolf survey. A number of fresh tracks were spotted from the air in fresh snow and, after landing and investigating, the tracks were tentatively identified as wolf. As the helicopter was lifting back into the air, a large gray wolf was spotted, and upon making a pass of the area for a closer look, a second large gray wolf was spotted near the first. The helicopter then landed again, and the tracks were inspected to confirm that the animals seen from the air had been wolves.

Due to the large number of tracks in the area, the ground survey was halted because the evidence indicated the presence of a wolf den — which wildlife officials did not want disturbed. Just three years prior to this event, and eight miles away, the manager of the Wall Creek Game Winter Range had reported that a pair of wolves were killing deer on the property. In 1971, a federal agent had heard wolf howls and took plaster casts of tracks of a pair of wolves near Black Butte, about eighteen miles from where the denning wolves were confirmed in 1975.

South of the park, on the Bridger-Teton National Forest, due to both reported sightings and personal experiences with wolves, forest supervisor Reid Jackson and forest wildlife biologist George Gruell concluded that a wolf population existed in the forest during the 1970s.

Gruell interviewed Don Larson, a WGF damage control warden, about an incident that took place in March, 1975, in the Gros Ventre area.[9] Larson explained that he and three other men had been snowmachining near Slate Creek when they observed two large canines at a distance of about one hundred yards. Gruell wrote:

"The snow was crusted hard, allowing ideal travel for snowmachines. Their primary purpose for being in the area was that of hunting coyotes, so they immediately made a run towards the animals. The terrain was gentle and covered by scattered aspen and conifers. According to Larson, coyotes would have little chance of escaping under existing circumstances. L. D. Hemert was in the lead and closed the distance to about 50 feet. His intention was to run down the animal, but when he saw its size he had second thoughts and veered away. This animal was the largest of the two and was gray in color.

"While Hemert was pursuing the gray animal, Larson, who was just behind, went after the smaller one which was very dark — darker and larger than any coyote Don had ever seen. This animal was approached within about 50 yards when its swiftness allowed it to escape into the trees. Don was particularly impressed with the speed of these animals. If it had not been for this speed the men would have killed them both. Upon reflecting over the incident later, the group was relieved that they had not destroyed what apparently were wolves.

"Agreement on identity was based on size of body, long legs, and size of tracks. Don said the tracks were the size of his hand. The animals had been hanging in the locality for some time as indicated by well-worn trails which had melted during earlier thaws. A group of elk had been wintering in the area and were apparently a primary food source."

Gruell voiced his opinion that this account was particularly significant in light of the fact that two years prior, while accompanied by a group of agency personnel, he himself had heard wolf howls in the same area. Gruell concluded, "Considering developments to date, it would appear that the lower Dalles Creek-Bear Paw Creek locality may be used for denning."

By the 1960s, public attitudes about the environment and environmental protection were changing. The nation began recognizing the need to conserve precious natural resources and the 1962 publication of Rachel Carson's *Silent Spring*, warning of toxic dangers, served as a wake-up call. Consequently, the 1960s and 1970s saw significant environmental protection laws enacted by the US Congress, including several that were designed to protect endangered species.

The Endangered Species Act (ESA), which became law in 1973, may be one of the most clear and comprehensive pieces of environmental legislation ever written. Congress declared that protection of endangered and threatened species was a national priority and that all agencies and departments of the US government were to take proactive steps by utilizing their authorities in protecting these species and the habitats on which they depended. In fact, the government was prohibited from undertaking activities that would harm these species.

Congress went further by defining a species to include "any subspecies of fish or wildlife or plants, or any distinct population segment of any species."[10] Thus, the listing of a species would apply to all subspecies as well.

In March, 1973, the Bureau of Sport Fisheries and Wildlife, which evolved into the present day FWS, published its *Threatened Wildlife of the United States*. The Northern Rocky Mountain Wolf, *Canis lupus irremotus*, was included in this publication, which noted that sighting reports indicated a scattered population of wolves existed in the Yellowstone region. "The best judgment is that they represent members of irremotus descended from those few individuals in that backcountry that escaped persecution in the thirties, forties, and fifties."[11] The significance of this detail is that it would be the basis for inclusion on the list of animals protected by the newly enacted ESA.

Consequently, on June 4, 1973, *Canis lupus irremotus* was added to the US list of endangered species.[12]

In June, 1977, FWS proposed to reclassify *Canis lupus irremotus* by delisting this subspecies and replacing it with the entire gray wolf species which would be listed as endangered in Mexico and the United States, excluding Minnesota, where wolves would be listed instead as threatened. "The Service wishes to recognize that the entire species *Canis lupus* is endangered or threatened to the south of Canada, and considers that this matter can be handled most conveniently by listing only the species name."[13]

According to the *Federal Register* notice, there was considerable concern among those reviewing the proposal that the listing of the full species would "jeopardize efforts to locate and maintain stocks of the various subspecies. The Service, however, can offer the firmest assurance that it will continue to recognize valid biological subspecies for the purposes of its research and conservation programs."

The proposed reclassification was finalized and enacted in 1978. The listing of *Canis lupus* included identification of the known distribution of the species, within which Idaho, Montana, and Wyoming were included.[14]

From 1974 through 1979, from two to eight sightings were recorded per year from people who reported seeing more than one wolf. The reports indicated that wolf activity remained in the northeast section of the park. In 1979, one report documented an adult wolf with pups, demonstrating that reproductive activity occurred in Yellowstone through the late 1970s.

In 1975, John Weaver was contracted by NPS to compile historic information on wolves in Yellowstone park and to determine their present status, which led to his often-quoted 1978 publication, *The Wolves of Yellowstone*, in which he provided a valuable record of historic wolf sightings in the park.

Weaver devised a point system for evaluating wolf reports, which he readily admitted was "subjective" and "designed to be conservative." While this point system was used by natural resource agencies for some time, the subjectiveness of the system led to its eventual dismissal. There is great danger of dismissing important data on rare species simply because of a lack of more detailed information, or because of the biases inherent in such a system or the evaluator.

In addition to his compilation of the historical record, Weaver's 1975 field work resulted in his discovery of two sets of large canine tracks and his hearing a series of howls that he was confident were made by a wolf. In his preliminary report, written in 1976, he stated: "I believe wolves inhabit two parts of the study area" and "Wolves have persisted in or near the park, mostly as singles or pairs, to the present . . . The Yellowstone wolf population has been 10 or less animals for the past 50 years . . . On September 20 at 1020 hours, one wolf howled three separate times in response to a recorded howl . . . Although no recording of these howls was made, I am confident the animal was a wolf. . . Based on this survey and other reported observations, I believe wolves inhabit two parts of the study area . . . Much more intensive research is needed, though, to determine numbers and productivity of wolves in these and perhaps other areas."[15]

Yet, in his final report, published in 1978, Weaver declined to even state the identity of the species or the genus, and referred instead to "some large canids in Yellowstone." And, where he had called for more research in the 1976 report, his final report called for wolf reintroduction.[16] Without any discussion of the reasons for the differences between his unpublished and published reports, questions arise about the basis for his final recommendations. Regarding management considerations, he wrote: "Two options are available for wolf management in Yellowstone National Park: [1] do nothing; or [2] attempt to restore a viable wolf population by introduction. The former alternative has been employed since 1927 when wolf control ceased in the park. Over the next 50 years, a viable population has not reestablished, and the wolf niche appears essentially vacant. Therefore, I recommend restoring this native predator by introducing wolves to Yellowstone." Weaver suggested using wolves from British Columbia or Alberta for this transplant.[17]

Weaver concluded that the reported wolf sightings "do not indicate a viable wolf population in the park."[18] This conclusion came as no surprise. By definition, there is no such thing as a viable population of any endangered species. Weaver's statement has since been misinterpreted to mean that no population existed in the park, a misleading and inaccurate interpretation.

John D. Varley, Yellowstone's chief of research, stated it best. "You'll note that we're very careful. When we talk about the absence of wolves in Yellowstone, we talk about the absence of a viable population. That's different from saying there's none here."[19]

Data collected after Weaver's report continued to demonstrate that a wolf population persisted in the park. In 1976, members of the Yellowstone grizzly bear research team reported seeing a dark wolf and finding wolf tracks. In 1977, a National Outdoor Leadership School winter expedition reported seeing a pair of wolves in the southeastern part of the park. One report in 1979 described an adult wolf with pups, indicating that reproduction was occurring as the decade ended.

But the push for reintroduction was underway. The wolves in the park were not fulfilling their expected ecological role. The elk population was booming, the park was being overgrazed, and NPS was being criticized by the public and non-governmental scientists. Something had to be done to control the elk population. Hunting inside the park was out of the question, and the firing line of hunters lined up just outside the park's northern border, shooting elk as they left the safety of the park boundary, had been halted by public outrage. The elk were destroying the park and some kind of control was needed. Reintroducing packs of wolves appeared to be the most acceptable solution.

The 1980s saw a decrease in reported wolf sightings in Yellowstone. Only eighty-eight sightings were recorded for the entire decade; seventy-six of the reports were of single animals and twelve were of packs ranging from two to five animals — four were of three animals, seven were of pairs, and one was of "two to four" animals. The reports indicate that in the mid-1980s one or two pairs of wolves were producing young in the north-central and northeastern sections of the park. An additional pair inhabited the Firehole area in the late 1980s. NPS judged one report of an elk calf being killed by two to four wolves in 1986 as probable.

Wolf researcher Dennis Flath suggested that the decrease in the number of wolf sighting reports in the park corresponded to an increase in reports of sightings on the nearby Beaverhead-Madison area outside the park. He suggested that the Beaverhead animals might have originated in Yellowstone.[20]

Another explanation for the decrease was that park officials had begun to behave like "Doubting Thomases," refusing to believe that people were actually seeing and hearing wolves, saying that these sightings were cases of mistaken identity. A double standard applied. When people reported wolf sightings in Montana, they were believed because the federal wildlife officials acknowledged that wolves existed in that state. Prior to the release of Canadian wolves into Yellowstone, if the public reported seeing wolves in Wyoming, they were accused of seeing coyotes and not knowing the difference.

However, when agency personnel and members of the public heard deep wolf-like howls, found large canid tracks at least four inches long, had livestock and big game killed by the large canids that left those tracks, found large canid scat, and saw eighty- to one-hundred-pound canids, there was a logical explanation for these collective experiences — wolves were in the area, a few cases of mistaken identity notwithstanding.

In 1981, Gary L. Day prepared a paper on the status and distribution of wolves in Montana as part of his graduate program in wildlife biology at the University of Montana.[21] Day reviewed 372 reports of wolves, the majority (261 of 279) of which referred to sightings made between 1967 and 1977. Day grouped the reports according to their location along a north-south axis and demonstrated that the observations were clustered in the north and south of his study area, with the middle section showing few if any sightings. The northernmost group centered around Bob-Marshall-Scapegoat Wilderness area, Glacier National Park, and Kootenai National Forest. The southern group included sightings in Beaverhead National Forest, part of Gallatin National Forest, and — extending into Idaho — Salmon and Targhee national forests. A ninety-mile strip that separated the main northern and southern clusters yielded only five reports of sightings, and no reported sightings were known from over thirty-miles of that strip. The gap separating the two clusters was not unexpected and was easily explained — poisoning was widespread in areas outside of Yellowstone and would have effectively hindered any wolf migration south from the Canada-US border region to the area near Yellowstone.

Day concluded, based on the eleven wolf reports recorded from 1974–1977 in the Gravelly Range area just west of the park, "Evidence seems very good that a pair of wolves use portions of this area, and that pups have been produced." Day further stated that "longtime residents in the Beaverhead area report that wolves have been present since early days, but were greatly reduced from 1910 to 1960." Citing a personal communication with C. Jonkel, Day also noted "a recent case of a small population of brown bears . . .

going unnoticed in Norway for about 100 years illustrates how easily a remnant population of elusive animals in rugged country can be overlooked."

Montana's Beaverhead National Forest had 118 wolf sighting reports from the early 1960s to 1992.[22] Of special interest are the reports of sightings that occurred east of Interstate 15, which includes the Madison and Sheridan districts of the Beaverhead. Of the thirty-eight reports recorded for these districts, four — two of two animals, one of four, and one of eight — were recorded in the 1960s. From 1970 to 1975, twenty-seven reports were recorded, with twelve reporting either one animal or no given number of animals and fifteen reporting two to ten animals. From 1981 to 1991, seven reports were recorded, with five of these either describing one animal or giving no number of animals. Two reports of three wolves were recorded in the Sheridan District during this same 1981 to 1991 time period.

Several reports from Beaverhead National Forest demonstrate that reproduction was taking place in populations located just north and west of Yellowstone. According to the unpublished reports found in the files of the Beaverhead National Forest, in 1974, a "pair of wolves raised five pups near Sam Grover's Ranch, 12 miles north of Spencer, Idaho. Seen again in spring of 1975. Bob Bridle, US Forest Service, looked at den." In the Madison District, in May, 1974, "Bill Baker, retired fish hatchery manager, found a den and saw two adults and three pups." In September, 1975, again in the Madison District, "Bob Storey saw a litter of wolves — one adult and three pups." A month later, in October, 1975, in the Sheridan District, it was reported that "Harry Allen saw a pair of wolves and four pups."

Day also detailed wolf occurrences reported near the Idaho-Montana border area west of Yellowstone. He recorded thirty-five reports dating from 1974 to 1977 in the area from Lemhi Pass south down the divide to Monida. He estimated that four to six wolves inhabited the area at the time of the reports.

Day recorded eleven reports dating from 1974 to 1977 in the Big Hole-Pioneer region. While most of these reports were of single animals, there were two reports of pairs.

From the Dillon District of the Beaverhead, a pair was reported during the 1960s, and of the twenty-five reports dating from 1970 to 1975, eleven ranged from two to eleven animals. Of the thirty-eight reports recorded for the period of 1981 to 1991, twelve were of two to five animals. In fact, in 1981, a USFS employee confirmed the presence of wolves in the Wild Cat Creek area.

Day concluded his study by stating that the management options available included increasing the wolf numbers by "transplanting, or, assuming a small resident population of wolves occurs in the Northern Rocky Mountains, by nurturing that population until it increases on its own." A study concluded a year later also suggested that more research was needed to determine the status of wolves in Yellowstone and adjacent areas of Idaho and Montana, but that reintroduction of wolves from elsewhere may be the only sure way to achieve wolf recovery in the region.[23]

A wolf recovery team meeting that convened at the University of Montana in March, 1986, began with one of Idaho Senator James McClure's staff members telling the group that the senator "did not object to reintroduction of wolves to Yellowstone National Park."[24] Yellowstone's John Varley then told the group about a possible kill of an elk calf by a wolf or wolves in the park the week prior to the meeting.

According to the notes of the meeting taken by Bart O'Gara: "John Weaver said that the chances of wolves recolonizing the park seemed remote even if one or two were there . . . Bart O'Gara questioned whether a few wolf sightings in the park would negate classifying the population as experimental if an introduction was made. Wayne Brewster (FWS) said sightings should not negate experimental classification because a viable population is not present.

"Dale Harms (FWS) related that none of the wolf reports in the Yellowstone Ecosystem during recent years had been confirmed. Timm Kaminski reported that dispersers, the wolves commonly involved in occasional reports, were usually young males and the chance of reproduction occurring was slight."

Kaminski would spend his career pushing the reintroduction program, serving as a biologist for USFS and the Nez Perce Tribe.

In 1986, Yellowstone's Mary Meagher wrote a "Summary of Possible Wolf Observations 1977–1986" in which she evaluated the reports received during that period, listing only nine occurrences as "possible."[25] Meagher concluded that if the animals reported actually were wolves, they were to be considered transients, even though a glance at the maps of wolf reports of previous years demonstrated that the reports of more than a single wolf recorded in the 1980s correlated with areas of the park where wolf activity had been documented for over fifty years.

Yet the reports of sightings outside the park during the 1980s were much more compelling (Figure 11). Reports of wolves on the southern Bridger-Teton National Forest had centered on one area for ten years, searches were being conducted, and agencies had received reports of up to four wolves having been killed in the area. In 1986, Bridger-Teton wildlife biologist Al Boss reported, "In total, the reports closely resemble sightings recorded in other regions of the West, where small, scattered populations of wolves are known to exist."[26]

The Green River Lakes area above Pinedale, Wyoming, generated wolf reports dating from 1977 through 1986. These reports were made primarily by local ranchers, outfitters, and WGF employees, and described the same group of animals being seen over a period of several years. The reports reinforced each other.[27]

A *Casper Star-Tribune* editorial written by Tom Bishop noted:

"Biologists have known for years that the wolf is migrating southward through the Rocky Mountain chain into the United States from Canada. The wolf is in Wyoming. For that matter, the wolf is reaching the southern end of the Wind River Range. The reason we don't hear much of this is because there aren't very many of them, and the wildlife population is abundant enough to sustain the present wolf population without their becoming a menace to livestock, or, for that matter, even being seen too often.

"As long as the migration of the wolf is natural, wildlife officials will be able to successfully manage the wolf," Bishop stated. But he also said that if wolves were reintroduced into the park, the

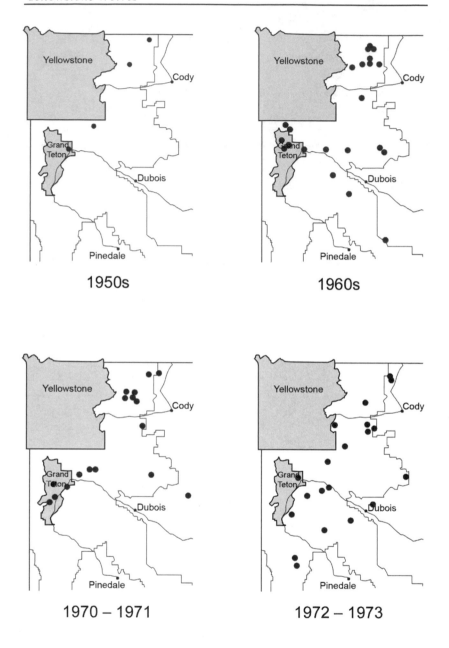

Figure 11 A. The location of reported wolf sightings in northwestern Wyoming: 1950s–1973.

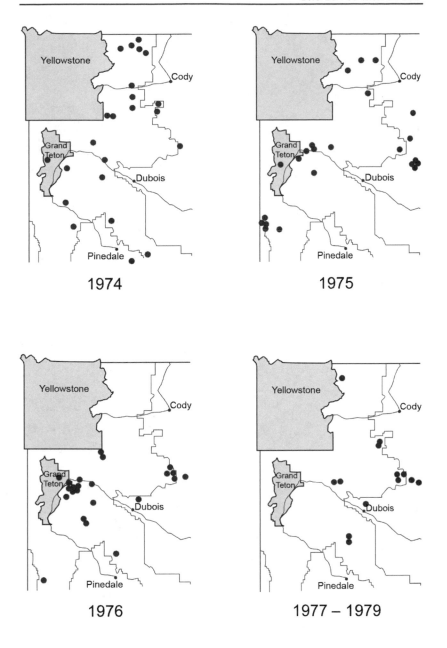

Figure 11 B. The location of reported wolf sightings in northwestern Wyoming: 1974–1979.

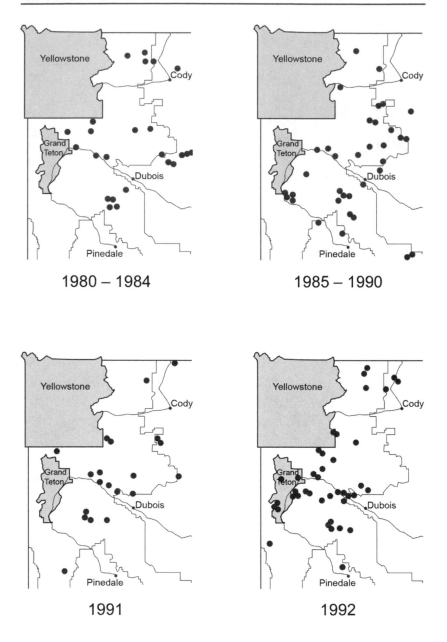

1980 – 1984

1985 – 1990

1991

1992

Figure 11 C. The location of reported wolf sightings in northwestern Wyoming: 1980–1992.

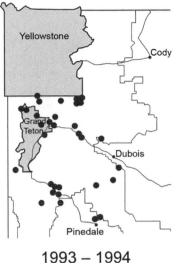

1993 – 1994

Figure 11 D. The location of reported wolf sightings in northwestern Wyoming: 1993–1994.

population level would get very high, and suggested instead to "let them come on their own."[28]

A *Jackson Hole Guide* editorial by Robert Steller endorsed the wolf reintroduction. "Proof of that is that we have had wolves in Wyoming since at least as far back as 1975, in more modern times, and they live and hunt here and now and they have not been bringing rack and ruin on our stockmen."[29]

In 1988, a male wolf was struck and killed by a vehicle just thirty miles north of Yellowstone.[30] FWS suggested that the animal was an escaped captive belonging to Jack Lynch, who lived in the area, but Lynch denied the allegation.[31] Montana statute requires that wolves kept in captivity be tattooed for identification, and this "Chico Wolf" had no such marks. FWS wolf taxonomy expert Ronald Nowak examined the skull of this male wolf and stated that it was "notably smaller" than those taken in recent years in the northwestern US, which were presumably Canadian immigrants.[32] Nowak proposed that the Chico wolf "looks more like a member of this original US population.

Its measurements fall mostly within the range shown by the subspecies *C. l. irremotus* of the northern Rockies."

Although it appeared that a specimen of Wyoming's native wolf had just been killed outside the park, the momentum to proceed with wolf reintroduction continued to build.

Chapter 6

Setting the Stage

After passage of the ESA and the resulting federal listing of wolves in 1980, an interagency team of biologists crafted the Northern Rocky Mountain Wolf Recovery Plan (WRP). The plan's purpose was to provide a roadmap to wolf recovery — to direct agency efforts toward facilitating the recovery of wolf populations so that federal protections would no longer be needed. Recovery would focus on three areas: Yellowstone, central Idaho, and northwestern Montana (Figure 12).

In 1987, FWS approved revisions to the WRP that called for the reintroduction of experimental populations of wolves into YNP and, possibly, central Idaho. The plan stated: "Despite the biases and limitations, wolf observations were consistently made in certain areas by well-qualified individuals. Some areas produced reports that corresponded in terms of color and number of animals involved. Such reports cannot be used to determine the actual numbers of wolves in the Northern Rockies but, if used carefully, they can indicate areas where wolves occur."[1] The plan outlined work to be conducted, with the first task being to determine the status of wolves in the northern Rockies and then, once the status of wolves in the survey area was determined, provided for the reintroduction of wolves. Nothing was stated about how the results of the monitoring efforts would affect subsequent aspects of the recovery plan. Interestingly, the monitoring effort to determine the pre-recovery status of wolves in the defined area was, itself, never completed.

In 1982, Congress amended the ESA to include a new subsection that would soon become the focal point of wolf recovery plans — the experimental population designation. This amendment allows the Secretary of the Interior to authorize the release of endangered or

Figure 12. Three wolf recovery areas that were identified in the Northern Rocky Mountain Wolf Recovery Plan consisted of northwestern Montana, central Idaho, and Yellowstone National Park. Wolves were present in northwestern Montana when this plan was devised, and populations from Canada were released in central Idaho and Yellowstone National Park in 1995. (After US Department of the Interior, Fish and Wildlife Service, 1994)

threatened species, with additional management flexibility, and species could be reintroduced into areas of their former range. However, Congress included a prohibition — that the experimental population could be designated as such "only when, and at such times as, the population is wholly separate geographically from nonexperimental populations of the same species."[2] Congress intentionally limited the use of this designation in order to protect natural populations of a species.[3] As the experimental population designation would become the cornerstone of wolf recovery efforts in Yellowstone, the "wholly separate geographically" limitation would become the key to challenging the reintroduction.

The legality of using the experimental population designation for Yellowstone wolves was discussed as early as March, 1986, as the recovery team met to prepare the revisions to the wolf recovery plan. The revised recovery plan defined a viable population as "a self-supporting population of wolves with sufficient numbers to ensure the species will not become threatened, endangered, or extinct,"[4] even though, by definition, there could be no viable population of an endangered species.

FWS Director Frank Dunkle had stalled approval of the recovery plan for over a year, so it was not formally adopted by the agency until 1987.[5] Dunkle had suggested that wolves would eventually recolonize Yellowstone on their own, or: "We could hurry it up with introductions. It would be more detrimental to the wolf if there is opposition to reintroduction."[6]

Dunkle, wearing a wolf-adorned necktie, told a Wyoming Wool Growers Association audience that NPS wanted to reintroduce wolves into Yellowstone to "undue the disastrous condition" of the park that was occurring as a result of overgrazing by herds of big-game animals, including the park's burgeoning elk and bison populations.[7] He reportedly told the group, "The only wolves that I will bring to Wyoming, or that I will sponsor to Wyoming . . . are on this tie."

Dunkle and NPS Director William Penn Mott, Jr., a champion of the reintroduction scheme, clashed heavily over the issue and the debate was widely publicized in the press.[8] Dunkle had the support of then-Secretary of the Interior Donald Hodel, who also opposed reintroduction.[9]

In an attempt to force the issue, Utah Representative Wayne Owens, a Democrat, sponsored legislation in Congress that would have directed NPS to restore wolves in Yellowstone within three years. Congress refused to enact the legislation.

Instead, in 1988, Congress directed FWS and NPS to cooperatively investigate and report on certain issues involving wolf reintroduction into Yellowstone, and appropriated $200,000 for the effort.[10]

Representative Owens again attempted to accelerate wolf recovery by introducing legislation mandating that an environmental impact statement (EIS) be prepared to analyze wolf reintroduction. Idaho's US Senator James McClure proposed legislation which would place three mated pairs of wolves within both the Yellowstone and central Idaho areas, but would delist wolves found outside of the core areas and allow them to be managed by the states. Congress rejected both the Owens and McClure proposals, but appropriated another $175,000 to continue investigations into the effects of a reintroduction.[11]

In announcing his support for a wolf reintroduction into Yellowstone, McClure said wolves could solve some big game management issues. "From my perspective, we have a problem with too many elk in Yellowstone," he said. "It's an unnatural condition."[12]

Control of the elk population by reintroduced wolves was a motive expressed by others. *Salt Lake Tribune* columnist Tom Wharton interviewed Yellowstone's research interpreter Norm Bishop and then wrote, "Bishop feels strongly that the wolf is needed to put a cap on those wildlife populations, which are rapidly growing due to fire control, lack of hunting and recent mild winters.[13]

In testifying before the congressional committee that was considering McClure's bill, Defenders of Wildlife (DW) Northern Rockies representative Hank Fischer said: "We want to emphasize, however, that Yellowstone is the only place in the Northern Rockies where reintroduction or an experimental population designation is necessary at this time. There is no reason for special action in either of the other two recovery areas in the Northern Rockies at this time. Natural recolonization is occurring in northwestern Montana, and wolf populations have been slowly increasing. For the time being, natural recolonization also seems advisable for central Idaho as well."[14]

Wyoming's US Senator Malcolm Wallop also testified at that hearing, stating: "I remain opposed to the reintroduction of wolves, and as a rancher, don't want these animals in my state. However, I also know that wolves could arrive in Yellowstone by natural migration. If that premise is inevitable, I would prefer to have the opportunity to manage these predators on terms and conditions that the residents of my state can live with — and not be shackled by the onerous provisions of the Endangered Species Act."[15]

Idaho Farm Bureau president Thomas Geary testified in opposition to the bill, noting that it would not reintroduce native wolves, but would instead introduce an entirely different type of wolf into the region.[16] "It is contrary to the Endangered Species Act to recover species in areas which are not their historic habitat," Geary testified. "It is also contrary to the management policies of the National Park Service which provide for the restoration of only native species."

Wyoming's US Representative Craig Thomas testified, "I have been and continue to be strongly opposed to wolf introduction, for a number of reasons."[17]

Wyoming's US Senator Alan Simpson testified: "Some wolf reintroduction proponents believe that the answer to this problem and many others is simply to classify the wolf as an experimental population. However, I am skeptical that this classification will result in the type of management flexibility that is needed to manage a large predator. So long as the wolf is listed under the Endangered Species Act, I do not believe that the federal and state land managers will be able to manage wolves properly."[18]

Although Simpson ran through a list of concerns in his testimony, he also stated: "I believe the McClure Bill represents a starting point for discussions which may some day lead to wolf reintroduction in a manner which will not decimate wildlife populations, restrict public access to public lands, cause excessive livestock predation, or disrupt local economies."

Meanwhile, the US Department of the Interior (USDI) saw some changes under the new George H. W. Bush administration, including the appointment of Manuel Lujan, Jr., as Secretary of the Interior and John Turner as Director of FWS. A former Wyoming legislator and operator of a guest ranch in Grand Teton National Park, Turner was a well-known Republican politico in Wyoming. In 1989, less than three months after being sworn in as director, Turner voiced his knowledge of wolf presence in the Yellowstone region and his view of the situation. He stated: "Although there is evidence of stray wolves wandering through Yellowstone in recent years, and even some suggestion that wolves were released in the park over the last few decades, there is no viable wolf population in the park at present. The sudden appearance of wolves in the park, by whatever route, before a decision is made on how to deal with them would not be in the best interest of any of the groups involved in the reintroduction debate."[19]

Turner served as FWS director from 1989 to 1993, then as president of The Conservation Fund before being appointed the Assistant Secretary of State for Oceans and International Environmental and Scientific Affairs. He finally returned to Wyoming in 2005.

In 1990, Interior Secretary Lujan questioned the need to save every endangered species. Lujan was quoted as asking: "Do we have to save every subspecies? The red squirrel is the best example. Nobody's told me the difference between a red squirrel, a black one or a brown one."[20] This was an unnerving statement from the man who was charged with implementing and enforcing the provisions of the ESA.

In October, 1990, Congress directed the Secretary of the Interior to form a Wolf Management Committee made up of government, agricultural, and environmental officials and charge them with the preparation of a wolf reintroduction and management plan for YNP and central Idaho. FWS Director Turner was credited with the idea to create the committee[21] which, once formed, included George Bennett of the Gem State Hunter's Association; Galen Buterbaugh of FWS; Jerry Conley of the Idaho Department of Fish and Game; K. L. Cool of the Montana Department of Fish, Wildlife and Parks; Tom

Dougherty of the National Wildlife Federation (NWF); Hank Fischer of DW; Jim Magagna of the American Sheep Industry Association; Lorraine Mintzmyer of NPS; John Mumma of USFS; and Francis Petera of WGF.

Although committee members questioned the legality of using the experimental population classification, and even had legal counsel advise them on the issue, they did eventually recommend the reintroduction of an experimental population.[22]

Magagna, one member of the committee, would later go on to serve as the director of Wyoming's State Lands Office and then as the chief executive of the Wyoming Stock Growers Association. Apparently his support of the wolf reintroduction program recommended by the committee did not hurt his future political aspirations, although he was strongly defeated in a run for statewide political office.

When Petera reported on the committee's activities in March to his state wildlife commission, he warned commission members that "more and more" reports of wolves in Wyoming were being recorded. He said: "We can sit here and wait and the wolves will come into the state naturally, or we can go along with the introduction now and manage them much as we do the elk if they go out of the park. I'd rather do it on our terms. I feel sure it's only a matter of time until the wolf is here."[23]

At its second meeting, held in February, 1991, in Cheyenne, Wyoming, the wolf committee had broached the legality of using the experimental population designation. Margot Zallen of USDI's Solicitor's Office in Denver explained the experimental population provision. The minutes of the meeting stated: "There cannot be an experimental population where there is already a population. There needs to be a geographic separation (but the spacing needed is not defined) . . . Biologists will have to determine what constitutes a 'population.'"[24]

Later in the meeting, the minutes reflected that: "The committee needs to determine if boundaries of an experimental population can be drawn to include Idaho, because wolves already may be in Idaho. The committee needs to have a definition of population. There is no evidence of reproduction or of the population being able to sustain itself, but there is very little data."

At the committee's next meeting, legal questions about using the experimental population designation were front and center once again.[25] Committee member George Bennett "observed that Ms. Zallen's dialogue raised the specter of litigation. Hank Fischer (of Defenders of Wildlife) offered that, to add certainty, the committee could suggest in the plan that the experimental population could be terminated if a successful legal challenge changed what all parties had agreed to." The minutes noted that Zallen agreed with Fischer.

Magagna played a key role in the Wolf Management Committee's final recommendation, according to Tom Dougherty of NWF.[26] But when the committee worked itself into a deadlock, John Turner stepped in to author a proposal that the majority of the committee would support.[27]

In May, 1991, after five months of deliberations, the Wolf Management Committee sent its recommendations to Congress. Those recommendations were adopted on an eight-to-two vote, with Hank Fischer and Tom Dougherty voting against the final recommendation and calling the terms of the wolf restoration "unacceptable." The plan would compromise the ESA, allow livestock producers to kill wolves at a level that would hamper recovery, and confine the outcome of the public participation process, according to DW.[28]

Defenders was concerned about compromising the ESA? The organization wrote: "The experimental population provision of the ESA does allow for relaxation of the law. But experimental populations can only be established where populations of the species are not present and the regulations for management of experimental populations must lead to recovery.

"There's no question that the committee's proposed experimental population boundaries intrude significantly on existing wolf populations. The committee's recommendation calls for management of the entire states of Wyoming, Idaho and Montana (with the exception of a small area around Glacier National Park) as an experimental population. To the extent that the FWS estimates that 40–50 wolves are present in northwestern Montana, and perhaps 10–20 in central Idaho, the committee's recommendation is clearly placing an experimental population designation on top of areas where wolves are already known to exist.

"This establishes a dangerous precedent," Defenders stated, adding that it was equally concerned about allowing livestock producers to kill wolves. "Such lenient taking restrictions could not only compromise a Yellowstone reintroduction, but they could also significantly harm ongoing natural recovery of wolves in northwestern Montana and central Idaho."

FWS Regional Director Galen Buterbaugh emphasized the management flexibility offered by the experimental provision, stating, "The basic point is, wolves are coming. Do you want to get out ahead of it?"[29] The Wolf Management Committee's controversial proposal would have made all of Idaho, Montana, and Wyoming into an experimental population area. FWS Director Turner reported that he and his staff authored the plan that was adopted by the committee.[30] Congress refused to act on the wolf committee's plan; it never came out of congressional committee. Turner was reportedly upset about the quagmire the proposal was in, and was quoted as saying: "We held hearings out here, and a majority of the people opposed the plan, which is their right. But it's certainly taking a risk because if wolves come (to Yellowstone) through any other mechanism, and I'm sure they will, they'll be under the full protection of the Endangered Species Act."[31]

Instead of approving the plan, Congress allocated money for an EIS to be prepared.

The Wolf Fund, a Jackson-area environmental group focused entirely on achieving wolf reintroduction, was led by executive director Renee Askins. Serving on the fund's board were wolf biologists L. David Mech and John Weaver, among others.

Turner and Weaver were good friends from long before. Weaver was researching coyotes back in the days when Turner was researching eagles. Turner even made a plaster cast of a large canid track and gave it to Weaver during this time period.[32] Weaver had recommended wolf reintroduction for Yellowstone in 1978.

The Wolf Fund newsletter gushed with support for Turner in its Winter–Spring 1991 issue. The newsletter noted that the Bush administration was willing to consider wolf reintroduction and Turner had already succeeded in getting Wyoming senators Malcolm Wallop and Alan Simpson to agree to discuss Turner's wolf recovery proposal.

"Turner is already under attack for his endorsement of wolf reintroduction," the Wolf Fund noted. "The Wyoming Farm Bureau is calling for his resignation from the Fish and Wildlife Service; local headlines claim he has gambled his political future on the wolf proposal, and letters to the editor demand that he never return to Wyoming. We need to give him support and urge him to continue to move forward."

The Wolf Fund noted in the same issue that Turner "is in a unique position to make Yellowstone wolf reintroduction a reality."

"On Sept. 19, 1990, in front of a congressional subcommittee on public lands, national parks and forests, Mr. Turner came forth with a strong position advocating wolf recovery. In a rather poignant personal statement he said, 'One of the things I'd like to hear before I die is the howl of a wild wolf in my home state . . . I'd also like to be able to return to my home state.'"

According to the Wolf Fund, "He is under tremendous pressure to back down and yet is committed to seeing wolves restored, for both personal and ecological reasons."

Tired of waiting for something to happen, DW filed a notice of intent to sue FWS for failing to institute a wolf recovery program in the northern Rockies.[33] The case was filed in federal court in Washington, DC. Defenders attempted to use the court system to force wolf reintroduction, but the court ruled that FWS should have the opportunity to move forward with its EIS without judicial intervention.

Defenders decided it would push for reintroduction in Yellowstone, but called for extensive survey efforts in central Idaho "to determine if wolves are present." If a wolf population was found, Defenders would urge that the animals be managed as an endangered population. If no wolves were found, reintroduction would be appropriate, Defenders claimed.[34]

Others were buying Turner's line. Wyoming Game and Fish Commissioner Dave Steger of Riverton wrote an editorial stating that in order to avoid problems with federal control of wildlife, "the State of Wyoming Game and Fish Commission is attempting to minimize the possible impact of the wolf on Wyoming by having him introduced as a nonessential experimental animal into the Yellowstone ecosystem."[35]

Director Turner voiced his agenda for wolf recovery early in 1991 in an editorial in Wyoming's only statewide newspaper, the *Casper Star-Tribune*:[36]

"Irrespective of our individual opinions, what must be realized especially by wolf opponents — is that there is a growing probability that wolves will return to the Yellowstone region without regard for the strong positions held by many in our state. The facts of the situation indicate that wolf recolonization may just be a matter of time . . . Whatever the time span, wolves are headed our direction.

"The most likely scenario is natural dispersion since it is an inescapable fact that wolves occur in increasing numbers and distribution in the Northern Rocky Mountain area."

Turner went on to explain that wolves recolonizing Wyoming would be given full protection under the ESA, and that "clearly, management flexibility would be extremely limited." Turner then described "a way to gain more flexibility" by using the experimental, nonessential designation. Turner explained the benefits, and the consequences of not using this designation.

"If, on the other hand, we sit back and wait for wolves to recolonize the Yellowstone area on their own, the opportunity to design locally responsible and flexible management strategies will be lost. Once they reach the area on their own, the experimental population option is foregone since the Endangered Species Act stipulates that an experimental population must be 'wholly separate geographically' from non-experimental populations of the same species.

"It is time to allow the reality of the situation to come into focus. Biological evidence and political realities have combined to suggest that wolves are headed our way. Two courses of action are open.

"The first is to let nature take its course and either hope the critters do not make it to Wyoming, or (depending on your perspective) pray they will. If we adopt this stance, we leave our fate to be swept along by outside forces . . .

"In my judgment, the wiser course of action is to take control while it is still available to us and reintroduce the wolf as an experimental and nonessential population in a carefully structured management program."

The total number of wolf reports recorded in YNP in the 1980s was lower than the total reports recorded in the 1960s and 1970s combined. This could have been a reflection of a population trend, but a more likely explanation is that an active monitoring and reporting system was not in place in the 1980s, and that, in fact, wolf reports were discouraged during the 1980s and early 1990s. Members of the public reporting wolf occurrence in the park were met with skepticism and many observations went unrecorded.

Chapter 7

Controlling the Message

Wolf reports increased sharply in the early 1990s. During the five-year period 1990–1994, the total number of wolf reports surpassed the figure for any decade in the history of YNP. Few sightings were recorded in 1990 (nine reports, each of one wolf) but they more than doubled in 1991 (twenty-four reports, twenty-three of one wolf each and one of three animals).

The increasing number of reports was parallel with, and perhaps a result of, a renewed interest in recording wolf sightings by NPS. YNP's Lake District Resource Management Coordinator Dan Reinhart reviewed several recent possible wolf sightings near Yellowstone Lake in early 1992 and relayed that information to Wayne G. Brewster of Yellowstone's research office. After summarizing the information he had on the matter, Reinhart wrote: "I hope this information is useful to you. You were right in that we should no longer discount reported wolf sightings as coyotes and must check them out when we can."[1] Reinhart offered to investigate any such sightings that might occur within his district so that he could "check out reports for tracks, scat or other sign for species confirmation."

But that was not the message Yellowstone's Research Interpreter Norman Bishop registered in a March, 1992, letter. He wrote: "The message inherent in the [Reinhart] memorandum is that although we continue to get reports from visitors who believe they may have seen a wolf, resource managers parkwide who are monitoring animal activity continually are seeing lots of coyotes, and haven't seen other large canids or signs of them."[2]

Of the thirty-three sightings of wolves recorded for YNP in 1990 and 1991, all but one of the reports had been of single animals. Most of these reports include accounts of observers seeing single large gray canines in various parts of the park. Several reports describe tracks that were observed, with one describing tracks 4 ¾ inches in length, and 4 inches in width, well within the size range of a wolf's track. One report from 1991 details three wolves in Hayden Valley. One of the three animals was described as being light gray in color, while its two companions were reported to be dark gray to black in color. The observer had worked as a federal wildlife agent in Alaska in the 1940s and was familiar with wolves.

In August, 1991, DW filed a lawsuit in federal district court in Washington, DC, in an attempt to force USDI to follow the wolf recovery plan and reintroduce wolves to YNP.

~

For a period of twenty-two months, from September 1989 to July 1991, my husband Jim, I, and others who shared our perspective on the issue had been trying to convince FWS to take action to conserve Wyoming's small surviving population of native wolves, *Canis lupus irremotus*. To accomplish this, we had dug through agency files, compiled all the reported wolf sightings, mapped the reports, and documented other stories about wolf encounters that were not in agency files. We filed Freedom of Information Act (FOIA) requests with various natural resource agencies to get all of their information, wrote articles about Wyoming's native wolf, did radio and newspaper interviews, and called and wrote letters to FWS on numerous occasions to try to get some action (Figure 13).

By July, 1991, our efforts to get FWS to act on preserving the local populations of *irremotus* having failed and, in the face of mounting pressure to proceed with the introduction of Canadian wolves, Jim and I filed a notice of intent to sue FWS. The agency responded with a letter signed by FWS Deputy Regional Director John Spinks, Jr.[3], which noted:

"Our long-term strategy is to promote reintroduction to Yellowstone while encouraging natural recolonization in the northwestern Montana and central Idaho recovery areas that were identified in the recovery plan.

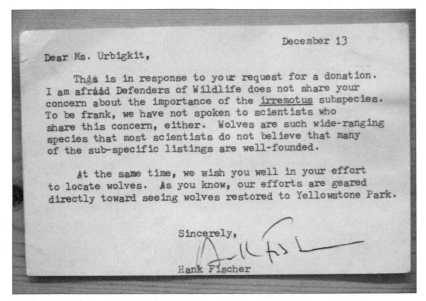

December 13

Dear Ms. Urbigkit,

Thįs is in response to your request for a donation.
I am afràįd Defenders of Wildlife does not share your
concern about the importance of the <u>irremotus</u> subspecies.
To be frank, we have not spoken to scientists who
share this concern, either. Wolves are such wide-ranging
species that most scientists do not believe that many
of the sub-specific listings are well-founded.

At the same time, we wish you well in your effort
to locate wolves. As you know, our efforts are geared
directly toward seeing wolves restored to Yellowstone Park.

Sincerely,

Hank Fischer

Figure 13. Defenders of Wildlife sent this postcard to the author in response to her request for assistance in documenting the occurrence of native wolves in Wyoming in 1988.

"In reality, the probability of natural recovery in Yellowstone is increasing as wolves naturally colonize from the northwest. Nonetheless, natural recovery probably is at least a few years away and, therefore, reintroduction is still a potential method of ensuring that a viable wolf population once again occurs within the area . . .

"The question of whether a remnant population of *Canis lupus* might now exist in the area is definitely of interest to the Service. However, it is fair to say that at this point, the Service is skeptical primarily because of the tendency for observations of coyotes or dogs (and occasionally captive-reared wolf-dog hybrids) to be reported as wolves . . .

"From a purely hypothetical standpoint, if a small remnant population of wolves does exist in the area, it probably has undergone a loss in genetic variability related to small population size and isolation from other wolf populations. Therefore it would not have the integrity of an original wolf population in the area; the genetic makeup of any small population still present would not be the same as that of the original population of wolves there. Another important consideration in this matter is that, even if no reintroduction to Yellowstone occurs, natural recovery will eventually occur. Through natural processes, expanding wolf populations now in Montana and probably Idaho will eventually reach Yellowstone. There is no reasonable and practical means by which the Service could or should desire to prevent that occurrence and thus hypothetically save any remnant population already there."

On November 15, 1991, Jim and I filed our first lawsuit against FWS. Judge Clarence Brimmer dismissed the case six months later, writing:

"It is important to note that the government has not taken a final stand on the issue of wolf reintroduction. Plaintiffs argue, however, that defendants have turned a deaf ear to their contentions that a wolf population already exists in the Greater Yellowstone Area and are proceeding as if reintroduction is a certainty . . .

"Plaintiffs' arguments are well-taken, but must be dismissed on the basis that these issues are not yet ripe for judicial review . . . Accordingly, the government is entitled to proceed with its draft environmental impact statement. The plaintiffs are entitled to closely pursue the process, and to remind the government of the true objectives of the Endangered Species Act. The government has assured this court that plaintiffs' viewpoint will be considered in the EIS, which assurances are not taken lightly by either plaintiffs or the court."[4]

The lawsuit filed in federal court by DW also was dismissed on grounds similar to ours.

On October 17, 1991, the US Congress appropriated $348,000 to FWS and $150,000 to NPS for use by the agencies to cooperatively develop an EIS pertinent to the reintroduction of wolves to YNP and central Idaho. In the appropriation's bill, Congress included the clause, "Provided, that none of the funds in this Act may be expended to reintroduce wolves in Yellowstone National Park and Central Idaho." Congress directed that the EIS was to cover a broad range of alternatives, and FWS began preparing a team to work on the document and solicit public involvement.

Congress had specified that it wanted an experienced wolf expert to head the EIS project. Steven H. Fritts had served as FWS's wolf recovery coordinator for the entire Northern Rocky Mountain area since 1989, and biologist Ed Bangs was appointed to head the EIS effort. Bangs had received a bachelor's degree in wildlife biology from Utah State University, then earned a master's degree in wildlife management at the University of Nevada late in the 1970s. He then worked for FWS as a biologist on the Kenai National Wildlife Refuge in Alaska, where he participated in a caribou reintroduction project. In 1988, he transferred to Montana where he worked as the project leader for wolf recovery in Montana until his appointment to head the EIS team.

While the EIS process served to push wolf reintroduction into the national spotlight, the wolves already present in northwestern Wyoming were making headlines of their own in the Wyoming press.[5] In mid-January, 1992, two Texas snowmobilers saw and videotaped what they believed to be a wolf near Fishing Bridge in YNP. In February and March, wolves were reported several times in the mountainous areas between Cody, Wyoming, and the Montana border, just east of the park. Two BLM scientists spotted a pair of large gray wolves running along Chapman Bench, and found large wolf tracks in the area the next day. A local hunter reported having seen a wolf in the same area just months before.

In February, 1992, Bangs responded to recent wolf sightings in the Yellowstone area by stating, "None of these have turned out to be anything real and certainly have not led to wolf packs, but the media has gone off the scale in reporting 'wolves are back,' complete with detailed analysis of what this means to the wolf recovery program."[6]

Early in April, 1992, a notice appeared in the *Federal Register* announcing FWS's intent to prepare an EIS for the reintroduction process, which included preliminary alternatives that would appear in the draft EIS (DEIS). The alternatives included a no-wolf option (not allowing wolves to recover), the Wolf Management Committee Alternative, reintroduction of wolves as experimental populations, a no-action alternative (natural recovery from other populations), and reintroduction of wolves as a fully endangered species.[7] Recovery of the existing wolf population was not listed as an option. A brochure detailing the EIS process and asking the public to help identify issues to be analyzed in the EIS, a legally required process called "scoping," was mailed out to about 12,000 people.

Throughout the month of April, 1992, FWS hosted open houses in twenty-seven communities in Wyoming, Montana, and Idaho in which the agency described the EIS process and requested the public to identify issues to be addressed in the EIS. While less than 2,000 people attended these open houses, FWS received about 4,000 responses to its request for public participation. But the open houses themselves were the subject of some controversy. Each of the open houses lasted about four hours, during which time people could come in and pick up a brochure, watch a ten-minute video about wolf reintroduction and recovery, and talk with agency personnel in attendance. No verbal comments or official testimony were recorded for consideration by the EIS team.

By May 1, 1992, members of Congress from Montana, Wyoming, and Idaho wrote to Secretary of the Interior Lujan and outlined the problem.

"Citizens, many of whom traveled long distances, were given no meaningful opportunity to express their views in a way that enabled others to hear them and respond. This is clearly not a setting that encourages the kind of spontaneous and meaningful dialogue that the US Fish and Wildlife Service needs to hear."[8]

Wolf Action Alert also carried the letter from the congressmen, which continued: "Needless to say, wolf reintroduction is one of the most politically sensitive and volatile issues in our region. As a result, it is especially critical that the general public have ample opportunity to meaningfully participate in all stages of the EIS process."[9]

In addition to the open houses, Congress asked for official hearings during which recorded testimony could be given.

DW was outraged when FWS announced that it would host a series of public hearings in the region for the public to have its say about wolves. Just a year earlier, Defenders had expressed a different view, stating, "These issues should be resolved through the environmental review process, conducted in the areas where the action is planned, with full unconstrained public comment."[10] Defenders said the hearings were called at the request of "anti-wolf western Republicans."[11]

At a Montana hearing, an aide to Montana Congressman Ron Marlenee gave his testimony for the no-wolf option and asked that FWS Director Turner resign.[12] A few years earlier, Marlenee had said "Montana needs wolves like we need another drought."[13]

The National Audubon Society (NAS) called on its members to take action on behalf of wolves.[14] Audubon's Brian Peck called for wolf activists to attend "these politically motivated public hearings." He wrote that the "anti-wolf elements," including "supporters in the Wise Use movement saw an opportunity to grandstand on this issue, while perhaps making some political hay." Peck wrote that the goal of the hearings appeared to be "to shout down wolf recovery once again . . . As conservationists, we can ill-afford to be out-maneuvered on wolf recovery."

Peck provided a series of talking points for wolf supporters, including one that said "the EIS process must in no way compromise the protection of wolf populations naturally recovering in Montana, Idaho and possibly, Wyoming. These are fully protected endangered populations and must remain so. Reclassifying these animals as part of an experimental population is unacceptable."

FWS Director Turner was also opposed to the congressional request for more public hearings, but the hearings were held anyway.

During this debate, a retired wildlife biologist from Alaska reported hearing a wolf howl on the South Fork of the Little Wind River in July.

DW sent out an action alert to wolf advocates that discussed the pros and cons of natural recovery of wolves.[15] The group concluded: "To the extent that the long-term success of a wolf recovery program may rest heavily on getting off to a good start, natural recolonization can be a risky business. A reintroduction to Yellowstone offers a golden opportunity to restore wolves with a minimum of conflict."

DW stated that wolves could first become established within the confines of Yellowstone park, and:

"As the wolf population grows, public support can grow along with it . . .

"With natural recovery, it's a roll of the dice. With reintroduction, chances for success are much higher.

"One other thought. It's interesting to observe that much of the push for natural recovery vs. reintroduction is originating with the agencies and the livestock organizations . . .

"It will be a far more important statement if Americans consciously embrace and support wolf restoration rather than just benignly let it happen."

The next stage of the EIS process was the selection of alternatives to be included in the document. While FWS had chosen preliminary alternatives, public input was needed before the final draft was prepared. FWS began the process of scoping — seeking suggestions from the public — for alternatives, with the mailing list quickly climbing to 20,000 people. Open houses were held again — and attendance dropped in every state. FWS then sponsored six public hearings where testimony was recorded. Speakers were selected hourly by random drawings and were given three minutes each to make his or her statement. Attendance levels rose, although not all who attended actually gave testimony.

Bangs was not happy with the actions of Wyoming's anti-reintroduction activists Arlene Hanson of Wapiti and Troy Mader of Gillette. At one of the first open houses, Bangs claimed Mader "showed up and badgered a few people who supported wolf recovery. He had to be asked to behave himself."[16]

A few weeks later, Bangs reported that Mader had sent a letter to various congressional representatives complaining about the way he had been treated at the open house. Bangs's response was, "As expected, the intimidation and personal attacks have begun and will surely get much worse."[17]

A "media tour" of Yellowstone, hosted by DW, was held in June. Bangs was presented as a panelist, and wolf recovery coordinator

Steve Fritts attended as well. Bangs reported: "About 15 wolf opponents led by Troy Mader and Arlene Hanson protested the meeting and the Defenders of Wildlife's wolf booth with placards. Defenders of Wildlife would not allow the wolf opponents to attend the meeting. The anti-wolf people suggested that the federal employees attending should not receive pay or per diem since the public couldn't attend."[18]

The complaints continued, with FWS receiving two more letters complaining about agency personnel attending the media tour. A month later, Bangs wrote: "These letters continue to come from the same individuals that have been writing such letters and demanding specific responses for years. Responding time and time again requires valuable staff time and seems to only stimulate another critical letter. These few individuals learned the technique of sending mail directed to the Secretary or Director with copies to a long list of elected officials. This situation is only the beginning of attempts to portray the Service or other government officials as less than honest."[19]

Mader seemed to be a constant source of irritation to Bangs. Mader called Bangs and told him that the date of the Cheyenne EIS hearing was not good — it was August 18, 1992, Primary Election Day in Wyoming.[20] Bangs said it was too late to change the date, but FWS eventually agreed to extend the hearing to noon on August 19 to give those voting in the primary time to get to Cheyenne to testify.[21]

Bangs seemed somewhat paranoid about his opponents and what possible action they might take. He wrote to his supervisors, saying, "Security is an issue that needs to be taken seriously."[22]

By November, the official EIS mailing list had grown to nearly 30,000 people, representing all fifty states and forty foreign countries.[23] The November elections brought in President Bill Clinton and, with him, Secretary of the Interior Bruce Babbitt and the first woman director of FWS, Mollie Beattie.

In 1992, wolf reports again began to increase. Of the sixty reports for that year, ten were of packs ranging from two to five animals each.[24]

In April, 1992, two reports of groups of gray wolves in the park were recorded. One sighting was of two wolves while the other was of four. The sightings were only ten days apart but at opposite sides of the park; one was south of the Old Faithful area, in the southwestern portion of the park, while the other was east of Tower in the northeastern part.

In June, 1992, two reports of two gray wolves each in Hayden Valley were recorded just a week apart. On August 2, 1992, a visitor reported watching a seventy-five- to one hundred-pound wolf attack a bison, only to be chased off. Five days later, on August 8, 1992, filmmaker Ray Paunovich, a cinematographer for Busch Productions, captured a wolf on film as it and a grizzly bear fed, side by side, on a bison carcass.[25] Paunovich was in Yellowstone filming a documentary on bears, and the day before he filmed the wolf, he had set up his camera on a rise overlooking a bison carcass.[26] He filmed several grizzly bears feeding on the bison, and when leaving the area, saw a large black canid running away from the carcass. Unable to capture the fleeing animal on film, Paunovich decided to come back to the site the next morning — and when he did, he found the wolf, along with three grizzlies, back at the carcass. He captured over ten minutes of the animal on film as it fed on the carcass and interacted with the bears (Figure 14). A Yellowstone park biologist returned to the area the next morning and found a wolf-sized track. Busch Productions released a short segment of the film to the major national television networks. While most biologists agreed that the animal was indeed a wolf, some, including Minnesota wolf biologist L. David Mech, deemed the footage "inconclusive" because, in their opinions, the animal could have been a wolf-dog hybrid. Mech added that he had never seen a wolf colored like the animal on the film[27] and argued further that even if it was a wolf, "there's no way to know if it got there naturally or somebody dumped it."[28]

Environmental groups that advocated wolf reintroduction scrambled to convince the public that Paunovich's sighting and film of the wolf was insignificant since it was only one animal, not a pack. They all urged that plans to reintroduce wolves into the park should continue.

Three days later, after the Paunovich filming, two gray wolves were reportedly spotted on Otter Creek in Yellowstone's Hayden Valley.

Figure 14 A. While the wolf reintroduction debate raged, filmmaker Ray Paunovich captured footage of a naturally occurring wolf, along with a coyote, grizzly bears, and birds, feeding on a bison carcass (see next page) in Yellowstone National Park. (Photos by Ray Paunovich/Busch Productions; use courtesy Busch Productions)

Figure 14 B. Wolf, grizzlies, and birds scavenged the bison carcass while being filmed by Ray Paunovich. (Photos by Ray Paunovich/Busch Productions; use courtesy Busch Productions)

Bangs updated his supervisors about the recent wolf reports:

"There are many reasons that extremists, both pro and con, might release domesticated or hybrid wolves into the park or central Idaho, even though these types of animals will never survive and reproduce successfully. Some extremists who support wolf protection and recovery could attempt to prevent an experimental population of Wolf Management Committee-type alternative by 'demonstrating' wolves have already made it to the park. Some extremists opposed to wolf recovery could attempt to prevent or delay any reintroduction by 'demonstrating' wolves have naturally recolonized or are about to naturally recolonize the park.[29]

"Either way, a situation could develop that these 'wolves' are never found again, but any type of management or progress toward resolving the wolf recovery and management issue is postponed another five to 10 years looking for something that was not real. Another 'study' is a real possibility. If the EIS process is delayed, it will only become more controversial."

Early in September, visitors to the Hayden area reported hearing howls of two wolves and found large canid scat in the area. Two days later, another report of a pair of wolves was recorded.

Steve Fritts briefed the regional FWS office by stating:

"There is a strong need to place the sighting of this animal in perspective . . . We especially need to minimize the significance of this incident to the EIS process.[30]

"If the filming of this animal were to raise expectations that natural recovery is imminent, turn opinion away from reintroduction, or stall a recovery option in favor of an extensive survey, it could easily be more detrimental than beneficial to wolf recovery in Yellowstone and central Idaho.

"The Service should resist pressure to capture and examine the animal."

On September 24, 1992, it was reported that an observer watched a mule deer doe being chased repeatedly in a marshy slough near Virginia Cascade. The observer noted: "The deer would head for deep water then turn and kick the swimming animal, while the deer reared on hind legs. Canid would get out and hide; deer would get out and the canid would reappear and water activity would repeat."

Late in August of 1992, a group of WGF fisheries biologists traveling in the remote Teton Wilderness just south of the park took photographs and measured tracks of an adult wolf at 4 ¾ inches long without claws, and 4 inches wide. They noted, "There appeared to be at least one set of pup tracks with the adult, but no measurements were made."

The following month, the existence of a wolf pack in the Teton Wilderness would become national news.

Chapter 8

Shooting a Dinosaur

Late September, 1992, was full of bright, sunny days, with temperatures ranging up into the seventies in northwestern Wyoming. Thirty-four-year-old Wyoming native Jerry Kysar and four of his Big Horn Basin-area hunting partners had packed in twenty-two miles on horseback to the Fox Creek area of the Teton Wilderness to set up camp for their moose and elk hunts. Jerry, a self-described redneck, views himself as an ordinary Wyoming man — "blue jeans, cowboy boots, own a dog, cuss a little, bitch a lot, that type."[1] Jerry and his wife Grace are the doting parents of four children, and Jerry is a cowboy poet and guitar picker.

On the morning of Wednesday, September 30, 1992, Jerry and partner Lynn Robirds separated from the rest of their hunting party and headed south on horseback towards Fox Park. The area they rode through had been burned by the Mink Creek forest fire in 1988. Riding down the trail, the hunters could hear coyotes howling on either side of them in the timber. Jerry mentioned to Lynn that he was tempted to shoot one of them. Killing coyotes in Wyoming is legal and Jerry estimates that he has shot a total of about a dozen coyotes in the past. With Lynn in the lead on the trail, the hunters crested a rise when Lynn said, "There they are!"

Jerry rode up and saw what he thought were three to five coyotes, two of them dark-colored as if they had rolled in the burn area. Jerry and Lynn bailed off their horses, with Lynn grabbing the reins to both mounts while Jerry dropped into a prone position and prepared to shoot. As the lead animal darted through the timber, headed up a ridge, Jerry fired a shot. The recoil from his 30.06 Parker-Hale knocked the sight off the rifle.

Jerry was still looking down trying to find his scope when Lynn told him the 250-yard shot had connected — the animal was down. The hunters rode to the kill and could not believe their eyes. Whatever the animal was, it was not a coyote. They debated whether it was a dog, a wolf, or some sort of hybrid between the two. Lynn said he thought if it was a wolf, it would have yellow eyes. Another look confirmed that the canid on the ground had both large feet and yellow eyes (Figure 15).

By then, two other members of their hunting party, hearing Jerry's shot, had ridden to the scene, and there the four hunters discussed their options, including practicing the "three Ss: shoot, shovel, and shut up." But Jerry had to do the right thing, he had to turn himself in. Taking a small piece of paper from his wallet, he wrote: "Please notify the Wyoming Game and Fish that we need a game biologist at the Fox Park hunting camp pronto! I accidentally shot what I believe is a wolf on Forest Service property. We need some advice on what they want me to do! Jerry Kysar."[2]

Figure 15. Jerry Kysar and the wolf he shot in the Teton Wilderness late in September, 1992. (Photo courtesy Jerry Kysar)

The note was tacked onto the door of the Fox Creek patrol cabin inside YNP, about two miles north of the kill site. The hunters took pictures of the animal, then moved it to get it out of the sun. They then covered the carcass with burned timber to keep ravens from pecking at it and returned to camp to wait for investigators to arrive.

At four the next afternoon, YNP ranger Mary Taber found the note on the patrol cabin door. Taber contacted the park's communications center and requested that WGF be notified of the situation. Because of the logistics of getting investigators into the area immediately, it was decided that NPS rangers, acting as deputized FWS agents, would investigate. Taber sent out a radio call to Michael Keator and Ann Marie Chytra, two other rangers patrolling the park boundary area. About half-an-hour later, the three rangers met up and headed toward Fox Park, but met two hunters from Kysar's camp on the trail near the Snake River crossing. The hunters agreed to take the rangers to the kill site. After sitting for a day and a half, rigor mortis had set in and the carcass was starting to bloat. The rangers were unable to get a horse to cooperate enough to pack the carcass out, so the women rangers — Taber and Chytra — tied the wolf onto a lodgepole pine limb and carried it the two miles back to the Fox Park patrol cabin, where they then secured it.

It was well after dark Thursday by the time the two women finally rode into Kysar's hunting camp to interview him about the incident. The scene was tense for both sides. For the rangers, they were riding into what they knew to be an armed camp in the dead of night to investigate a man who killed what may prove to be an endangered species. For the hunters, they wondered if the rangers would understand the incident had been an accident, or would they try to hang Kysar out to dry on a federal felony charge? As the rangers conducted the interview, their radios would squawk every few minutes, with the communications center checking in on the situation. It was 11:30 that night before the rangers arrived back at the Fox Creek patrol cabin inside the park to get some sleep.

Meanwhile, that evening Wayne Brewster of YNP put in a telephone call to Steve Fritts in Helena, Montana, to apprise him of the situation. Joel Scrafford with FWS Law Enforcement and Steve Fain of the FWS Law Enforcement Forensics Lab in Ashland, Oregon, were consulted several times throughout the evening. It was decided that the entire carcass should be brought out of the wilderness and placed in an evidence freezer in Mammoth, then FWS would take possession and put it on an airplane to the Oregon lab on Monday.[3]

Friday morning, October 2, 1992, was the start to another beautiful fall day. Ranger Michael Keator wrapped the wolf carcass in canvass and loaded it onto a packhorse, passing it on to Ranger Matthew Vandzura, who then packed the animal out the long Pacific Creek Trail. Rangers Taber and Chytra went back to the hunting camp to continue their investigation. The rangers met with Kysar and Robirds, and went back to the kill site, where the hunters explained how the incident had occurred. Tracks of the wolf were found, measured and flagged. Kysar turned over his roll of exposed film and the spent round casing from the bullet he used to kill the wolf.

The wolf carcass finally made it to Mammoth Friday evening where it was measured, weighed, examined and placed into the evidence freezer. It was a ninety-two-pound male, probably between two to five years old (Figure 16). It was obvious from the difference in coloration that this was not the animal filmed in the park a month earlier. Word that a wolf had been shot south of the park was broadcast on the Friday evening television news before the carcass ever reached the freezer (Figure 17). By this time, word that the animal was shot out of a pack had reached Yellowstone's chief ranger's office, but that information would not make it to the research division, or to FWS, for several more days.

On Saturday morning around nine o'clock, rangers Michael Keator and Mary Taber would have an experience that seemed to substantiate Kysar's claim that the wolf was a member of a larger group.[4] Taber reported hearing an unusual canine-like howl from the vicinity of the Fox Creek patrol cabin. Taber and Keator went out to a meadow near the cabin and there saw several canids. Taber's written account referred to two animals, one that was "black in color with silver grizzling on its face, sides and tail" while the other "appeared to be the

Figure 16. A close-up view of the wolf killed in the Teton Wilderness by Jerry Kysar. (Photo courtesy Jerry Kysar)

color of a bleached out stump" with a "black-tipped tail which he held straight out parallel to the ground." Taber went into the cabin to retrieve a set of binoculars in the middle of her observation. Keator described seeing one large, mostly black-colored canid, and watching a second, light gray canid walk out of the timber. Three smaller canids with black-tipped tails accompanied these two animals.

Jerry Kysar finally filled his moose tag on Saturday. On his way to hang the carcass, he met rangers Taber and Chytra on the trail. Later in the day, the rangers rode back to Kysar's camp to get written statements from the members of the hunting party regarding the wolf killing and information regarding any firearms they had in their possession. On Sunday morning, Kysar met the rangers on the trail once again, this time giving them his written statement on the wolf, then he headed out of the wilderness toward home. The newspapers that day noted that federal officials would determine whether Kysar would face civil or criminal charges for killing an endangered species. If found guilty, Kysar could face up to a year in prison and fines of up to $100,000.

On Monday morning, Steve Fritts left his Montana office and headed to Yellowstone to get a look at the wolf carcass before it was sent to the Oregon lab. He was planning on taking a look, then heading back north to Missoula to help recapture a wolf from the Nine Mile area of northwestern Montana. When Fritts arrived at Mammoth, he finally learned that the wolf had been shot out of a pack, and that Yellowstone's Wayne Brewster wanted Fritts to accompany him on a backcountry search for the other animals. Up until this time, Fritts had not been notified that the wolf had been seen with others, or that park rangers had also reported seeing a wolf pack in the same area. Fritts, completely unprepared, borrowed some clothes from Brewster, bought some groceries, and prepared for the trip.

Figure 17. You shot Big Foot! (Cartoon by Greg Kearney; © 1992 and 1993, *Casper Star-Tribune;* reprinted with permission)

The search party, up at 4 A.M. Tuesday, wrangled horses and headed out of the park. By 8 A.M., snow began to cover the park and park officials were restricting vehicle traffic. The search party hit the trail on horseback about noon, and rode most of the twenty miles in a heavy, wet snow. Four other park service representatives, as well as a representative from WGF, accompanied Fritts and Brewster. They arrived in the Fox Park area that evening, where the group split to accommodate the two cabins a few miles apart.

The front-page headlines of many Wyoming newspapers on Wednesday, October 7, 1992, reported that a wolf pack had been spotted in the Yellowstone area. An editorial in *Jackson Hole Guide* on that date noted: "The rangers' sighting of the pack was, for some reason, not revealed until Tuesday, at which time it also came to light that park visitors, rangers and concessionaires have made at least six such reliable sightings during the past two months. The most recent of those was within the last two weeks . . . Interestingly enough, neither the Park Service nor the Fish and Wildlife Service found it necessary to tell taxpayers — who are in the process of doling out money for an environmental impact statement that contemplates reintroducing gray wolves to Yellowstone — that the animals, had, indeed, found their way back . . . It was like pulling teeth to get information about last week's sighting and, even then, the information was incomplete. It's time for the US Fish and Wildlife Service and Park Service to be up front with the public and tell us what they know, because the implications of a wolf pack in Yellowstone are far-reaching."[5]

On Wednesday the search party split into three groups, each going a different direction from the kill site. By then, it had been a full week since the incident had occurred. Search efforts on Wednesday and Thursday were fruitless, so the searchers left the area early Friday morning (Figure 18).

The Thursday edition of the *Casper Star-Tribune* ran an article with the headline, "Worland man faces possible prosecution." It reported that a federal agent said that once the investigation into the wolf shooting was completed, the report would be turned over to the US Attorney's office in Cheyenne for a decision on whether Kysar

Figure 18. Wrong wolf pack! (Cartoon by Greg Kearney; © 1992 and 1993, *Casper Star-Tribune;* reprinted with permission)

would face criminal charges. Jerry waited out this storm at home. Even though he had an unlisted telephone number, his telephone was constantly ringing, sometimes with calls from reporters wanting his story and sometimes with obscene messages from people enraged that he had shot a wolf. All the time while wondering if he was going to be prosecuted, he was also both cooperating with investigators and fighting to get the negatives from his roll of film — which had been turned over as evidence — back from FWS.

US Attorney Richard Stacy announced on Friday, October 8, that he would not pursue criminal charges against Kysar. Stacy stated that Kysar had been very cooperative with investigators and, because wolves had long been absent from the region, Kysar could not have known he was shooting at a wolf and not a coyote. It was reported that FWS concurred with Stacy's decision. Kysar could breathe a sigh of relief.

It would turn out to be a short sigh. The FWS investigation would continue. If biological testing were to determine that the animal was a wolf, the investigator's report would then be turned over to USDI's Office of the Solicitor, which would then determine whether to file civil charges against Kysar. If he were found guilty in a civil suit, Kysar would not do jail time, but could still be fined up to $10,000. Kysar's case would be in limbo until after federal officials determined whether the animal was a full-blooded wolf. Sharon Rose, a FWS spokeswoman, said the test results should arrive within a week, and within two weeks the agency would decide whether to file a civil suit against Kysar. Rose was wrong. Numerous delays would hold the release of the test results up for weeks, then months (Figure 19).

An editorial in the November 18, 1992, issue of the *Jackson Hole Guide* accurately reflected the frustration many members of the

Figure 19. Well, it's big! (Cartoon by Greg Kearney; © 1992 and 1993, *Casper Star-Tribune;* reprinted with permission)

public felt over this hold-up. It reported that FWS law enforcement officials stated that in order to win a civil suit, two things must be demonstrated. The first was to prove that the animal was a pure wolf. The second was to prove that Kysar knew that the animal he was going to shoot was a wolf. The *Guide* editorial responded to these statements:

"How is it that the Fish and Wildlife Service — our federal wildlife experts — can expect Kysar to have known he shot a wolf when they already have spent more than six weeks in their laboratories trying to figure it out, and still don't know what it is they're dealing with?

"If the Fish and Wildlife Service wants to consider filing a civil suit against Kysar, it should — at the very least — be able to do what it is asking him to do in terms of identifying the animal.

"And it should have begun sharing information about the numerous recent suspected wolf sightings in the area of Yellowstone National Park before it came down to identifying a carcass. Maybe then there would have been reason for a hunter to suspect what he was shooting.

"It's another sign of the need to demand full disclosure of 'public' information from 'public' officials and agencies."[6]

Members of the media had a heyday with FWS's apparent stalling with the release of test results on the animal. Political cartoons by Wyoming cartoonist Greg Kearney addressing the wolf situation appeared regularly in the *Casper Star-Tribune* as the various issues concerning the wolf matter unfolded (figures 17–21).

Bangs did not like the coverage of the wolf shooting incident that appeared in the *Jackson Hole Guide*. He wrote: "Actually, it is surprising that it has taken so long for the 'conspiracy' theories to be brought up. Unfortunately, this is another typical wolf-hysteria type event where people want to believe there is more to an incident than there really is."[7]

"The wolf shooting spawned the usual level of wolf hysteria and rumor," Bangs wrote.[8]

Sierra Club Legal Defense Fund attorney Doug Honnold said that the Teton wolf could make the experimental population destined for YNP illegal. "I think you can have a population of one,"[9] he said.

Figure 20. We're baaack! (Cartoon by Greg Kearney; © 1992 and 1993, *Casper Star-Tribune;* reprinted with permission)

FWS Director Turner disagreed, stating, "In my interpretation, a population is one that can sustain itself."

Bangs said the chance of the Teton wolf being a survivor of a remnant population were extremely remote, but conceded: "This raises the potential a little bit, but we're still talking one in a million. It's always possible, but I'd say it's still highly, highly unlikely."[10]

Fritts again briefed his supervisors, writing: "Someone has to keep calm throughout this commotion and it might as well be us! We are witnessing one more example of wolf hysteria, complete with media hype, reporters suspecting a government plot and seeing more in a story than is really there, wolf advocates trying to facilitate matters but only complicating communications, everyone expecting more from wolf-dog taxonomy than current techniques can give, and the media and the public failing to understand the uncertainty we deal with in situations such as this. It is entirely possible that we will never know whether the animal was a pure wolf, where it came from, how it got to its final location, and whether it was with other wolves when shot."[11]

Figure 21. Go on, shoot! (Cartoon by Greg Kearney; © 1992 and 1993, *Casper Star-Tribune;* reprinted with permission)

Fritts said one of the reasons FWS was reluctant to even call the animal a wolf was "the high potential for someone to attempt to manipulate the recovery/EIS process by seeing to it that a wolf shows up in the park at this time. A cautious approach has served us well in the past and should be continued." He urged his agency to "use every opportunity" to explain that "one wolf does not equal recovery, nor necessarily indicate process toward recovery. We especially need to minimize the significance of this incident to the EIS process, while avoiding creating the perception that we do not want to find wolves in the Yellowstone area — as a *Time/Life* reporter concluded this week."

Fritts included nearly a full page of "similar words for the media when similar incidents occur in the future," adding, "and they will."

In November, 1992, the Associated Press (AP) reported that Robert Crabtree, a wildlife biologist involved in a long-term study of coyotes in YNP said that there was mounting evidence that wolves and coyotes were "associating" in the park. The AP report quoted Crabtree as saying "it looks to me as if there is some association between these two species of predators" and "something is going on there that should raise a lot of questions."[12]

In an attempt at damage control, FWS tried various tactics. At first, agency officials admitted that the emphasis of the EIS could shift from reintroduction of Canadian wolves and "could focus more on the process of natural recovery."[13] FWS then backtracked, shifting toward trying to downplay the significance of the event. Bangs was quoted by the AP as saying "hey, it's interesting stuff, but let's not go overboard" and "I've been in situations where a wolf report is considered absolutely, positively guaranteed. But by the time you get through with it, it turns out to be nothing more than a Labrador retriever."[14] FWS also publicly pondered whether the animal might have been a released captive, or a wolf hybrid. Bangs stated, "In Yellowstone, there's so much dead stuff lying around that you could drop wolves off there that are half blind and three-legged, and a hybrid could probably scavenge enough off dead stuff to make it for a while."[15] Some FWS officials publicly pondered whether someone attempting to influence the outcome of the EIS process might have released the animal. But FWS Director Turner said that it was unlikely. According to a press account, "He noted the numerous unconfirmed wolf reports over the years, and said that could indicate a population has been there for some time."[16]

Bangs said, in October, "It's important to know whether this is just a dog-wolf hybrid that was essentially someone's pet and got kicked out the door, or an indication of natural wild wolves moving that far south."[17] A month later, Fritts changed tactics again, stating that it was not important, regardless of the results. "I don't see why there should be an effect on the EIS one way or another regardless what the animal turns out to be."[18] Wolf-reintroduction advocate Renee Askins of the Wolf Fund proclaimed that both the animal killed by Kysar and the animal filmed in the park a few months earlier were wolf-dog hybrids, not wild wolves.[19]

The *Jackson Hole Guide* attended a press conference held by FWS Director Turner in December, after which they ran the headline,

"Turner: Dead wolf is insignificant."[20] The *Guide* quoted Turner as saying "whatever that thing is has absolutely no bearing on our responsibilities." The *Guide* reported, "Turner criticized the media, and particularly the *Jackson Hole Guide*, for insinuating that the many delays in issuing test results from the animal might have amounted to the agency's trying to hide information."

In mid-December, 1992, FWS announced that the tests were inconclusive, it could not determine whether the animal was a full-blooded wolf, and that they would not pursue a civil suit against Kysar. Then, late in January, 1993, FWS announced that the animal was in fact a wolf. But contrary to claims that the case against Kysar was closed, the FWS Law Enforcement Division never actually closed the case against Kysar until September 7, 1993, over eleven months after the incident occurred.

While FWS tried to fight back from the bad press it was getting, it would soon be taken to the mat again. On December 30, 1992, the *Jackson Hole Guide* printed both a front-page article and an editorial based on a biologist's view that wolves had persisted in the Yellowstone area. George Gruell had worked as a wildlife biologist on the Bridger-Teton National Forest south of Yellowstone from 1967 to 1978, and had documented over fifty wolf sightings in the area by people he viewed as very credible sources. Gruell asserted that some of the sightings were accompanied by very compelling evidence. Both Gruell and Bridger-Teton National Forest Supervisor Reid Jackson had heard wolf howls on the forest and both men maintained that a remnant population of wolves had persisted in the Gros Ventre area south of YNP at least through the 1970s. Gruell's editorial was scathing in its criticism of the FWS contention that northwestern Wyoming contained no wolves. Gruell wrote: "Until I see evidence to the contrary, I'm convinced that Fish and Wildlife Service personnel will continue to discount the presence of wolves. Once an agency is committed to a cause, it is extremely difficult to steer a new course. You don't question established policy. After all, personnel of Yellowstone Park and the Fish and Wildlife Service have been telling us for the past 20 years that the only way to have wolves is to reintroduce them."[21]

Kysar, not knowing that he was the subject of a pending investigation, decided to publicly challenge FWS statements that there were no other wolves in the Yellowstone area. He and a business friend produced a black-and-white poster showing him in mountain-man garb, holding a rifle, standing next to a horse with a wolf pelt draped over the saddle. It read, "Wyoming: Remember, there ain't no wolves in Wyoming, Clinton won't raise your taxes, and Elvis lives in Jackson Hole." Kysar installed a toll-free telephone line to accept reports of wolf presence, and began organizing backcountry horsemen to aid in the search for Wyoming wolves. However the public interest in wolves was directed more toward the EIS process and Kysar's project fizzled — but not before animal rights activists spoke out in outrage, with one stating: "Talk about the fox guarding the hen house. Wolf found, wolf killed (again)."[22] Then a man named Walt Eisenstein told a reporter that Kysar had told him that he knew he was aiming at a wolf when he shot that fateful day in the wilderness.[23] Eisenstein, not knowing the case had never been closed, requested that it be reopened. Federal officials, stating that they had no evidence to substantiate such an allegation, publicly declined.[24] Animal rights advocates mailed letters to federal law enforcement officials protesting the decision not to prosecute.[25]

Chapter 9

Discounting Reports

The wolf sighting reports in YNP had increased dramatically from 1991 to 1992. Sightings of more than one animal jumped from one to ten within a year. The reports of more than one animal, based on the descriptions of numbers of animals seen, their physical characteristics, and the time of year and area of occurrence reinforced each other.

The increase in sightings of more than one wolf (one–ten) and the number of total wolf sightings reported (sixty) indicated that wolves were inhabiting YNP and that reproductive activity had taken place in the park and adjacent wilderness areas to the south in 1992. It seemed that the wolf population in Yellowstone was still producing young, and reports supporting this conclusion continued into 1993.

A sharp increase in wolf reports occurred in 1993, almost tripling the number of reports from 1992 (increasing from sixty to 162).[1] One-hundred-forty of the reports in 1993 were of single animals and the remaining twenty-two reports were of two to four animals. Of particular interest were the reports of sightings in the southeastern section of the park, just north of where Kysar had killed the wolf the previous fall. A pair was spotted in this area in August, and eight to ten baritone howls by "multiple animals" was also recorded for the area that month. That fall, rangers stationed at the Thorofare and Cabin Creek cabins reported hearing howls of multiple wolves in the area.

The search for Wyoming wolves had been sporadic over the years, but the people who had done the search knew very little about the subject of their efforts. Very little research had been done on Wyoming's native wolf and wolf biologists based their views of the animal's probable behavior on wolves in other locations that had been studied more extensively, such as those in Minnesota and Canada.

Consequently, the behavior of wolves that had migrated south into Montana from Canada became the basis for the FWS monitoring program in Wyoming. The idea that Wyoming's wolves might behave differently than their neighbors to the north was never considered in the reintroduction program.

FWS relied extensively on a three-phased procedure for locating and monitoring gray wolves in the northern Rockies.[2] The approach included detection, confirmation, and monitoring by radiotelemetry. Detection included soliciting reports of wolf activity from agencies and the public. When the detection system revealed a cluster of reports in an area, suggesting wolf pack activity, the confirmation phase would begin. Wolf identification teams would be sent to an area to search for wolves and wolf sign in an attempt to determine wolf presence and the number of animals in the population. The monitoring phase would begin after the presence of a breeding pair was confirmed. Once a breeding pair was confirmed, animals would be captured, radio-collared, released, and monitored via radiotelemetry.

While this monitoring strategy was successful in northwestern Montana, it was proven to be ineffective in the Yellowstone region of northwestern Wyoming. Failure in the first phase, coupled with agency skepticism of wolf presence and the assumption that Wyoming wolves would behave like Canadian wolves, rendered the procedure useless in determining the status of wolves in the Yellowstone region.

Phase 1 of the program, the detection phase, solicited the aid of the public in reporting wolf activity. Distribution of wolf identification cards and posters, news releases and publications, and live presentations by agency personnel were all used to encourage people to report wolf activity. Natural resource agency personnel were trained in wolf identification and recovery.

This detection phase was used extensively in Montana, but few if any of its parts were used in the Yellowstone region until just prior to the actual reintroduction of wolves took place.[3] Wolf identification cards and posters were not distributed until the early 1990s. Relevant publications and presentations were non-existent in the Yellowstone region until work on the EIS began early in the 1990s. Agency personnel were trained in wolf identification only after a lawsuit was filed against FWS for failure to conduct wolf conservation activities in the Yellowstone region.[4] News releases encouraging people to report wolf activity did not appear until after Jerry Kysar killed a wolf in the Teton Wilderness in the fall of 1992. To the contrary, in 1990, a reporter was asked to leave an interagency meeting convened to discuss wolf sightings because, according to Steve Fritts, the participants "were very concerned about publicity about wolves generating sightings."[5] Apparently the agencies feared that the public would actually begin to report wolf sightings.

Ideally, when a member of the public observed a wolf or wolf sign, he or she was supposed to immediately notify the closest natural resource agency. The person who reported the sighting would be interviewed and the information would be systematically recorded. FWS would then be notified of the report, and the report would be both examined independently and compared with other reports for possible correlations, via computerized information and/or mapped occurrences. If the report merited a search, a field investigation would be conducted, and efforts to trap and radio-collar the animal would be made.

But individuals encountered substantial difficulty in reporting wolf activity to natural resource agencies in Wyoming. Members of the public attempted to report wolf activity, only to find the agency personnel apathetic and unwilling to record the information. As a result, valuable data were lost. If an individual subsequently observed other wolf activity, he often remembered the indifference encountered during the earlier attempt to report the information, and would or might not attempt to provide information again.

On several occasions, members of the public were instructed to keep the information to themselves, that it should not be reported. A 1985 account suggested that a sheepherder killed two wolves that had gotten into his herd. The herder notified the local USFS office, only to be discouraged from reporting the event. He was warned that if he did report the occurrence, he would have to face the penalty for the federal offense of killing an endangered species. The herder retreated, the account was left unrecorded, and the carcasses were not recovered. When law enforcement learned of this encounter, it was far too late for the investigation to be fruitful.

Members of the public were often met with skepticism when reporting wolf activity. A December 18, 1985, memo to the Bridger-Teton Forest Supervisor Reid Jackson from District Ranger Robert Riddle stated: "No sightings have been made by reliable sources, nor have any sightings been substantiated. Until a confirmation is made, wolf reports should be discounted."[6]

Interestingly, a few months earlier, the local wildlife biologist from WGF had written a letter to the head of the Wolf Recovery Team stationed in Montana and presented a very different view.

"I am convinced there are wolves or wild dogs people are mistaking for wolves, living in the area. I have interviewed many people who believe they saw wolves or heard howling and I am not prepared to call them liars. From my interviews it seems likely that two wolves were killed here in the past 10 years and two more may have been killed by a sheepherder this July. I hope this material will convince you of the possibility of there being wolves in the area."[7]

FWS employees working on wolf recovery were also guilty of this skepticism. According to Steve Fritts: "Sometimes chasing wolf reports, it's kind of like chasing flying saucers. People often see coyotes and think they're wolves."[8] Ed Bangs, in a discussion with a member of the media concerning wolf reports and the existence of a wolf population in Yellowstone, said, "And maybe they'll get Bigfoot too."[9] FWS Regional Director Galen Buterbaugh compared locating single wolves based on wolf reports to "chasing ghosts."[10]

Controversies involving other endangered species also had an impact on the amount of information volunteered to the agencies by the public. Near Meeteetse, Wyoming, where the last wild colony of endangered black-footed ferrets was discovered, people seemed reluctant to report sightings of protected species for fear of land-use restrictions that tend to accompany federal protection of endangered species. One federal wildlife biologist wrote: "There is a rising tide of reluctance to report any wolf observation due to the impacts of the ferret area. Wolf observations are not uncommon, but are second- and third-hand, and very difficult to get meaningful evidence of any sort. The air of suspicion is high and saying nothing is the rule for most folks down here."[11]

Likewise, it was suggested that one natural resource agency, WGF, had experienced such difficulty over grizzly bear recovery that the department did not want to know anything about wolf presence in Wyoming. Jim and I have talked with several people who, upon reporting wolf presence in the Wyoming Range area, were told by game wardens that they better keep their mouths shut about the matter, because if FWS found out about the wolves, the hunting seasons and grazing leases in the area would be severely reduced or eliminated entirely.

When agency personnel did conduct interviews and record information, it was not done consistently from agency to agency, or even office to office. Some reports were merely hand-written memos for the file, while others were recorded on forms that vary within each agency and among agencies. Most reports did not record the legal description of the location of the sighting and some did not include any description of the location at all. Others omitted dates, name or address of the observers, or even number of animals seen. After recording the specifics of the sighting, FWS often was not notified of the report. Research found more wolf reports in other agency offices than in FWS files. Few agency offices forwarded their reports to FWS. Although a few agencies did send the reports on to FWS, few contacted FWS within forty-eight hours of receiving the report. Most agencies mailed the reports on a monthly basis, but sometimes only annually.

When FWS was notified of reported wolf sightings, the reports should have been examined both independently and compared with other reports, for any correlations, via computerized information and mapped occurrences. This, however, was not done. The FWS computer database, aside from being extremely limited in regards to data entry, had many mistakes. FWS had been negligent in entering and maintaining data. One printout of wolf sightings reported during the early 1990s from the FWS system omitted more reports than it contained. Data from individual reports were not entered correctly. The most visible error noted is that most site locations were not put in the system. This most critical bit of information rendered all other data on the system completely useless. It did no good to know that a pack of three animals was seen, if no one knew where the sighting occurred.

Thus with the wolf occurrences unmapped and not cross-referenced, no correlations or comparisons could be made. Without comparisons, FWS had no way to evaluate whether an area did or did not warrant field research — and, therefore, few field searches were made.

One WGF biologist observed late in 1991: "Over the past two decades I have received dozens of wolf sightings . . . Many of these sightings were made by very reliable observers, but in no instance did the FWS follow up on these observations or send personnel to the area to verify the sightings. In fact, I do not believe they ever even called the observers to obtain additional information."[12]

When field searches were conducted, methods used in the process were often shoddy.[13] One search of the southern Bridger-Teton National Forest consisted of fourteen people (family groups) on snowmachines for six hours, searching for wolves while checking roads. Other searches involved dragging a deer carcass behind a snowmachine and the use of time-lapse cameras. Search parties included untrained, inexperienced individuals who did not have a clear idea of what to look for or what search methods should be used. Most searches were conducted weeks or even months after wolf activity was reported. Most of the initial search efforts yielded nothing and further research was rarely conducted.

Further, FWS resisted efforts to conduct field searches, even after a series of wolf sighting reports was recorded. After two BLM employees sighted what they believed to be wolves on two occasions in 1990 near the Washakie Wilderness, Steve Fritts stated: "The sightings, however reliable, are still not an indicator of important wolf activity in the Yellowstone region. It's too far from any breeding population to mean much."[14] Months later, after receiving several reports of wolves in the Wood River area, Steve Torbitt of FWS reported that his agency "has no plans to send people into the field to verify the sightings. Even with a verified sighting, the agency must consider that an all-out search effort is expensive and still may not succeed."[15] In December, 1990, Fritts again reported that the agency had no plans to launch a search for wolves in Wyoming. "Reports of wolf sightings must be viewed with skepticism . . . I'm not saying these people in Wyoming are not seeing wolves, because a few of them may be."[16]

In August of 1991 an interagency team entered the Dunoir area in a search for wolf presence. Attending were Tom Ryder and Doug McWhirter of WGF, Renee Askins of the Wolf Fund, Sharon Kearney of USFS, and John Varley and Wayne Brewster of NPS. The following information has been extracted from a trip report written by Doug McWhirter.[17] The group entered the area on Thursday evening, August 1, 1991. Friday morning, while riding into the area on horseback, the group stopped in a meadow. "Wayne and Renee howled and received an immediate response. Time was 8:38 A.M. Although coyotes were heard at this time also, the very first response was considered to be of non-coyote origin. Everyone in the group was genuinely convinced of the uniqueness of this howl." The group then split into two groups. No further howls were heard, but two canine scats were collected.

According to McWhirter, the group met back at camp where unsolicited howling began at approximately 7 P.M. "One set of vocalizations was determined to be coyotes, but the other was much lower and very unlike that of a coyote. At about this same time, the wrangler from an outfitter camp on the West Fork of the Dunoir told us he had heard wolf howls that morning at sunrise. At 11 P.M., unsolicited howling began to the north of the cabin. These howls also were unique and thought to be different from that of coyotes. There were 2–3 different episodes between 11 and 11:15 P.M."

On Saturday the group rode to Dundee Meadows where it encountered a group of hikers who said they had heard wolf howls the night before. Several sets of large canid tracks were found in the area. "Once again at 11 P.M. unsolicited howling began north of the cabin. Wayne got the best reception of this episode and felt confident that the low, single howls which lasted for approximately 15 seconds was not a coyote."

The group left the area Sunday morning, with no other experiences to report.

In total, the group heard howling four times, found two sets of tracks, and collected two scat samples measuring 27 mm (1.1 inches) in diameter. Yet FWS biologist Jane Roybal was quoted as saying, in reference to the field search, "There was nothing found to indicate wolves were actually there."[18]

After yet another search early in 1994, FWS issued a news release that wolf specialists had just returned from a ten-day, 1,300-mile search for wolves in northwestern Wyoming and "found neither wolves or wolf sign."[19] While it sounded good for the agency's position, it was not. Actually, seven days, not ten, were spent in Wyoming. Included in the search were the 258 miles from Helena to Red Lodge, Montana, miles that were not even in the state of Wyoming. Nine hundred miles were spent in a vehicle on a road, most often a blacktop highway, but these miles were counted as search miles. One-hundred-seventy miles were spent on a snowmobile, which is a good way to familiarize a person with an area, but staying on a well-used snowmobile trail is not likely to increase the chance of encountering a rare endangered wolf. Very few miles were spent on foot, which is reasonable, considering the season. In total, sixteen miles were surveyed on skis on January 26, 1994, a wise way to spend search time. In this search, Jim Till of FWS skied into Berry Creek with two others. They found evidence that "strongly suggests the presence of a lone wolf."[20]

FWS consistently resisted public pressure to capture and radio-collar wolves in Wyoming during those few opportunities it had to do so. As previously mentioned, in August, 1992, a wolf was filmed alongside a grizzly bear feeding on a bison carcass in YNP. The tape, taken by professional cinematographers, was released to several national television networks. Public interest in the animal was high. FWS seemingly had confirmation of wolf presence, yet did not make any effort to capture the individual. In fact, one memo stated: "We especially need to minimize the significance of this incident" and "The Service should resist pressure to capture and examine the animal."[21]

Two months later, after Jerry Kysar's wolf was shot just south of the park, Fritts stated: "We may be called on to conduct a broad scale search for wolves in the Yellowstone area. An extensive survey would not be a wise use of Service funding or personnel."[22]

The reports of wolf presence inside and adjacent to YNP demonstrated the continuity of wolf sightings in the area from the last days of the predator control era to just prior to the release of Canadian wolves into the park. The available record indicated that a few wolves had survived in the area, and that both NPS and FWS confirmed the presence of wolves during this time.

Documenting wolf occurrence in an area where most people viewed wolves as extinct should have been of great scientific value. Zoologist and wolf taxonomy expert Ronald Nowak, when speaking of the possibility that the wolf killed in the Teton Wilderness may have been a survivor of a remnant population, stated, "It would be one of the major zoological finds of the century."[23] It would have given us a chance to learn about an animal of which we knew relatively nothing.

Chapter 10

Planning Process

Early in February, 1993, an elk feeder working for WGF saw four wolves on the Dell Creek elk feedground northeast of Bondurant, Wyoming. The feeder was riding a snowmobile into the feedground when he saw the four large, heavy-bodied black canids. The feeder then went to a nearby ranch, the Little Jenny, and ranch managers Dennis and Karen Allen went back to the feedground and saw canid tracks they knew were larger than those made by coyotes in the area.[1] Wolf reintroduction team leader Ed Bangs deemed the fact that the media got word of the incident "unfortunate."[2]

In mid-March, 1993, FWS announced that it had determined that the animal shot south of YNP by Jerry Kysar was indeed a wolf, probably one that had dispersed into the area from the northern Montana population.[3] This announcement only stirred the controversy over the true identity of the Yellowstone-area wolves further. By mid-November, photographs of the wolf appeared in newspapers throughout the West. The photos were vivid — the animal was obviously a wolf. The official announcement by FWS was anticlimactic, except for the inference that it was a Montana wolf. Many people simply felt that FWS was lying. It had taken FWS over five months to decide that the animal was indeed a wolf, and the minute that determination was made, FWS suddenly knew where it came from. It was unbelievable.

The *Billings Gazette* discussed the findings with Jerry Kysar, and reported him saying, "It is hard to believe that [he] happened to run into and shoot the only wolf to find its way to Yellowstone."[4] But that is precisely what FWS claimed. Bangs retorted, "You finally got a wolf making it all the way to Yellowstone, and it got whacked in a matter of months."[5] Another account quotes Bangs as stating: "It took 50 years for wolves to get to Yellowstone. One finally did and now it's dead."[6]

FWS had more problems. Robert Ream, a wolf expert with the University of Montana, challenged the FWS notion that the animal was a lone disperser. According to AP reports, Ream asserted that the wolf was probably not the only one in that area. Ream also stated that FWS should conduct search efforts in northwestern Wyoming for wolves, and pressed for natural recovery over wolf reintroduction.[7]

Bangs kept up the front. "These lone wolves occasionally pop up. But people shouldn't confuse a lone wolf that is now dead with any kind of population recovery. Other than the fact that it's kind of a novelty, it really doesn't mean anything to the EIS."[8]

Late in May, 1993, naturalist Jim Halfpenny of Gardiner, Montana, discovered a set of wolf tracks in YNP. He made plaster casts of the tracks from which his later statistical analyses determined were indeed made by a wolf.[9] His findings were carried by the AP in newspapers throughout the West.

Following a series of reports of wolf sightings between Jackson and Dubois, which FWS's Joe Fontaine said appeared to be from "a single, dispersing wolf," Wolf Fund director Renee Askins cautioned that tracks in the area could be from a dog or a hybrid.[10] She said, "We have to be careful of inferences made from a single track."

WGF issued a caution to hunters.[11] "In previous years, this type of reminder was largely unnecessary, since no wolves were known to exist in the state," read a press release in the *Casper Star-Tribune*. But with the killing of a wolf by a hunter the previous fall, the state wildlife agency cautioned shooters to positively identify their targets before pulling the trigger.

Of the Teton wolf, Askins proclaimed:

"One wolf, a dead wolf, is a far howl from wolf recovery . . . Some opponents are indeed delighted with the dead wolf and not just because it is dead. The dead wolf, they assert, demonstrates that a process of natural recolonization is under way and all this reintroduction nonsense can stop.[12]

"With a wink they say to each other, 'Natural recolonization has worked great for 50 years!' Meaning they can shoot, shovel and shut up faster than Canis lupus can disperse to Yellowstone."

Askins said wolf opponents were pushing the claim that Yellowstone already had wolves so that reintroduction plans should be dropped in favor of natural recolonization.

"What's going on here? Have wolf opponents become wolf protectors overnight?

"No.

"What people now face is a cunning strategy that is intended to further confuse and divide an already confused and divided public. The opposition has created a fog of misinformation to stall, subvert, and sabotage the Endangered Species Act, the gray wolf environmental impact statement and the goal of wolf recovery . . .

"There is no question" that single wolves or perhaps even pairs of wolves have been present in the park during the last 50 years, but "it is absurd to assume that a population of wolves could survive undetected in the Yellowstone region . . .

"Let's recognize this situation for what it is — another ploy by opponents to sabotage wolf recovery."

On June 2, 1993, EIS team members Wayne Brewster and John Varley followed up on a report of wolf tracks in the northern portion of the park and managed to locate a set of wolf tracks. Bangs reported "It is likely [that the tracks are from] the wolf photographed last summer. Last week lone wolf tracks also were discovered in the Hayden Valley. It is a continuing battle to keep the public (and some agency people) focused on breeding wolves or wolf populations rather than an occasional loner."[13]

With the release of the environmental impact statement pending, *Casper Star-Tribune* writer Dan Neal joined the fray, predicting:

"While the plan likely will satisfy most wolf supporters, expect opponents to demand more hearings, no matter how many are planned. It's just part of their never-say-die approach of trying to talk wolf reintroduction to death.[14]

"Then we can expect the really rabid opposition to heat up the conspiracy theories. They'll start pushing the idea that Fish and Wildlife and National Park Service biologists are hiding evidence that Yellowstone already holds a population of reproducing wolves. Watch for sighting reports to jump this spring and summer."

Finally, in July, 1993, the DEIS was released. The FWS mailing list had grown to almost 45,000 people. The DEIS was the subject of public review and comment until late November. FWS held sixteen official hearings, twelve of these in the three affected states, and four others in cities in other states. Nearly 1,500 people attended the hearings and almost seven hundred testified. By the time the public comment period closed, FWS had received over 160,200 comments in the form of letters, resolutions, petitions, hearing testimony, form letters, and post cards.

The Northern Great Plains Regional Chapter of the Sierra Club sent out a memo to "all wolf activists and supporters," stating that FWS "is promoting a plan which responds to the political rhetoric of wolf opponents, rather than good science." Sierra Club wanted wolves reintroduced under full ESA protections.[15]

The Wolf Fund, as predicted, endorsed the experimental reintroduction proposal. Two Idaho-based groups took another tack by asking for more monitoring in Idaho. Both the Wolf Recovery Foundation and Idaho Conservation League stated their belief that Idaho already harbored wolves.[16]

The Greater Yellowstone Coalition (GYC), a regional environmental advocacy group, denounced the reintroduction plan because of its reduced protections for existing wolves in Idaho and Montana.[17]

NPS Director Roger Kennedy proclaimed that reintroduction was the preferred route to recovery, not natural extension of wolf range.

"Are these indigenous, already occurring, self-introduced, or is the . . . process a tightly managed one?" Kennedy pondered.[18]

FWS refused to evaluate several very important issues in the DEIS, including the issues of existing wolves and wolf subspecies. The DEIS was based on the assumption that, while a few lone wolves may inhabit the area, "wolf populations do not currently exist in these areas"[19] and "no evidence exists that wolf population persisted in the Northern Rocky Mountains of the US to the present time."[20]

Yet, later in the DEIS, FWS presented evidence in direct contradiction to these statements. It discussed breeding activity in the park in the late 1960s through the early 1970s and breeding activity adjacent to the park from the late 1960s through the late 1970s. Locations of den sites found in 1974 and 1975 were discussed,[21] although elsewhere in the document it stated, "The likelihood of wolf populations persisting at a low level without evidence of pack formation . . . is extremely remote." Pack formation and reproduction had been confirmed in southwestern Montana and Yellowstone and was documented in the DEIS.[22]

In one part of the DEIS, the text stated that the Kysar wolf was the first wolf killed close to the park since 1926, yet later in the document was text that stated that a wild wolf was known to have been killed in the Yellowstone area in 1944.[23] Evidence indicated that numerous wolves were killed in the Yellowstone area over the years, including a road kill of a single individual just thirty miles north of the park in the spring of 1988.

Public opinion surveys conducted by Alistair J. Bath in 1987 revealed that 29.1 percent of the Wyoming general public agreed that wolves currently existed in YNP.[24] Another survey by Bath revealed that thirty-four percent of the Idaho and Montana general public agreed that wolves existed in the park.[25] These surveys were conducted before wolf occurrence in the park really became a publicized issue, before Ray Paunovich filmed a wolf and Jerry Kysar killed one in 1992.

In the DEIS, FWS dismissed the idea of providing an alternative that would allow for the recovery of existing wolves.[26] The agency dismissed this alternative based on two false allegations — that no pack activity had been documented in the Yellowstone area since 1926 and that an intensive monitoring effort was underway that would have detected the presence of any wolves in the study area.

The first statement was false and was refuted in the DEIS itself. Wolf packs and dens with pups were documented in the Beaverhead National Forest just west of Yellowstone in the mid-1970s. Glen Cole also reasoned that wolf reproduction was occurring within Yellowstone in the late 1960s.

In its decision-making rationale as presented in the DEIS, FWS had clearly abandoned scientific standards. FWS started with the assumption that wolves had been extirpated in the region and, consequently, in practice would consider only evidence that supported this assumption. If the recovery of the existing wolf population had been considered in depth in the DEIS and if evidence to support the possibility of an existing population had been accepted or evaluated, a different conclusion on this alternative likely would have been reached.

FWS also used wording in the DEIS to create a definition of what constituted a "wolf population." Federal regulation already defined a population to be "a group of fish or wildlife in the same taxon below the subspecific level, in common spatial arrangement that interbreed when mature."[27]

But in the DEIS, FWS proposed, "Wolves would be reintroduced into either or both the Yellowstone National Park or Central Idaho recovery areas unless a wolf population (defined as two breeding pairs, each successfully raising two or more young for two consecutive years in a recovery area) has been documented." The reintroduction had already been scheduled for October, 1994. FWS had no intention of actually finding any qualifying, breeding wolves that might meet the standards of a population as defined in the DEIS. Hence, the outcome of the monitoring program was predetermined, as defined by the timetable.

In the DEIS, FWS claimed with "the listing of all wolves (Canis lupus) in 1978, regardless of subspecies, any past or potential future subspecies designation is not relevant to wolf recovery in the western US at this time."[28]

FWS's own expert on wolf taxonomy, Ronald Nowak, took issue with his agency's treatment of wolf subspecies in the DEIS. Nowak was a scientist with FWS Office of Scientific Authority, and was recognized as a world authority on canid taxonomy when he addressed the fact that the document did not come to grips with the issue of native wolf survival.[29]

"If there were actually a surviving population of the original Yellowstone wolf, every effort should be made to maintain its purity and to avoid bringing in other wolves . . . In any case, the document [DEIS] improperly suggests that the original Yellowstone wolf is not substantially different from wolves that would be reintroduced. My own work indicates a subspecific distinction . . .

"There is a difference between that and other populations . . .

"Again, there is the misleading suggestion that the original Yellowstone wolf has affinity with the wolves that would be reintroduced, when in fact there is a pronounced subspecific distinction. It is wrong to state that the 1978 listing made subspecies irrelevant. A big part of the conservation of a full species is to ensure that its component subspecies and populations remain intact and in place, and that over-all diversity and evolutionary potential are maintained."

Earlier, Nowak had proposed that five subspecies of gray wolves occurred in North America (Figure 4).[30] *Canis lupus irremotus*, an older name for the subspecies of wolves that naturally occurred in the Yellowstone area, had been synonymized with and belonged to a southern group of wolves named *Canis lupus nubilus*. *Canis lupus occidentalis*, the subspecies of wolf from Canada that was to be used in the reintroduction program, belonged to another, more northerly group. Nowak's classification of the Yellowstone wolf had been accepted by most taxonomists and had been supported by the research of other scientists, all of which suggested that a major north-south division of wolf subspecies existed along the Canada-US border in western North America — *C. l. occidentalis* to the north of the border and *C. l. nubilus* to the south.

While calling the reintroduction "damn foolishness," US Senator Malcolm Wallop admitted he was considering sponsoring legislation to mandate an experimental wolf population.[31] "I think most people in the West have had a belly full of US government and its ability to keep its word," Wallop said.

US Senator Alan Simpson joined Wallop in stating he might support the experimental reintroduction.[32] Simpson said: "If we're going to have it shoved down our throats at least . . . they should come in as an experimental population . . . For a guy that has distaste for the whole thing, this is about the best we'd be able to do with the threat of litigation and the present administration."[33]

Wyoming Governor Mike Sullivan, nearing the end of his term of office, said of the FWS plan:[34] "Our support will continue to hinge on approval of reintroduction with adequate safeguards as outlined in the impact statement . . . It appears that reintroduction of experimental populations is an effort to reach a balanced solution, offering us more control and greater safeguards than passively waiting for natural repopulation, which I believe is inevitable and which would leave us with the worst of all worlds — wolves with no controls."[35]

Only Wyoming Congressman Craig Thomas remained steadfast in opposition to the reintroduction.

As part of our research on Wyoming wolves, I systematically filed FOIA requests with most federal natural resources agencies in the Yellowstone region, seeking "all information" in their files related to wolf occurrence. That way, we could compile the information available from various agencies into a more comprehensive and accurate record. We knew that if we did decide to take the reintroduction plan to court, it would be an administrative record review case, so we wanted to have all the wolf reports together, ready to file with our comments on the EIS to become part of that administrative record.

In response to my request for all wolf sighting reports in the WGF files, agency Director Pete Petera sent the packet of information along with a cover letter stating: "The information that you have requested is anecdotal at best. Wolf sightings in Wyoming have not been confirmed. Follow-up observations of such sightings have resulted in the identification of everything from coyotes to domestic dogs."[36]

Submitting FOIA requests was a time-consuming process that worked very well, until FWS decided to withhold some of the information. We argued that the withholdings were a violation of FOIA and FWS granted us more of the information, but continued to deny some of what we had requested. I appealed the withholding, which again led to only partial success. I knew that what they were doing was illegal and felt it was an attempt to stonewall our research, so I hired an attorney and we filed a FOIA lawsuit in federal court in Wyoming on August 16, 1993.[37]

With the effective representation of Jackson Hole attorney Steve Jones, Federal Judge Alan Johnson agreed with our arguments in whole, issuing his decision on May 31, 1994, and ordering FWS to promptly release the information. The withheld information ranged from embarrassing "talking points" for handling the media in order to discredit wolf sightings that made the news, to withholding the identity of those reporting wolves and locations of wolf sighting reports.

FWS tried a variety of tactics during the lawsuit to avoid having to release the information. One such tactic involved the agency sending letters to people who had seen wolves to learn if those people opposed having their names and addresses released. The letter opened with the statement that "the United States Department of Interior is currently involved in a lawsuit with an individual who is seeking the identity and address of persons making wolf sighting reports from 1990 to the present."

While Johnson did not rule on whether it was proper for the letter even to have been sent, he did note: "It does not appear to this court that the letter which was actually sent was designed to solicit unbiased responses when the letter suggested that respondents could somehow be involved in pending litigation. It is likely that such letters are of dubious value."[38]

Johnson ruled that the information I had requested should be released because "the public interest will be served in that it brings the activities of FWS with respect to the duties imposed on it by the ESA into public scrutiny and may contribute to public understanding of the operations and activities of that government agency."[39]

While our FOIA case was making its way through the legal system, YNP officials declined to release the same type of information to me, although it had done so in the past. I filed an appeal and won the appeal for the Yellowstone records that fall as well.

Chad Baldwin of the *Riverton Ranger* was not surprised that FWS continued on its single-track experimental reintroduction program. He wrote:[40] "What's most disturbing, however, is that neither the shooting of a wolf in the Teton Wilderness last fall, nor the filming of an apparent wolf in the park last summer, could deter the agency from its plotted course. Backed by 'pro-wolf' groups that are just as narrow-minded as those in the anti-wolf camp, the FWS is proceeding with a reintroduction plan that essentially disregards the possibility that wolves already inhabit the Yellowstone area."

Baldwin pointed out that logically, the pro-wolf groups should be pushing to find any existing wolves before any transplants took place, but: "Instead, the organizations are pushing for accelerated reintroduction and are branding those who dare to suggest that wolves may already live around Yellowstone as 'wolf haters.'. . . The FWS and 'pro-wolf' groups are hell-bent on reintroduction, and it'll take court or congressional action to stop them."

Wolf advocate Robert Hoskins editorialized about wolf haters. "In prattling about wolf DNA or subspecies to keep wolves out of Yellowstone . . . those who deal in hate steal the wolf's dignity and express contempt for its ancient gifts of knowledge of life and death."[41]

In November, 1994, Renee Askins of the Wolf Fund just could not take all the attention that wolf sightings and other alternatives to reintroduction was getting, so she wrote an editorial to the *Jackson Hole Guide* complaining about that paper's coverage of the issue and of our views. She spoke of "misguided (if not well meaning efforts) of people who don't understand the basics of wolf ecology."[42]

Apparently if you disagreed with her views, you were simply ignorant.

The final EIS (FEIS) was released in May, 1994, and it was no better than the earlier version in that it again failed to analyze several important issues and reach conclusions that were based on balanced, scientifically derived assessments, including the effect of the action on the naturally occurring wolves in the Yellowstone area, the need for more research on the naturally occurring wolves, and the issue of wolf subspecies. FWS dismissed these issues from consideration in the FEIS for one main reason — that wolves had been extirpated from the area by 1930, so it claimed. The FEIS stated: "No evidence exists that wolf populations persisted in the northern Rocky Mountains of the US to the present time or that the lone wild wolves occasionally reported in these areas are other than dispersing wolves from Canadian populations."[43]

Of course, the available record indicated that a few wolves had survived in the Yellowstone area, and that both NPS and FWS confirmed the presence of wolves during this time. So why was this issue lied about in the FEIS? There could only be one answer — to allow the wolf reintroduction to go forward. It was no secret that NPS had pushed for a wolf reintroduction program since the late 1960s. Regardless of the reason, the fact remained — FWS was dishonest in its treatment of the issue in the EIS process. FWS stated that "no evidence exists" that wolves had persisted in the Yellowstone area when, in fact, the evidence to the contrary was plentiful.

A second issue important to the legality of conducting this reintroduction was the mandated responsibility, as part of the ESA, to protect and conserve subspecies. The FEIS dismissed this issue without analyzing the relevant data in detail because, again it argued, no evidence existed that any wolves, of any subspecies, had persisted in the Yellowstone area. FWS also argued that subspecies are irrelevant to wolf recovery, ignoring the ESA mandate that subspecies *are* relevant.

As the preparation of the EIS proceeded, one scientist was learning how FWS reacted to its critics. In August, 1993, *Petersen's Hunting* magazine published an article called "Wolves in the West: What the government does not want you to know about wolf recovery," written by Charles E. Kay of Utah State University. In the article, Kay claimed that the federal government proposed a recovery goal of about one hundred wolves "knowing that would not be enough to meet requirements of minimum viable population size, and environmental groups did not object, knowing that 100 wolves would raise less political opposition than 1,500 wolves."[44]

Kay said the one-hundred-wolf proposal was developed with little or no scientific evidence, thereby rendering invalid all subsequently derived reports, population models, and other studies regarding potential impacts of the plan. "They represent not science but a masterful job of deception," Kay wrote.

Kay's article indicated that wolves would limit ungulate populations, hunting opportunities would be reduced, and wolf control would be unlikely. He also called on the public to get involved in the

EIS process and "demand that the government stop spreading misinformation and begin telling the public the true impacts of wolf recovery."

Ed Bangs was not happy with Kay's article, calling it "inaccurate and misleading."[45] In a report to the FWS Regional Director, Bangs wrote: "Dr. Kay's allegations were absolutely not true . . . A rebuttal was prepared for the magazine. After attempts to contact Dr. Kay failed, the dean at his department (Institute of Political Economy) at Utah State University was contacted to try and resolve the issue. Hopefully, Dr. Kay will print a complete retraction and apology."[46]

Bangs later reported to the regional director that, "Comments from Utah State University contacts indicated that Dr. Kay has done this type of thing (misinformed accusations) before, has a tendency to believe in plots, and is his own worst enemy."[47]

Bangs wrote a letter to the editor of *Petersen's Hunting* protesting Kay's article.[48] In addition, he sent letters, copies of Kay's article, and contact information for both *Petersen's Hunting* and Utah State University to all the EIS team members and reviewers, to twenty-three contacts in all, "asking for your assistance."[49] The letter went on:

"I hope that you will also write a letter to the editor and send a copy to the President of Utah State University, to provide your thoughts on Dr. Kay's allegations regarding preparation of the draft EIS on the reintroduction of gray wolves to Yellowstone National Park and central Idaho.

"I believe that Dr. Kay's allegations were far beyond just his opinion or a professional disagreement over data interpretation or philosophy, and thus must be directly addressed. I hope you can add any concerns you or your agency might have about Dr. Kay's allegations, to mine."

There were calls for Bangs to resign from the EIS team as his actions were viewed as an assault on Kay and served to try to get Kay fired.[50]

Troy Mader of the Abundant Wildlife Society of North America in Gillette was outraged at Bangs's attempt to censure Kay, "who dared to expose the errors and deceptions involved in the government's promotion of wolf recovery here in the West."[51]

Wyoming Wool Growers Association executive director Carolyn Paseneaux wrote to US Senator Alan Simpson, "Bangs' actions are clearly that of a witch hunt for an individual who happens to disagree with his views of reintroduction of wolves to the Yellowstone area, even enlisting others to help him in his cause."[52]

California Forestry Association director of wildlife ecology Robert J. Taylor wrote a letter to the deputy director of FWS, stating: "I write not to defend Dr. Kay but to question the propriety of a federal employee engaging in a clear attempt to suppress the opinions of a scientist who has established his research credentials. I am particularly troubled by Mr. Bangs' attempt to influence the president of Utah State University."[53]

Utah State University Institute of Political Economy Director Randy Simmons wrote FWS Deputy Director Richard Smith that Bangs had called him to complain about Kay's article. His letter stated:[54] "He claimed Fish and Wildlife Service employees lives would be threatened by Idaho neo-nazis because of Dr. Kay's claims. He also suggested organizing a university committee to review Dr. Kay's work and, if possible, censure him . . . Mud-slinging and attempts to silence critics are not appropriate ways to deal with scientific controversies."

Predictably, FWS defended Bangs. In its response to Senator Simpson, FWS Deputy Regional Director John L. Spinks, Jr. called Bangs "an honest and dedicated federal employee and is highly respected both within and outside the government" and said that he "does an exemplary job[55]. . . [but] Unfortunately, in this capacity, Mr. Bangs is vulnerable to accusations from any source displeased with the Service's goal of recovering the gray wolf. . . There is no truth to the allegation that Mr. Bangs requested that Dr. Kay be fired, [I believe Bangs] handled this situation in a professional and appropriate manner [and] The Service believes the situation should be laid to rest."

Late in November, 1994, FWS published the final rules establishing the experimental population status for both the Yellowstone and central Idaho areas (Figure 22). This was the last step in the legal process to conduct the reintroduction.

Figure 22. The Draft Environmental Impact Statement proposed two nonessential experimental population areas into which experimental populations of Canadian wolves would be released and monitored. (After US Department of the Interior, Fish and Wildlife Service, 1994)

Perhaps the greatest folly for the experimental population rule centered on the agency's definition of a wolf population and what that meant in terms of wolf recovery in the Yellowstone area. FWS, in the proposed experimental population rule, used "populations as defined by wolf experts" to justify the claim that no wolf population — "at least two breeding pairs of wild wolves successfully raising at least two young each for two consecutive years in an experimental area" — existed in the Yellowstone area.

In developing the definition of what constituted a wolf population, FWS had sent a written survey to wolf experts. In the cover letter accompanying the survey, FWS admitted, "This is a critical legal question because reintroduced wolves cannot be designated as an 'experimental population' if they are placed into an area where a population already exists."[56] Even with this prompting, the opinions of the respondents varied greatly. While a few agreed with the definition proposed by FWS, most preferred their own definitions, many of which included descriptions of a 'viable' population, indicating they really did not understand the problem set forth in the survey. Some of the comments are worth noting.

Mark Boyce, for example, stated, "If accepting your definition would imply that a population doesn't exist and therefore you have free reign to carry on with a release program, I would reject your definition."[57] Diane Boyd, citing recent evidence of wolf activity in the Yellowstone area, advocated natural recovery and stated, "Even one or two wolves should be considered a population for potential recovery in lieu of [an] artificially reintroduced [one]."[58] Other experts associated with universities provided comments that varied from how "unfortunate" the wording of the ESA is[59] to calls for enhancing viability by reintroducing animals "unless there is some reason to think that a small number of isolated individuals is genetically unique."[60]

Some of the comments by wolf experts employed by FWS were appalling. Mike Phillips proposed a more conservative population definition because he felt "a more lenient definition would provide opponents to recovery too great an opportunity to prevent introductions by invoking the geographical separation requirement."[61] Although

Phillips understood what Congress intended with the ESA mandate, he disagreed. Michael Nelson actually suggested that FWS's Steve Fritts should "pick or create the 'legal' definition that favors (in your opinion) the interests of the wolf."[62]

While FWS was the lead agency charged with implementing the ESA, it seemed some of its employees were choosing to circumvent the act rather than implement it.

Both the EIS and the experimental population rule background information recognized that *yes*, a few wolves did occur in the area, but *no*, a "wolf population" as defined by experts, did not exist. The wolf population definition was nothing more than politically convenient biology.

FWS's claims that subspecies were not important and that there was no subspecific difference in wolves were false claims, unsupported by the record before it. The agency continued to make unfounded claims that were essential to the legality of the decision. Litigation was soon to come.

Chapter 11

Taxonomic Distinction

Congress had declared that the purpose of the ESA was to provide a program for the conservation of endangered species and "to provide a means" whereby the ecosystems upon which these endangered species depended would be conserved.[1] Congress's stated policy was clear: "It is further declared to be the policy of Congress that all federal departments and agencies shall seek to conserve endangered species and threatened species and shall utilize their authorities in furtherance of the purposes of this chapter."

The ESA included definitions of terms used throughout the text of the act. An endangered species was "any species which is in danger of extinction throughout all or a significant portion of its range . . ." "Fish or wildlife" was defined as "any member of the animal kingdom, including without limitation any mammal, fish, bird . . . and includes any part, product, egg, or offspring thereof, or the dead body parts thereof." "Species" "includes any subspecies of fish or wildlife or plants, and any distinct population segment of any species of vertebrate fish or wildlife which interbreeds when mature." And, the terms "conserve, conserving and conservation" "mean to use and the use of all methods and procedures which are necessary to bring any endangered species or threatened species to the point at which the measures provided pursuant to this chapter are no longer necessary."

On June 4, 1973, the subspecies of wolf native to the Yellowstone area — the "Northern Rocky Mountain Wolf, *Canis lupus irremotus*" — was added to the United States List of Endangered Native Fish and Wildlife.[2]

In 1977, FWS proposed to change the gray wolf listing. The proposed rulemaking, which appeared in the June 9, 1977, issue of *Federal Register*, proposed that four listed subspecies of the gray wolf, including *C. l. irremotus*, would be removed from the endangered list and, instead, the entire population of gray wolves in Mexico and the lower forty-eight states would be listed as endangered, with the exception of those in Minnesota, which would be listed as threatened.[3] The 1977 proposal stated: "This listing arrangement has not been satisfactory because the taxonomy of wolves is out of date, wolves may wander outside of recognized subspecific boundaries, and some wolves from unlisted subspecies may occur in certain parts of the lower 48 states. In any case, the Service wishes to recognize that the entire species *Canis lupus* is Endangered or Threatened to the south of Canada, and considers that this matter can be handled most conveniently by listing only the species name."

The *Federal Register* addressed the factors determining the species' endangered status. Under a section addressing "The present or threatened destruction, modification, or curtailment of its habitat or range," it stated: "The gray wolf once had a range that included most of Mexico and the 48 conterminous States of the United States. The species now occurs in only a small fraction of this range, and is very rare in most places where it does exist . . . In the northwestern United States the wolf is restricted to remote parts of the Rocky Mountains, though some individuals may wander from this region, or from Canada, into other areas."

Included in the gray wolf's known range, in revisions to both the proposed and final listing, were the states of Arizona, Idaho, Michigan, Montana, New Mexico, North Dakota, Oregon, Texas, Washington, Wisconsin, and Wyoming — and Mexico.

On March 9, 1978, the final rule changing the classification was published. Several comments received from the public and agencies expressed concern for the protection of subspecies.[4] According to the *Federal Register*:

"The US Forest Service supported the reclassification . . . but requested assurance that biological subspecies would continue to be maintained and dealt with as separate entities. The Fish and Wildlife Service can give this assurance . . . The National Park Service also favored continued recognition of the different wolf subspecies, and in general supported the proposal . . .

"The North American Wolf Society . . . questioned the elimination of subspecific differentiation in listings, suggesting that such elimination could jeopardize efforts to locate and maintain stocks of the various subspecies. The Service, however, can offer the firmest assurance that it will continue to recognize valid biological subspecies for purposes of its research and conservation programs."

The 1978 change remained in effect until FWS published special rules in the *Federal Register* establishing experimental populations of gray wolves in central Idaho and Yellowstone in 1994.[5]

Recognizing the mandate to protect subspecies, on May 28, 1980, FWS approved the first Northern Rocky Mountain Wolf Recovery Plan, noting: "Although there is a trend among taxonomists to recognize fewer subspecies of wolves, the Northern Rocky Mountain wolf is still considered a distinct subspecies by the US Fish and Wildlife Service . . . However, this plan only deals with the subspecies *irremotus*."[6]

To address the issue of subspecies, it is helpful to take a step back and look at the larger picture. Zoology, simply put, is the biological study of animal life. Aristotle, born in 384 BC in Greece, arranged animals into natural groups based on their characteristics. Years later, Carolus Linnaeus, born in 1707 in Sweden, devised a system of classification into which every living thing could be fitted. Linnaeus's system, which was based on shared characteristics and natural relationships, is the basis of the current system of biological taxonomy. Linnaeus classified the gray wolf as a species, *Canis lupus*, and later scientists, working with significantly more information, recognized subspecies — morphologically distinct populations that occurred in geographically distinct areas — within the gray wolf. *Canis lupus irremotus* was one among several subspecies of gray wolf that came to be recognized. Stanley Young and Edward Goldman became early authorities in the arena of gray wolf taxonomy.[7]

More recently, progress in the field of molecular genetics has contributed to differences of opinion, and sometimes disputes, among taxonomists and others whose work depends upon taxonomy. Some geneticists have suggested, based on molecular analysis, that there is little genetic difference or variation among all wolves in North

America, and have used this perspective to argue that "augmentation plans need not be concerned in detail with the locality of origin of gray wolves."[8]

However, others in the field of zoology, notably Thomas E. Dowling and Ronald Nowak, have challenged the techniques used in these analyses and their implications for conservation.[9] Indeed, mitochondrial DNA (mtDNA) analysis has failed to show genetic differences between brown bears and polar bears, or mule deer and white-tailed deer, yet found distinct differences between small- and large-bodied subspecies of the Canada goose.[10]

Although morphological differences traditionally had been recognized by FWS as a valid basis to define and differentiate subspecies, Jerry Kysar's shooting of a wolf south of Yellowstone in 1992, prior to the scheduled wolf reintroduction, brought about a change in this policy.

Young and Goldman's *The Wolves of North America* maintained that the subspecies of wolf native to the Yellowstone region was *Canis lupus irremotus*,[11] "a light-colored subspecies of medium to rather large size, with skull having a narrow but flattened frontal region." In the same work, *Canis lupus occidentalis*, the subspecies of wolf from western Canada that FWS eventually released into the Yellowstone area, was described as "the largest of the North American wolves, with a large and massive skull." Young and Goldman noted that *irremotus* differed from *occidentalis* in its "decidedly smaller size." In addition, after examining hundreds of wolf skulls, they noted that cranial abnormalities in the large number of specimens were few, but did find an abnormality that was specifically associated with the subspecies *irremotus*. "The small posterior lower molars may be absent, and the small anterior premolars may be lacking in either jaw." In contrast, they found an abnormality in only one skull of *occidentalis* — the specimen had an additional upper premolar.

More recent taxonomic work has resulted in the recognition of fewer subspecies than had been recognized by Young and Goldman. Nowak proposed that wolves in North America belong to only five subspecies.[12] As stated earlier, he placed *C. l. irremotus* among a southern group of wolves named *C. l. nubilus* while *C. l. occidentalis* was retained as another, more northernly group. Nowak's classification of the Yellowstone wolf was not contested by other taxonomists, and was supported by studies of other researchers, all of which suggests that a major systematic north-south division of wolf subspecies existed along the Canada-US border in western North America. This body of work demonstrated that Yellowstone's native wolf, *C. l. irremotus*, was substantially different than *C. l. occidentalis,* the subspecies that was eventually released into the area by FWS.

Nowak sent a letter commenting on the DEIS concerning the wolf reintroduction, and very clearly pointed out to FWS that the wolves native to Yellowstone were "substantially different" from the Canadian wolves, that there is a "subspecific distinction" between the two, and that the DEIS improperly suggested otherwise.[13]

FWS knew that wolves had survived in the Yellowstone region. FWS also knew there was a pronounced subspecific difference between the native wolf, *C. l. irremotus*, and the released northern wolves, *C. l. occidentalis*. It should have come as no surprise that the wolf killed by a vehicle just north of the park in 1988, according to Nowak, "looks more like a member of this original US population. Its measurements fall mostly within the range shown by the subspecies *C. l. irremotus* of the northern Rockies."[14]

Nowak had examined the skull of this male wolf and stated that the skull was "notably smaller" than those taken in recent years in the northwestern US, presumably immigrants from Canada.

The wolf that Jerry Kysar shot in 1992 had several skull abnormalities, and Nowak could not determine, with certainty, its subspecies. After examining the skull of this animal, Nowak commented that, based on cranial measurements, it was "considerably smaller than what would be expected for a male wolf of the current population in western Montana." Nowak again pointed out that his analysis indicated the Canadian wolf population migrating into northwestern Montana represented a subspecies of wolf that differed from the smaller subspecies that occurred to the south. He proposed several possibilities for the taxonomic and geographic history of the Teton Wolf, including that it might have been "a member (somewhat inbred) of a population that had survived in the wild in the Yellowstone area."

Nowak did, however, note a specific cranial abnormality in the Teton wolf. "The right third lower molar tooth is not present and seems never to have erupted."[15] This is the abnormality described by Young and Goldman in 1944 as occurring in the native wolf, *C. l. irremotus*. The Cody wolf, killed by FWS in 1997, also had the same dental abnormality. One of the lab reports stated, "Gross examination of the skull indicates an adult individual with no visible abnormalities, except a missing right lower first premolar."

Bangs said, of the Cody wolf, "It looked a little short-legged and small-footed to me but otherwise very much like a wolf and likely within the physical variation found in wild wolves."[16] These characteristics were also attributed to a wolf discovered in the wild near Kemmerer in 1998 by USDA Wildlife Services agent Merrill Nelson.[17]

While a wolf roped and captured by a rancher near Boulder early in 1999 was held in a pen in YNP, Yellowstone biologist Doug Smith had the opportunity to observe the animal.[18] "It looks an awful lot like a wolf," Smith said. "It's pretty wary of us, which is pretty typical wolfish behavior." But he also said that the female wolf's body frame looked small in comparison to that of the Canadian wolves that had been released in the park.

The FWS National Fish and Wildlife Forensics Laboratory in Ashland, Oregon, was given the task of determining through DNA analysis whether the Teton wolf was a wild wolf. Lab director Ken Goddard sent a memo to FWS's regional law enforcement office providing an update on the comparison of the Teton wolf to three wolves from Montana.[19] He wrote: "The mitochondrial DNA of three of these wolves have been extracted, isolated and compared. These three wolves are identical. The subject animal is not identical to these three wolves; however, so far, the questioned specimen is most closely like these wolves. The mitochondrial DNA of four more of these wolves is in the final stages of analysis this morning. If these four wolves turn out to be identical to the first three, then the questioned animal is not of this population."

Five days later, Steven Fain, the scientist conducting the DNA work, wrote that he had completed the analyses of mtDNA of the Teton wolf and seven Montana wolves, and concluded, "The genetic analyses indicate that the evidence animal did not originate from the Glacier National Park, Montana wolf pack."[20]

Genetic work continued, and late in February, 1993, Fain prepared a draft serology report which stated that the mtDNA of the Teton wolf had been compared to that of eight wolves from Montana, five wolves from Alaska, one Mexican wolf, one coyote, one red wolf, two coyote-gray wolf hybrids, and six domestic dogs, including one each of a husky-wolf hybrid, elkhound, shepherd, Labrador retriever, rottweiler, and collie.

The analysis proved fascinating, with the result being the sorting of the gray wolf and dog specimens into five distinct lineages. The first lineage comprised the collie, retriever, and rottweiler while the shepherd represented the second lineage. The third and fourth lineages both contained gray wolf samples from Montana and Alaska. But the fifth lineage comprised "the evidence animal, gray wolves from the Nine Mile Valley, Montana, as well as the Elkhound and Husky-wolf dog references."

Fain's conclusion was that: "Of all the reference samples, the evidence animal was most similar to the Nine Mile Valley animals. One animal was identical and the second differed by only a single substitution."[21] His final report stated that the Teton wolf was "identical to that of a radio-collared animal from the Nine Mile Valley wolf pack in Montana."[22]

Fain's work demonstrated that, while the Teton wolf was related to some but not all of the wolves in the Nine Mile Valley of Montana, the wolves from this area fell into a lineage that was distinct from the Glacier National Park wolf population. This was very interesting information since the Nine Mile pack was founded by wolves first discovered near Marion, Montana. While FWS suspects that these wolves came from Canada, their actual origin has never been determined. The mtDNA analysis indicated that Montana had two distinct lineages of wolves, a circumstance that suggests subspecific distinction.

The available evidence indicated that *C. l. irremotus* had survived in the Yellowstone region through 1992. No reintroduction should have occurred prior to the unraveling of this canid identity issue. Again, going back to the ESA, Congress included in the species definition "any distinct population segment of any species." With DNA testing proving that there were two distinct lineages in the Montana wolf population, that threshold had been met.

FWS claimed that the "reintroduction of wolves into the park will enhance wolf population viability by increasing the genetic diversity of wolves in the Rocky Mountain population." In reality, the reintroduction of Canadian wolves into Yellowstone would indeed send a unique gene pool into extinction. Contamination of the gene pool through interbreeding could lead to the extinction of a distinct population of this endangered species, and would, in fact, decrease the genetic diversity of wolves in the Rocky Mountain region by eliminating an entire genetically distinct population.

Many years of intensive predator control could have led to the relative isolation of wolf pack demes, or small breeding populations. Whatever the cause or causes, a few small wolf packs could have survived in isolated areas in and adjacent to Yellowstone, and with restricted gene flow among the demes, conspicuous variation in the morphology of demes could have developed.[23] However, with a low population density, the wolf population would have had a high dispersal rate, increasing the genetic interchange between semi-isolated demes. Thus, interbreeding — the crossing of different varieties within a group, but different than inbreeding, which is breeding within the group — would occur on a moderate level, given the situation. One researcher stated, "It is the subdivision that results from interbreeding in small semi-isolated demes that best generates and maintains significant species-wide variability as a hedge against environmental flux."[24]

What this discussion indicates is that a subspecies can consist of semi-isolated packs. Breeding between the packs within that subspecies would help to maintain genetic variation within the subspecies, while maintaining the subspecific distinction. A species that comprises multiple subspecies has greater variability than a monotypic species.

There may have been more than just a physical difference between *irremotus* and *occidentalis* — there may also have been a behavioral difference. *Irremotus* may have been more similar in behavior to another southern gray-wolf subspecies, the Mexican Wolf, than to wolves to the north. In the Mexican Wolf Recovery Plan, the behavior of this wolf subspecies, *Canis lupus baileyi*, was described as being very different than Canadian wolves. "Mexican wolf packs may contain fewer individuals and be less cohesive in nature than is the case reported for northern subspecies of wolves . . . Mexican wolves are found singly or in very small packs of two or three animals and never in the larger packs reported for wolf subspecies of Canada, Alaska and northern United States."[25]

The behavior of the Mexican wolf is similar to the behavior of the Yellowstone wolf. Sighting reports of wolves in Yellowstone from 1836 to the 1990s paint a picture of wolves without cohesive pack behavior. In the early 1900s, federal trapper Vernon Bailey reported that there were never more than two old wolves at a den site, and that the wolves he tracked in western Wyoming were usually found in pairs. Bailey wrote of his visit to the Upper Green River Valley in March, 1906:

"Fresh tracks were seen almost every day, usually of wolves in pairs, but in one case a band of nine. Between March 24 and April 21, 1906, four dens, containing 32 wolf pups, were found, with two old wolves at each den; and evidently there were two or three other dens in the valley.[26]

"Men who have made a business of hunting wolves for the bounty assert that they are usually able to shoot one or both of the old wolves at the den by watching the trails, or hiding near the den early in the morning before the wolves return from the night's round. These statements are fully corroborated by my own experience. While watching dens in Wyoming I could easily have shot the male who was doing sentinel duty; for although he watched from a high point from which he could see a man long before being himself seen, still in his anxiety to decoy me away he often came within rifle range."

Of the 148 reports of wolves in Yellowstone from 1836 to 1926, where the number of animals could be determined, only ten reports were of six or more animals together. Nine of these ten reports occurred late in the year, and could be explained as an adult pair with their pups of that year. In one extraordinary report, a pack of "about 16 wolves" was reported in February, 1918. This was the largest group of wolves ever reported in the Yellowstone area and only one such report was recorded.

In addition, all of the 881 reports of wolf occurrences in the park from 1927 through 1993 were of one to five animals. In summary, the large pack cohesiveness reported as common in Canadian wolves was not reported for the wolves native to YNP.

Is this lack of large pack size or pack cohesiveness a result of human pressure on the population causing a broken social pattern, or is this a behavioral characteristic unique to this subspecies? Canadian wolves, although hunted, retain the larger pack size.

How could it be that such a large predator could survive nearly undetected for so long? The answer might lay within the wolf, within its elusive nature, its ability to learn, to adapt. And the answer can be framed by turning the question around. The only way this wolf could have survived was to remain virtually undetected.

In other areas of the world where wolves have been relentlessly persecuted, they have adapted and survived. Wolves still hang on in small numbers in Spain, Italy, Eastern Europe, and Israel. Studies of the wolves in Italy are particularly interesting. These animals have not only survived, but do so in close proximity to fairly dense human populations.[27] These wolves frequently feed at garbage dumps on the outskirts of cities. Not only have they adapted their diet to survive in a modern environment, but they have learned to stay out of sight and to remain virtually undetected by the general human population. For years the only evidence of these wolves came with the loss of sheep in mountain pastures during sudden storms that obscured visibility and allowed the wolves to do their killing unseen. It is easy to believe that if wolves could survive extermination efforts in a nation with over fifty-five million people in only 116,000 square miles, then wolves could have survived in Wyoming, a state with only half a million people in 98,000 square miles, into the mid-1990s.

Wolf researcher Dennis Flath has stated that "wolves are highly social animals with a very strict set of social standards. The concepts of pack cohesion and territoriality are essential to their well being."[28] Referring to the low number of wolf reports that contained descriptions of three or more wolves together, indicating pack activity, Flath stated: "If the animals involved are actually genetically pure wolves, this pattern implies an extremely low and probably insecure population. Under such circumstances breeding would be sporadic and it is doubtful the population could maintain itself without some additional recruitment."

Flath, in describing an "extremely low and probably insecure population," is describing an endangered population, as we maintained was the case with Yellowstone's native wolf population. Although there was reproduction occurring, there did not appear to be a cohesive pack structure. Flath further stated that "territorial boundaries are not maintained by wolves in the absence of pack associations" and "the result is a broken social pattern which can only work to the detriment of the wolf, partly because opportunities for breeding are minimal or nonexistent."

Flath demonstrated that an endangered population of gray wolves has behavioral characteristics that differ from secure, nonendangered populations. Thus, it would be reasonable to assume that opportunities to detect wolf pack activity in an endangered population would be extremely low.

Many researchers have reported on the very elusive nature of the wolf. L. David Mech wrote "Anyone who has spent much time in wolf country will verify that the wolf is one of the wildest and shyest of all the animals in the northern wilderness. Many an experienced woodsman has lived a lifetime without even glimpsing a wolf in its natural surroundings. I hiked approximately 1,400 miles during four summers in Isle Royale National Park, which harbors one of the highest wolf densities known, and saw wolves on only three occasions during that time. In all cases, the animals ran off so quickly and silently that

I was left wondering if I had really seen them."[29] Mech's statement was similar to Glen Cole's report that, while he worked in Yellowstone, he saw wolves on only two occasions.

The odds of seeing a wolf are comparable to the odds of seeing a mountain lion in Wyoming. Although there are breeding populations of mountain lions throughout the state, they are rarely seen. From this perspective, it is surprising that so many people have reported seeing wolves over the years.

In federal court, FWS claimed that recent studies on genetic variation in gray wolves had concluded that there was very little genetic difference between subspecies, but did not cite a source or sources supporting this assertion. Rather, what FWS cited was a literature review paper written by two biologists — one employed by FWS, the other by YNP — not taxonomists. The authors of the paper admitted they were not experts on the subject, as revealed in a memo in which they discussed the issue:

"If we really want to be brave we could . . . say in our paper that there should be no subspecies of gray wolf in North America. Or (and I might actually go for this) suggest there should be two, i.e. Nowak's northern group and his southern group. Since Ron is saying in his new paper there should be five, I suppose this would be unfair to him. We might want to at least mention, albeit timidly, that one option would be a classification system with either one or two subspecies in North America (the latter idea would be consistent with our role as reviewers of the subject, rather than taxonomy experts)."[30]

These "reviewers" seemed to have an agenda of their own, making suggestions not based on the taxonomy literature they were reviewing.

Even the biologists writing the taxonomic review admitted that "Only a real expert measuring many skulls can distinguish among most races."[31] The statement acknowledged that different races, or subspecies, do indeed exist, though it takes an expert to distinguish them.

⌒

Jim and I sent Ron Nowak a packet of information about Wyoming's wolves. He responded saying:

"It seems as if you have put together a good case for persistence of the original wolf population.[32]

"The theory (as supported by Leopold and by experience with wolves in other countries) that the remnant animals in the Rockies may be behaving differently from most wolves (with regard to seasonal movements and social structure), together with the continuation of reliable records through the 1940s–1970s until present, while not conclusive, does make your case deserving of serious consideration. It would be tragic to ignore or perhaps lose a unique wolf population, valuable both in the zoological and historical sense, especially if such occurred through carelessness or political maneuvering."

Chapter 12

Reintroduction and Litigation

Just three days after FWS published the final rule establishing the experimental population status for wolves that would be released into YNP and central Idaho, the Wyoming Farm Bureau and its fellow chapters in Idaho and Montana, the national Farm Bureau, and the Mountain States Legal Foundation filed a lawsuit in US District Court in Wyoming seeking to have the reintroduction declared illegal.

Although both British Columbia and Alberta governments had agreed to supply wolves for use in the reintroduction program, British Columbia officials required written confirmation that the applicable state wildlife management agencies were "on side" with the transplant.[1]

Each state provided the letters of approval to FWS. WGF Director John Talbott wrote: "Please accept this letter as documentation of the Wyoming Game and Fish Department's commitment to the reintroduction of gray wolves to the Yellowstone ecosystem. Pending approval of the proposed rule, we will proceed with development of a state wolf management plan to be submitted to the Secretary for approval."[2]

FWS biologists headed to Alberta, Canada, and began working with provincial wildlife officials in efforts to capture wolves, paying Canadian trappers $2,000 for every wolf captured and another $500 for every one of these wolves that was actually transported and released in the United States. The Alberta government also received a lump sum of $25,000 for its cooperation. At the same time, British Columbia officials backed out of the reintroduction effort, saying that they needed funding from FWS to plan how and where wolves would be taken from their province, due to concerns from the Canadian public about the welfare of their wolves.[3]

FWS reached an agreement with the Farm Bureaus to not release any wolves until after the first of January, 1995, in order to give

Judge William Downes an opportunity to hear the Farm Bureaus' request for an injunction. Downes denied the Farm Bureaus' motion on January 3, 1995. By January 10, trappers had captured fifteen wolves in Alberta and the Farm Bureaus asked the US Court of Appeals in Denver to grant an emergency injunction pending a decision of its appeal of Downes's denial. By Wednesday, January 11, the wolves kept in shipping crates had left a Canadian airstrip headed for the US when the US Court of Appeals issued an order preventing their release from their cages.

Injunction or not, Secretary of the Interior Bruce Babbitt was on hand to participate in the reintroduction effort and stated that if the delay lasted, "Those cages will be coffins."[4] During his first two years at the helm of USDI, Babbitt had initiated what some saw as his "War on the West." Babbitt proposed grazing reform for federal lands that many ranchers felt was designed to drive them from the industry, and that in fact would allow decision-making about the use of federal lands to be conducted at higher levels, not by local officials familiar with nearby range conditions, which can vary substantially from year to year. Babbitt reportedly clashed with Republican Wyoming Governor Jim Geringer over both grazing reform and wolf reintroduction.

Under the reintroduction plan, the wolves that had been shipped to Yellowstone were to be held in acclimation pens inside the park. Those that had been shipped to central Idaho would undergo a hard release that provided instant freedom.

The wolves destined for Yellowstone completed their five-hundred-mile journey early Thursday morning, January 12, 1995. Members of the news media had been camped out in local hotels waiting for the court decision that would allow the wolves to be released. As a result, they were available to take advantage of the photo opportunity offered by Secretary Babbitt and FWS Director Mollie Beattie as they helped to carry a wolf, still locked in its crate, to a holding pen in the park.[5] That evening, the appeals court lifted the stay, and, at about 10:30 P.M., park employees released the first six wolves into their holding pen at Crystal Bench and another two into a pen in the Rose Creek area. After all of the anticipation, however, this was not quite the publicity event that officials had hoped for — no pomp and ceremony, just the opening of the cage doors in the dark of night.

On Saturday, January 14, 1995, the first four wolves were released into the wilds of central Idaho.[6]

On Monday, Governor Jim Geringer requested Babbitt to order that the wolves being held in pens in the park remain there until the legal issues had been resolved and the state had prepared a management plan for any wolves that might wander outside of the park. Babbitt refused.[7]

By Thursday, January 19, another fourteen wolves had been captured in Alberta and flown to the US. One additional wolf had been killed accidentally during capture when a tranquilizer dart punctured its lung.

Soon after the start of the Wyoming state legislative session in January, the Agriculture Committee of the Wyoming House of Representatives approved Representative Roger Huckfeldt's proposal for placing a $500 bounty on wolves that might stray outside of the park, while acknowledging that the measure probably violated federal law and would encourage the illegal killing of wolves. After weeks of debate and negotiations, a bill providing a $1,000 bounty was passed, but Governor Geringer vetoed the bill before it could become law.[8]

Idaho's Lemhi County Sheriff Brett Barsalou had heard rumors that some opponents to the wolf reintroduction in Idaho planned to be in the release area with weapons when the wolves and their captors arrived. On Friday, January 20, Sheriff Barsalou, fearing an armed standoff, blocked the road near the Yellowstone Mine northeast of Challis and barred biologists from releasing the wolves in the area. Instead, the eleven wolves were flown into the Middle Fork area of the Salmon River and released. Another six wolves were placed in pens in Yellowstone. Meanwhile, the Sierra Club Legal Defense Fund, representing several environmental groups, filed suit in federal court in Idaho, asking for full legal protection for the wolves of Idaho and for the experimental population designation to be declared illegal.

On Sunday morning, January 29, seventy-four-year-old rancher Gene Hussey found a dead wolf on his ranch about twenty-five miles

149

south of Salmon, Idaho.[9] The female wolf, one of the first released, had been shot in the chest and a dead calf lay nearby. Neither Hussey nor his ranch hands had shot the wolf. Hussey promptly called Idaho Cattlemen's Association board members, asking for advice on how to handle the situation — a dead endangered species lay on his land, over his dead calf, with a bullet hole in it. Hussey was advised that he had twenty-four hours to notify authorities, and that he should attempt to secure his own documentation of the situation in that time. This he did, calling in Sheriff Barsalou and the state veterinarian.

On Monday morning, FWS was notified that two wolves had been killed in Idaho over the weekend, just two weeks into the reintroduction effort. One was the female shot on the Hussey ranch, while another was killed by M-44 poison set by USDA Animal Damage Control (ADC) personnel in the Idaho Panhandle. The poisoned individual was a naturally occurring wolf that FWS did not know was in the area. Tracks of a second wolf were observed near the poison set.

By Monday night, FWS and ADC officials had visited Hussey's ranch and concluded that the wolf had indeed killed the calf and had been feeding on it. They would later retract this statement. ADC voluntarily suspended poison control activities in Idaho's Panhandle area.

On March 8, 1995, three armed federal agents went back to Hussey's ranch with a search warrant to conduct further investigations, mainly looking for shell casings from the weapon used to kill the wolf. Hussey requested that the agents wait until Sheriff Barsalou arrived to conduct their search and when the agents resisted, seventy-four-year-old Hussey gently lobbed rocks at the agents until the sheriff arrived minutes later. Barsalou arrived and while a physical confrontation did not take place, a verbal altercation ensued. The agents threatened to arrest the sheriff for obstruction of justice. Barsalou withdrew his cooperation from the federal investigation, saying that the agents attempted to intimidate Hussey and their manner was "dangerously close to excessive force." Idaho Governor Phil Batt stated that the FWS agents' actions were "totally unreasonable and overreaching." Lemhi County Commissioners called the actions "high-handed" and demanded an apology from the agents. The Idaho

Congressional delegation, within two days of the incident, scheduled a public hearing to be held in Idaho, and another hearing before the US House of Representatives in Washington, DC. FWS Director Mollie Beattie defended the agents' actions, commending them for preventing a violent confrontation. FWS issued a $5,000 reward for information about the killing of the wolf and retracted its earlier declaration that the wolf had killed the calf. Now, the agency said, the wolf had not done so.

By early April, 1995, a bill was being drafted for consideration by the US House of Representatives that would require federal law enforcement agencies to consult with the local sheriff before commencing any operations within that jurisdiction.

⌐

Jim and I filed our lawsuit challenging the reintroduction program on January 31, 1995, and shortly thereafter filed a motion for an injunction. Along with our quest for an injunction, we filed affidavits from experts expressing their views that wolf populations already existed in the Yellowstone area.

Reid Jackson was the Forest Supervisor for the Bridger-Teton National Forest from 1975–1986. He swore in an affidavit filed with the court that, based on the wolf-sighting reports compiled while he worked for the forest, and because he had heard wolf howls in the late 1970s, he felt that "there was a resident wolf population inhabiting the Gros Ventre region of the Bridger-Teton National Forest . . . I believe that wolves may still inhabit portions of the Greater Yellowstone Ecosystem of northwest Wyoming."[10]

Former Bridger-Teton National Forest wildlife biologist Al Boss signed an affidavit as well. He had worked on the forest from 1984 to 1989. He wrote:

"From the late 1970s to 1986, there were recurring reports of large wolf or wolf-like animals on the Bridger-Teton National Forest. The reports were a combination of actual sightings of animals, tracks and howls over this time period. Several of the wolf sighting reports came from individuals whom I believed to be reliable observers.

"Although wolf presence on the Bridger-Teton National Forest was not verified, the reports closely resembled sightings recorded in Idaho, where a small, scattered population of wolves was known to exist. In my opinion, it is possible that wolves did exist on the Bridger-Teton National Forest as recently as 1985."[11]

George Gruell signed yet another affidavit. Gruell had served as a biologist on the Bridger-Teton forest from 1967 to 1978 and, during that time, he compiled a list of fifty-two reported wolf sightings. He stated: "In my opinion, many of the observers reporting wolf occurrence on the Bridger-Teton National Forest were reliable observers, and a majority of the reports were of such quality that they could not be easily discounted."

"I feel that the US Fish and Wildlife Service has in the past, and continues today, to discount the evidence of the presence of wolves in Wyoming from the public," Gruell stated. "Based on my personal expertise as a wildlife biologist, I believe that evidence indicates that a wolf population has survived on portions of the Bridger-Teton National Forest in the mid to late 1970s, and strongly suggests that a wolf population may still occur in the Greater Yellowstone Ecosystem of northwest Wyoming today. It is my opinion that this naturally occurring wolf population may have been expanding since the mid 1970s."[12]

On Monday, March 20, 1995, Jim and I received word that we had lost the injunction, but that Judge Downes had ordered FWS to have radio collars on all the wolves when they were released.[13] Audubon's case was transferred to Wyoming and the three cases were consolidated, to be heard together, with the Farm Bureaus' being the lead case.

Wyoming Senator Alan Simpson wrote to me early in 1995, saying: "I admire your zeal and energy. Keep scrapping, my friend." While his letter offered encouragement, it appeared he had resigned himself to accepting the reintroduction.[14]

⤳

Twenty-four hours before the scheduled release of the first wolves from their holding pens in the park, Wyoming Governor Jim Geringer

held a news conference announcing the state's temporary management plan for wolves that might leave the park.[15] The keystone of the
plan called for wolves caught menacing private property to be trapped
and held by WGF officials until the federal agents retrieved them for
relocation back within the boundaries of the park. If the federal agencies failed to claim the wolves within twenty-four hours, state officials would transport them back to the park for release and bill the
federal government for their efforts. Geringer stated, "If you want
wolves on your terms, keep them in the boundaries of your park." In
a letter to Bruce Babbitt, Geringer wrote: "To date, your approach to
the reintroduction of the gray wolf has been by unilateral action and
blatant disregard of the partnership you so often espouse. It's time for
a change."[16]

On Tuesday, March 21, 1995, the door was opened at the Crystal Creek pen in Yellowstone and the wolves were free to move into
the wilds of the park. But the six wolves did not leave the pen.[17] The
next afternoon, the door of the pen at Rose Creek, where three wolves
were being held, was opened. These wolves also refused to leave their
pen. That night, Jim and I received a telephone call letting us know
that a wolf had been photographed on Sunday near the North Fork of
the Shoshone River. It was not a released wolf.

On Thursday, FWS decided that the wolves were associating the
area around the pen door with human presence, thus avoiding that
part of their pen. FWS then cut four-foot holes in the sides of two
pens, but the wolves still did not leave. The next day, biologists cut a
hole in the remaining pen at Crystal Creek. Having decided to cut
another larger hole in the other two pens, biologists approached the
Crystal Bench pen, only to hear a wolf howl behind them. The alpha
male had wandered three hundred yards outside the pen, but the others remained inside.

It was not until almost a week later that the wolves still inside
the pens began to venture outside. By Thursday, March 30, the pack
of six wolves at Crystal Bench began exploring within a third of a
mile from their pen and fed on a nearby elk carcass. The pack of five
at Soda Butte stayed within five miles of its pen, but the Rose Creek

pack — a female wolf, her daughter, and an unrelated male — moved fifteen miles north of its pen to an area outside of YNP. Two days later, this pack moved back into the park. The Soda Butte pack remained in the vicinity of its pen, and five members of the Crystal Bench pack were located in the Cache Creek drainage, while the sixth, a large male, was in a different area three miles south of the pen. By Monday, one of the packs of five had killed and partially consumed a bison.

On Friday, April 7, 1995, the last wolf remaining in the pens ventured out. The other five members of the pack had spent the past six days along the Lamar River with very restricted movements and park biologists began hoping that they were preparing a den site. The Soda Butte pack was located outside the park boundary in the Cooke City, Montana, area and the Rose Creek trio could not be located.

On Thursday, April 13, 1995, the Rose Creek trio was located five miles north of the park in the Gallatin National Forest in Montana, and the Soda Butte Pack came back to the vicinity of its pen. By April 25, however, only one wolf remained in the park, a young male in the Lamar River vicinity. One pack of five was located southeast of Red Lodge, Montana, in Custer National Forest; another was located fifteen miles north of the park in the Stillwater, Montana, area; and the Rose Creek trio was a few miles north of the park.

On Sunday, April 16, the Cardwell Wolf was found dead on a roadside near El Paso, Texas.[18] This wolf had been first discovered in August, 1994, in a coyote trap within the Yellowstone experimental population area, and was radio-collared and released from the trap. After being closely monitored for several months, FWS made a preliminary determination that the animal was likely an escaped captive and began formulating plans to take it out of the population. Then, mysteriously, the animal disappeared, only to wind up, six months later and nearly 1,000 miles to the south, dead and still wearing its government-issued radio collar.

On Wednesday, April 26, 1995, the Rose Creek male's dismantled radio collar was located in a metal culvert along a road east of Red Lodge, Montana. The wolf itself could not be located, and, suspecting foul play, FWS immediately issued a $1,000 reward for information leading to the conviction of those responsible for the disappearance of this wolf. The reward was promptly increased to $11,000 by conservation groups. Ed Bangs noted that biologists planned to recapture the Rose Creek adult female and relocate her back within the park, lest she remain in an area inhabited by "goons with guns."[19] This plan was abruptly abandoned soon after. The younger female of the Rose Creek trio had separated from the adult pair and remained near the park. Meanwhile, the Crystal Bench pack had come back into the park, while the Soda Butte pack remained north of the park in the Stillwater area.

A week later, on May 4, 1995, FWS announced that the Rose Creek adult female had given birth to eight pups on private land east of Red Lodge. FWS officials decided to begin feeding the female, since she no longer seemed to have a mate to help her hunt and care for the pups. On Thursday, May 18, the female and her pups were recaptured and moved back into the Rose Creek holding pen in the park, where officials began feeding the pack. Meanwhile, on May 7, a horn hunter discovered the carcass of the Rose Creek male and FWS quickly charged Chad McKittrick, a man from Red Lodge, Montana, with the shooting. FWS had been tipped off by McKittrick's bear-hunting buddy who allegedly was with him when he killed the animal, and on May 17 federal agents had found the head and hide of the male wolf in a cabin located on McKittrick's property. McKittrick was found guilty in a federal court months later, and sentenced to six months of imprisonment.

By late May, the Crystal Creek pack had settled comfortably into the Lamar Valley, with their antics being viewed nightly by tourists lined up along the roadside. The Soda Butte pack, which remained in the Absaroka-Beartooth Wilderness of Montana, north of the park, produced one pup that spring.

Throughout the summer, the Soda Butte pack wandered back and forth along the northern border of the park, with the new pup in tow. The Rose Creek female and her pups, while still being held in the pen, were visited in August by President Bill Clinton and his family. On October 11, the Rose Creek family was released and was soon joined by a young male from the Crystal Creek pack. The Rose Creek female's daughter, wandered alone in northern Yellowstone, killing elk and generally fending for herself. The Crystal Creek pack, now numbering five animals, continued to entertain visitors in the Lamar Valley throughout the fall of 1995.

By December, 1995, the Soda Butte pack had killed a hunting dog near Fishtail, Montana, north of the Absaroka Wilderness. Local ranchers were upset over the government's failure to notify them that the pack was in the area. Later in the month, one of the Rose Creek female's pups was hit and killed by a delivery truck in the park.[20] Late in December, an adult male wolf left the Soda Butte pack and began wandering on his own. Within two weeks he was spotted along the South Fork of the Shoshone River, fifty miles southwest of Cody, Wyoming. Three days later, he was seen within a mile of Dubois, Wyoming. The rest of the Soda Butte pack remained near Absarokee, Montana, and the Rose Creek female, her new mate, and her remaining seven pups stayed in the Slough Creek drainage of the park, while the Crystal Bench pack remained in the Lamar Valley.

Early in January, 1996, a young male wolf from the Crystal Bench pack killed two sheep on a ranch near Emigrant, Montana, and was captured and moved back into the park. He was placed in the Rose Creek pen for ten days and then re-released farther into the park. Later, he again killed sheep and was destroyed.[21]

By January 20, the Beartooth Stockgrowers, a group of livestock producers centered in the area just north of the park where the Soda Butte pack roamed and already fed up with the reintroduction,[22] requested the government to move the pack back into the park to protect their livestock — which were due to begin calving. The government refused. While this was happening, FWS biologists were in northern British Columbia overseeing the capture of more wolves to be released into the Yellowstone and Idaho areas.[23] As opposition to the reintroduction program built in the United States, it also grew in British Columbia. A British Columbian group called "Friends of the Wolf" offered a $5,000 reward to anyone who could find where the captured Canadian wolves were being held and free them prior to their export to the US.[24]

On January 25, 1996, the Montana Stockgrowers Association, Beartooth Stockgrowers, and Fishtail, Montana, rancher Vern Keller went to federal court in Billings, Montana, and requested a temporary restraining order against FWS in an effort to halt the reintroduction in both the Yellowstone and central Idaho areas until its content and implications were fully analyzed.[25] The stockgrowers requested that FWS be required to evaluate the impact of the releases on the naturally occurring wolf packs in Montana, in light of the fact that the naturally occurring wolf population there was at an all-time high and livestock losses in the area could be devastating to individual producers. US District Court Judge Jack Shanstrom, refusing to decide the case himself, sent it to the Wyoming court early in February. Within another four months, Fishtail Rancher Vern Keller began suffering wolf predation on his sheep. The lawsuit eventually failed.

By the end of January, 1996, FWS placed another seventeen Canadian wolves into four pens in YNP and released twenty into the wilds of central Idaho.[26] Controversy erupted again. A bar on the cage of one wolf had been bent, and biologist John Weaver, attempting to bend the bar back into place, was bit by the animal inside.[27] The protocol for the wildlife agencies involved required that if a wild animal injured a person, the animal must be killed and its brain tested for rabies. Dave Hunter, a wildlife veterinarian with the Idaho State Department of Agriculture, immobilized the wolf, transported it to Idaho with him, and euthanized it. FWS identified the wolf as B-21. The event made the front-page headlines throughout the West. Dave Hunter received some negative feedback from the public about the incident, although the decision to kill the wolf was not his since public health laws in all three states involved demanded the same outcome.[28]

In late December, 1995, and January, 1996, articles and letters from people opposed to the reintroduction effort and concerned about the status and survival of the native wolf were sent to editors and published in several Wyoming newspapers. Late in January, 1996, an article appeared in the *Cody Enterprise*, describing author Bob Meinecke's experience, just a week before, of watching two large buff-colored wolves on Bald Ridge near Cody, Wyoming. Meinecke had wondered whether he was watching released Canadian wolves or native Wyoming wolves, but from his description, it would seem they were natives.[29]

⟜

Oral arguments in the three lawsuits were set to be heard in the federal courtroom in Casper by Judge William Downes early in February, 1996. One day before the hearing was to start, the Sierra Club dropped out of the lawsuit, but left its legal team, the Sierra Club Legal Defense Fund, to represent the environmental groups in their fight for full protection of the naturally occurring wolves in Idaho.

A federal court, in reviewing agency action, must make several findings, based on the record before it; the agency's action must be supported by the facts in the record and the facts underlying the challenged action must be supported by substantial evidence in the administrative record. Evidence is not substantial if it is overwhelmed by other evidence or if it constitutes mere conclusion.

In the case of this suit, statements and findings included in the wolf reintroduction EIS must be supported by evidence found in the administrative record. The administrative record consists of those documents the agency cites in the EIS, or considered in conducting the EIS process, to make its decision. The agency itself decides which documents constitute the administrative record. For the decision regarding wolf reintroduction, the administrative record consisted of about thirty file boxes of documents.

Jim's and my brief reminded the court that Congress enacted the ESA to save species from extinction — to preserve the nation's biological diversity and to require federal agencies to protect those species and, if possible, facilitate their recovery.

Wyoming's native wolf, *C. l. irremotus*, was listed as an endangered species because it was critically close to extinction. That Congress intended to preserve subspecies is clear; that intent was written into the act, as was the protection of distinct populations of those subspecies.

Protection of subspecies was not mandated by Congress as an option, as FWS claimed. Congress did not state that federal agencies "may" conserve endangered species, nor did Congress state that species "may include" subspecies and distinct populations. To the contrary, Congress was explicit, stating "federal agencies shall" conserve endangered species, and then defined species to include "any subspecies . . . and any distinct population segment of any species."

In listing several different subspecies of gray wolf as endangered in 1973, FWS had not provided for the protection of all gray wolves, so the agency changed the listing in 1978 to protect all subspecies of gray wolf, wherever those wolves occurred. This change was never characterized as a delisting of any subspecies and did not include the necessary status review for such an action.

In our opinion, we told the court, FWS was attempting to rewrite history and federal legislation by, in essence, delisting *C. l. irremotus*. FWS had developed a grand scheme to conduct an experimental reintroduction of a large predator into the northern Rockies. The wolves that were most abundant elsewhere — in Canada — could be used for the experiment. The agency simply did not show concern that this reintroduction would violate the ESA and would necessitate circumvention of the National Environmental Policy Act (NEPA).

Jim and I maintained that the administrative record before the court demonstrated that the Yellowstone area harbored wolves prior to the development and introduction of FWS's wolf reintroduction program, and that FWS was violating the ESA by failing to protect and conserve these animals.

Alternatively, FWS chose a path intended to permit the recovery of "gray wolves" in general, regardless of which wolf subspecies "recovered." This action resulted in changing the status of the naturally occurring wolves from endangered to experimental, a move that was contrary to the stated purposes and intent of the ESA.

In order to allow for the reintroduction, FWS created new definitions of commonly used terms to circumvent the intent of Congress and, in violation of federal law, failed to discuss issues of significance in the FEIS for the reintroduction program.

Some of our arguments were very similar to those put forth by the Wyoming Farm Bureau Federation and its allies, but our reasons for wanting the reintroduction declared illegal were vastly different from theirs. We were not livestock producers at that time, although years later we would become sheep ranchers. Our objective was simple — we wanted wolf recovery in the Yellowstone area to be based on the native wolf population. We despised the reintroduction proposal and all that it meant for native species.

We worked hard on our briefs and were fairly pleased with the outcome, since we represented ourselves and did not have an attorney. We thought the Farm Bureaus' brief was well done, but were surprised and angered by the dishonesty and lack of effort in the briefs done by the intervenors, which were NWF, DW, Wyoming Wildlife Federation, Idaho Wildlife Federation, and the Wolf Education and Research Center. These groups had intervened in the case to ally themselves with the federal government in support of the reintroduction program. Tom France of NWF was their lead attorney and he included inaccurate claims and information from the current headlines rather than focusing on the administrative record before the court. For example, one statement claimed, "One of the Idaho wolves was shot by a rancher who claimed the wolf had killed a lamb." In reality, the identity of the person who shot the wolf had not been determined, and the dead animal was a calf, not a lamb.[30] I always figured France was more interested in the philosophical reasons for promoting wolf reintroduction rather than the legal interpretation of the case at hand. In the same brief, France stated that the Farm Bureaus, Audubon, and the Urbigkits represented extremes and termed the case an "odd coupling before this court. They agree on very little."[31] But later in the same brief, France wrote that these three parties "offer a series of closely related and narrowly drawn arguments."[32] France's brief argued our case was completely without merit, and was critical of NAS for its stance also. He claimed "the wolves NAS argues are not being protected are more wolves of the imagination than of reality."[33]

Clinton appointee David Freudenthal was the US Attorney, and lead local attorney, defending the federal government in this case, although federal attorneys from Washington, DC, appeared to be doing all the work. Freudenthal would later become governor of Wyoming and once again become embroiled in the wolf debate. Other notable Wyoming names were involved in the case as well, albeit briefly. Kim Cannon and Kate Fox of the Davis and Cannon law firm were the attorneys for the intervenors led by NWF, but they both withdrew from the case about nine months into the process.

The Sierra Club also became a casualty. Over a year into the case, and a few days prior to oral arguments in a federal courtroom, Sierra Club bowed out of the lawsuit, to which it had joined with NAS, Predator Project, Sinapu, and the Gray Wolf Committee.

Sierra Club was dismissed from the case "based on Sierra Club's agreement that it will not bring or join any challenge to the US Fish and Wildlife Service's reintroduction of wolves to Central Idaho or YNP that Sierra Club might have brought in this case or any other court."[34]

In June 1997, the Sierra Club Legal Defense Fund, which had represented National Audubon and its counterparts, changed its name to Earthjustice.

At least three separate times during the litigation in federal district court in Wyoming the Farm Bureaus tried to have the court order the removal of Yellowstone wolves, but Downes refused to issue the order.

Chapter 13

Judicial Howlings

The hearing started a little after 9 A.M. on Thursday, February 8, 1996. Set before Judge William Downes and his courtroom staff were two tables. Seated at the table to the right of the courtroom were attorneys for the US government, some from Washington, DC, and others from Colorado and Wyoming. Joining them were Ed Bangs and Thomas France. Accompanying France was his local counsel, Megan Hayes of Laramie, Wyoming. Lead counsel for the US was Christiana P. Perry, a US Department of Justice (USDJ) attorney from Washington, DC.

At the table to the left sat two attorneys representing livestock interests — Rick Krause with the American Farm Bureau Federation of Park Ridge, Illinois, and Steve Lechner with the Mountain States Legal Foundation of Denver, Colorado. Joining them at the table were three attorneys with Earthjustice: Doug Honnold, Jim Angell, and Susan Daggett, all of Bozeman, Montana. Jim and I completed this mixture of diverse interests sitting around one table, united only in opposition to the US government. Judge Downes noted early in the day that: "It's an interesting group of people sitting at that table. The irony has not been lost on me."

Downes summed up the arguments against FWS by stating: "It has not, contrary to the law, done a good-faith analysis of the existing wolf population in the affected areas. And that as a consequence, all of your work over the last fifteen years is inherently flawed. I mean, that's the bottom line. But if there is common ground between these two very divergent groups of people, there it is, that the government has not followed the procedures that they're supposed to follow."[1]

In legal briefs filed prior to the oral hearing, USDJ attorney Perry had questioned the livestock groups' right to file an ESA suit, calling the action "antithetical" to their true interests. Rick Krause, representing the Farm Bureaus, opened the arguments. Krause quickly expressed disagreement with the federal claim that agricultural organizations really are not interested in protecting the environment and that, therefore, the organization lacked standing to pursue the matter under NEPA.

Downes replied:

"I guess the government is suspicious about your client's professed concern for indigenous population of wolves pre-existing in the Yellowstone ecosystem. I think that's — they used the word 'antithetical' a lot; your interests are antithetical to that of the reintroduction of wolves or the sustaining of the existing populations of wolves.

"But I agree with you, Mr. Krause . . . but at the heart of your concern, of course, is not the well-being of existing populations of wolves within the ecosystem."

Krause acknowledged, "The heart of our concern is the protection of the interests of our clients."

Downes pressed the issue: "In fact, Mr. Krause, your clients are making a studied guess that there is no population of indigenous wolves, and that if this court does not think that the Secretary has appropriately used his authority given by Congress, then in effect there will be no wolf population in the ecosystem. That really is at the heart of your strategy, is it not?"

Krause replied: "Your honor, our strategy, we believe that there are indigenous wolves in both Yellowstone and Central Idaho. We think that the record's replete that there are. We don't think that the reintroduction is warranted."

Krause pointed Downes to the administrative record and documents indicating that FWS had been aware of a wolf in the Kelly Creek area of central Idaho, and had, in fact, monitored that wolf for three years. But Bangs discounted the importance of this animal, because it was only a single wolf.

Krause said: "The sightings that have been made by the general public which defendants have asked for now mean absolutely nothing. The federal government is looking for wolf packs and ignoring individual and pair sightings."

Downes suggested that many of the sightings are cases of mistaken identity anyway.

Krause pointed to other documents written by Bangs to federal personnel stationed in Idaho. One letter to Chuck Lobdell stated: "We should avoid giving the public a false sense of optimism about natural recovery being imminent by voicing our independent opinions about the reports of possible wolf activity, rather than what the data actually document about wolf breeding groups and attaining the Service's progress toward wolf recovery as defined in the 1987 recovery plan and restated in the EIS."

Downes said, "It suggests to me that Mr. Lobdell is being taken to the woodshed for not speaking the party line."

Krause responded, "Yes, Your Honor. I certainly think that's a fair interpretation." Krause argued about subspecies as well, calling attention to the fact that the Canadian wolves being released into YNP were of a different subspecies than the one native to Yellowstone. He stated:

"Now defendants say, Your Honor, we don't recognize subspecies of *Canis lupus* anymore, that a wolf is a wolf is a wolf. Well, they forgot to tell the people down in the southwest who were trying to reintroduce a particular subspecies of Mexican wolf, which is *Canis lupus baileyi*, and they also forgot to tell the people in Minnesota, who have a recovery plan for the eastern timber wolf, *Canis lupus lycaon*.

"So in fact, Your Honor, subspecies of wolves are recognized. They're just not recognized where the government chooses to ignore it."

Christiana Perry gave the rebuttal argument on ESA issues for the federal defendants. She agreed that a wolf is a wolf is a wolf, saying, "So there is no such thing as the Mexican wolf or the eastern timber wolf, for purposes of the Endangered Species Act."

"There are no recognized subspecies," Perry said. "This is really a red herring. It's really not relevant, that taxonomic dispute."

Perry experienced some difficulty during questioning from Downes as she attempted to explain and justify that single wolves do not a population make, what constitutes the historic range of a wolf, that there is no such thing as subspecies, and how numerous wolf biologists had been polled to come up with the definition for the word "population."

Downes interjected, "It's worth noting that some of the biologists seem to have their own agenda beyond science."

Perry riled. "I think that — I don't know if that's true or not. I've seen — I know there's statements in there that you could interpret that way."

Downes responded: "I don't know what other interpretation you could give it. I mean, one of them blatantly says, pick a definition which bests protects the wolf reintroduction plan, in essence."

Perry said biologists should promote species recovery, to which Downes responded, "What might be offensive, though, to the whole process is if that biologist's definition is clouded by his own opinion about whether the wolves should or should not be reintroduced." He continued: "What I'm getting at is that all of the plaintiffs attack the integrity of the assessment. They basically, if you want to summarize their view, is that all of them believe that the Fish and Wildlife Service approached this evaluation of existing population with a view of obtaining a desired result, and that is, finding none, because in finding none, and in defining what none would be, is the only way that 10(j) can be implemented."

Perry disagreed with the argument.

The court adjourned for lunch and reconvened about 1:30 P.M. Downes called Perry back to the podium to talk about a document that described a wolf being filmed in YNP and wolves reported in other parts of the ecosystem. He also sought information relative to some talking points about why the Yellowstone animals might not have been wolves and how insignificant the presence of a wolf would be.

Downes said: "Reading this document, one could get the impression that folks really didn't want to confirm that that high-quality film was a wolf. I got the impression that people are almost frightened to conclude that that was a wolf."

Downes quoted the FWS memo: "If the filming of this animal would have raised expectations that natural recovery is imminent, turn opinion away from reintroduction, or stall the recovery option in favor of an extensive survey, it could easily be more detrimental than beneficial to wolf recovery in Yellowstone and central Idaho."

Downes continued, "Hear no wolves, see no wolves, is that what the message is?"

Perry replied, "I don't think so." She said that every statement expressing skepticism about a wolf sighting could be subject to the charge that federal officials do not really want to find the animals.

Federal attorney Sandra Zellmer was up next and gave the federal government's arguments dealing with NEPA. Downes showed little interest in this portion of the case and did not ask any questions. NWF attorney Tom France then gave a short presentation in support of the reintroduction program.

Jim was up next. Dressed in a western suit, hands trembling, he approached the podium, carrying his notes and a box full of exhibits. Downes, noting Jim's nervousness, told him: "All right. Mr. Urbigkit, let me just tell you, and I know you're a little nervous about this, but take a deep breath, and I'll simply make the observation at the outset that while you and your wife are not lawyers, your briefing in this case is far better than some members of the bar — not ones here present — who have filed briefs in this courthouse, and it shows quite a bit of scholarship, very candidly, and some legal scholarship."

Jim responded. "I'm not nervous. I'm terrified." He then jumped right into the issues, telling Downes, "There's no such thing as a viable population of an endangered species."

Downes once again raised the issue of wolf reports and possible misidentification. "One of my problems . . . is that a lot of the fair-minded and good people who come down on both sides of this issue are being awfully subjective in what they see or what they don't see, when it comes to the presence or nonexistence of wolves in Yellowstone and central Idaho."

Jim then led Downes through a review of wolf reports, keying on a report written by Glen Cole of YNP which concluded that small numbers of wolves had been present in the park since the 1930s and that they were reproducing. Jim said:

"The point of this is that in the early 70s, the presence of wolves, of a breeding population of wolves in Yellowstone was accepted as fact and was recognized as representing the native wolf *irremotus*. We went from having wolves, *irremotus*, in the park in the early 70s, to them being extirpated by 1930, according to the conclusions of the decision.

"There is nothing in the administrative record that supports their assertion that these wolves became extinct by 1930. In fact the record supports our conclusion that the wolves survived."

Jim then told the court that FWS was lying when it claimed that wolves were not present. Downes questioned, "Why?" while noting the discussion had gone outside the record of the case at hand. Jim explained that Cole had felt that wolves had been protected in the park since the 1930s and still had not managed to increase to appropriate numbers, so population augmentation was necessary to achieve a recovered population of wolves.

Downes questioned, "Now, is that referenced anywhere in the record?"

Jim said that it was not, but I quickly approached the podium and handed him an exhibit from deep within the boxes of files.

Downes said:

"Let me read into the record the information that your wife handed you in a timely fashion . . . The subject is a trip report, first interagency meeting for the management of the Northern Rocky Mountain Wolf, Mammoth, Yellowstone National Park, Wyoming, October 6, 1971.

"The program began with Glen Cole, Yellowstone park biologist, discussing his program and knowledge of the wolf. He estimated a population of 10–15 wolves in and close around the park. The park has a record of observations in the park for a number of years. Clifford Martinka, biologist in Glacier, says that there are five to 10 wolves in that park. The range of the wolf now extends from Grand Teton park through Yellowstone and nine national forests to Glacier National Park, possibly some BLM land is included. Cole suggests in all likelihood, our population estimates are low. He said that it is wrong to confine this present meeting to a consideration of the wolf in the park alone.

"Cole is also concerned about the Yellowstone gene pool and wants to strengthen the pool by natural influx of wolves into the park. The Park Service wants to preserve the biological community of Yellowstone in its natural association for its educational and scientific value. The park has the food necessary for the wolf to expand its numbers. Elk in the park will be left to adjust their numbers by natural devices, including predation.

"Now the park needs an unknown number of wolf packs to control these ungulates. Possibly 30 to 40 wolves in the north Yellowstone area could be accommodated. Cole indicated that the park would accept live trapped wolves, even though they might disrupt some of the existing packs."

Next, Jim went into the issue of subspecies, telling the court: "Protection of endangered species is — goes to the heart of protecting evolutionary lineages. And what we're on the verge of losing here is an evolutionary lineage of thousands of years."

Jim then walked the court through claims made by the federal government in its EIS and the evidence in the record that clearly contradicted those claims.

Perry rebutted Jim's arguments, stating, "I think the parties are in agreement about a lot of evidence, and the dispute is really what is the significance of that evidence."

Downes asked Perry to respond to Cole's claims that Yellowstone had a wolf population in 1971, "yet the Fish and Wildlife Service opines subsequent to this that there has not been a population of wolves, the wolves have been extirpated since 1930."

Perry said: "Well, the response I have to that — and this is just based on my recent discussion with Mr. Bangs, so I'll hope he'll correct me if I'm wrong — is that this — this was — this was what was believed at the time. There was never any evidence, physical evidence, of this population."

Bangs himself interjected to tell the court that a photograph of a wolf had been taken, "But at the time, they believed that there were wolves everywhere south of Yellowstone, all the way to the Canadian border. That's why Dr. Weaver was hired."

Jim stood and voiced his objection to Bangs giving testimony. He said: "This should have been discussed in the record. If it's left out of the record, then the record's incomplete, and this needs to be remanded back to the agency for correction." Downes sustained Jim's objection.

Perry paused to confer privately with Bangs, then re-approached the podium, telling Downes that Weaver's work was the result of the issues raised by Cole and that Weaver did not find any evidence of persistent wolf activity during the 1970s.

Downes noted that Weaver's findings were at variance with Cole's.

Downes said, "We're dealing with one of the most remote areas in the lower 48, where conceivably a population of wolf could have maintained a lifestyle there in that park unbeknownst to biologists and wildlife specialists."

Perry said: "I think that's conceivable. I don't think it's incredibly likely, given what we've discussed about the large range of the wolf pack."

Downes grilled Perry:

"What I'm wondering is, were Mr. Cole's observations just discounted? And if so, why? Because what we're talking about in this 1971 report is doing just what has been going on for over a year, introduction of trapped wolves from other areas; but this memo supports the Urbigkits' contention that people like Mr. Cole had a notion that this should be done to strengthen an existing Yellowstone gene pool of wolves.

"My question is this. Was this historical information ignored in the EIS and other documents that lead up to its production, or was it addressed and dispelled?"

Perry stammered. "I — I'm going to have to get back to you on that. I'm sorry. I just don't know."

Perry never did answer the question, and instead turned to the issue of subspecies. Downes was taken with her argument, stating: "Am I mistaken, the Secretary elected, as I think is his right, to address subspecies in the reintroduction of Mexican wolves? Isn't that true?"

Perry said: "Yes, I think he elected to do that. He elected to address the issue here too. Legally, he's not required to do that."

Downes responded, "I understand that."

As for the whole notion that FWS was trying to avoid finding wolves, Perry said: "[I]t would have been much easier to find a population and then not have to go through all this, and we wouldn't be here today. So, I guess the question is, what purpose did all this serve?"

Downes responded by explaining what he called Cole's theory of concealment. "Mr. Cole doesn't think that the indigenous population is sufficiently large and strong enough, its genetic pool isn't strong enough to allow long-term sustenance of the species in Yellowstone park. So the best way to deal with it, as alluded to in the 1971 memo, is to invigorate that species of wolves with introduced species. And you can't do that, of course, if you're going to have the full protection under the Endangered Species Act. So the theory would be, don't find any indigenous population of wolves, and bring in the new ones, and if they strengthen the gene pool, all the better."

Perry said that 1971 was prior to the passage of the ESA, "so none of that was legally relevant at the time that memo was written . . . We could just go introduce them anyway."

Downes adjourned the hearing for the day.

Doug Honnold, representing NAS and its counterparts, was first to speak the next morning. He sought to clarify his clients' position.

"[W]e have not challenged in any way the Yellowstone wolf reintroduction program . . . National Audubon Society plaintiffs challenge only the defendants' failure to protect Idaho's natural wolves. We do not say you can't translocate wolves to Idaho. We do not say you can't invoke 10(j) in translocating wolves to Idaho. What we do say is that you can't translocate wolves to Idaho, use 10(j), and drop the full legal protections for the wolves that are there on the ground, or the so-called natural wolves."

Honnold explained that his clients wanted the court to declare that Idaho's natural wolves could not be stripped of their endangered status, and that the issue be remanded back to the agency to be dealt with.

Downes responded: "It's not going to be that simple. The government proposes to destroy the wolves if I order them removed."

Honnold said that Canadian officials had indicated that they would take the reintroduced wolves back if necessary. Regardless, he said, the relief his group was asking for was full protection for naturally occurring wolves.

Downes agreed that if Honnold could establish that wolves are present in central Idaho, "They have, the full protection of the Endangered Species Act applies to them."

Downes said: "Let me tell you at the outset, my feeling on it is, I have some real trouble with the Urbigkits' position about the evidence of naturally occurring wolf populations in the Yellowstone ecosystem, but the documentation that you have supplied to me and which is part of the administrative record is more problematic. There are even estimates by the Interior Department's own employees that wolf packs would reoccur naturally within five years . . . Now that stands in marked contrast, it seems to me, with the state of facts in the Yellowstone ecosystem."

Honnold pressed that 10(j) could still be used, but if the reintroduced wolves came into contact with naturally occurring wolves, full protection applied to all the wolves. "The irony here is that acts of nature are catching up with and overturning the acts of man," Honnold said. "The race against time is to put wolves on the ground and hope that those wolves repopulate an area more rapidly than the natural wolves come down and do the job themselves."

Downes said that what Honnold was suggesting was that he overturn a congressional enactment. "I mean, you package it very attractively, like a good advocate should; but aren't you really asking me to do a retrospect of assessment of what Congress did and tell them it's a nullity? Because wolves are migrating in ways you hadn't envisioned, 10(j) cannot apply here in any respect," Downes said. "Is there a circumstance where a judge has to make those findings? Yes. But nobody put me on the bench here to legislate from this bench, if I can avoid it."

Honnold responded. "[W]hat Fish and Wildlife Service would like to do is interpret this in such a way from a flexibility standpoint, they write this law right out of existence. Essentially what they want this language to say is, we don't care what congress said. What we want to do here is a good thing. We think that this will help recover the wolves in the Northern Rockies. It's a good objective, and we're going to twist and turn and interpret every phrase and word in this definition, in this statute, in the 10(j) statute, so that we can get the job done."

Honnold said that, although compromise may have been the intent in other portions of the statute, never was it a consideration when it came to protecting naturally occurring populations of endangered species.

Downes said:

"[Y]ou know, I have to confess that the compromise even has some attractiveness to a federal judge. It is less likely, for example, that a Wyoming rancher will stand in front of me indicted for having shot a wolf depredating on his sheep.

"[F]or a farmer or rancher who comes before me, under this 10(j) provision, if he shot that wolf depredating on his livestock, I said it before and I'll say it again, he won't stand indicted in this courthouse. And woe to the United States attorney who brings it. But under your plan, of course, he'll stand indicted. I'll have to give him his day in court, won't I?"

Honnold responded: "Well, Your Honor, the sad truth is that there are hundreds if not thousands of instances where threatened and endangered species are illegally taken and the government does not choose to prosecute. There is a question of prosecutorial discretion."

Turning the focus once more to his core argument, Honnold said, "Our argument is that under the language of the statute, it's only those wolves that were transported and released, or offspring arising solely therefrom, that can ever be considered an experimental population."

Honnold then presented to Downes a newspaper article that originated the day before in the Spokane *Spokesman-Review*. When Perry objected because it was not part of the record, Downes said: "It's not in the record, Ms. Perry, but I'm not a mushroom. I won't die if I hear it. The record is what I'll be guided by, Ms. Perry, so relax."

The article indicated that a reintroduced wolf had produced off-spring with a naturally occurring wolf in Idaho. Honnold pressed that the offspring of such a mating must be treated as fully endangered animals, not part of the experimental population.

After perusing the article, Downes handed it back to Honnold, stating, "It's interesting, anecdotal material, but it's not part of the record." Downes called for a break, with court reconvening a half-hour later with Perry once again at the podium.

Downes asked Perry: "Doesn't any federal judge, reading the environmental regulations and laws of this country, particularly the Endangered Species Act — am I not required to give a wolf not released by the Secretary the full protection of the Endangered Species Act? Isn't that what Congress intended?"

Perry responded, "Um, I'd like to respond to that by saying that you're required to judge this controversy based upon the facts that are before you in the record and at the time the decision was made," adding that anything else was speculative. Perry pressed that the record demonstrated that there were no wolves known to occur in Idaho at the time the decision was made.

Downes pointed to documents written by wildlife biologists which stated that there had been many wolf sightings in the area where the experimental population was to be placed. Perry pointed out that one of the documents stated "no wolf packs are known to occur in Idaho."

Downes replied: "Yeah. The word is packs."

Perry continued: "Right. Then it says, wolves occur in Idaho. It doesn't say, doesn't specify a factual basis for that statement."

"But," Downes said, "there's another reference in here that seemed to imply criticism that there was not enough discussion about the increase in wolf population or at least the wolf sightings in Idaho in the record." Downes then read aloud from the memo sent to Bangs from the Idaho office. "It is apparent that you did not use most of the information my staff provided for inclusion. You have since explained that you were under tight deadlines at the time. In the future, we suggest that it would be much safer to default to include information provided by the office responsible for overseeing the program in question."

Downes concluded by saying, "I took that as a gentle back of the hand."

Perry said: "But I think that the question for the court and for the plaintiffs' claim that they're bringing is, where is the evidence that there was even one wolf in the area at the time of the decision . . . if what they're talking about is protecting an individual wolf, they have to show us that that wolf exists and that we owe it some protection."

Downes responded: "But isn't this letter admitting as much? . . . I mean, does he have to go out there and get the wolf in hand?"

Perry said, "Well, they do mention, when there has been a wolf, they refer to it by name." Perry maintained that Honnold should have to prove that there was a wolf in the area on the date the decision was made to reintroduce wolves. "What I'm trying to convey is, at the time the decision was made, there's no confirmation that there was even one wolf in the Idaho area."

Downes grilled Perry on the argument, since she insisted that the plaintiff should have to prove that there was even one wolf in the area that FWS was obligated to protect. He asked Perry about the court's obligation to protect all wolves under the ESA. "Is it a legitimate exercise of executive authority for the Secretary to prepare a plan that would dispossess a wolf of that endangered protection?"

Perry asked, "An individual member?"

Downes said, "Yes."

Perry replied, "Yes."

Downes told Perry: "Assume for the sake of our discussion that one wolf is there today . . . and the Secretary didn't bring it in. Is that wolf entitled to the full protection of the Endangered Species Act or isn't it?"

Perry replied: "I think it's not. If the Secretary establishes an experimental population there, which I think he has the authority to do, if there's no existing population, then that wolf is not entitled to the protection, the full protection of the Endangered Species Act."

Perry turned the floor over to France, who once again gave a glowing overview of the road to wolf recovery, until Downes interrupted him to break for lunch.

When court reconvened, Downes did not give France the chance to start talking again, but said: "Well, Mr. France, let me hit you with the $64 question. How did it come to pass that two prominent advocates for wildlife conservation are sitting at two different tables? How did we get to this point in this discussion, this debate on the 10(j), when we come to that place? It's really a remarkable event, you'd have to admit. Very seldom I think in the courthouses of this country would we have recognized advocates for wildlife conservation so diametrically opposed to one another on such an issue."

France responded, "Your Honor, I don't want to dwell too philosophically here, but I suspect there have always been different strains in the environmental community." He suggested that there are preservationists and conservationists, suggesting that his clients were of the conservationist strain. As for reduced protections for individual wolves in the area now, France said, "We acknowledge that there will be some losses perhaps because of this judgment. But in terms of the overall benefit, and this conservation duty, and this notion that we are managing a population towards recovery, we find that choice is — the benefits more than offset the possible harm."

Krause gave his rebuttal, letting the judge know that there was no conflict in the record that the Canadian wolves were not the same type of wolf native to the area. He noted that if it were mainly a difference of opinion on taxonomy, "the duty of the government, as so-called experts on the issue, Your Honor, is to evaluate the evidence and to make a decision on it, not to duck the issue entirely."

I was next to take my turn at the podium. I read from the federal government's brief that "no evidence exists that wolf populations persisted in the northern Rocky Mountains of the US to the present time or that the lone wild wolves occasionally reported in these areas are other than dispersing wolves from Canadian populations."

I then responded, "We know that the evidence [documenting the presence of wolves in these areas] is there in the administrative record." I then proceeded to review some of that information with the court, showing Downes two three-ring binders containing more than 1,200 wolf-sighting reports. I used a flip chart that Jim and I had prepared early that morning to demonstrate where in the administrative record Downes could find evidence of wolf depredation on livestock and wild ungulates, as well as reports of wolf activity made by agency personnel. As I went down the list, Downes quickly discovered that his copy of the administrative record was lacking the relevant reports and asked me for copies of the documents I was citing. The government had redacted embarrassing pages from the court's copy of the record.

"I guess my main point here, what I was doing with listing these things, is that any — was just showing that any assertion that this type of evidence does not exist for the Yellowstone area or for Wyoming is false," I said. "It's there. It's in the record."

I reviewed the Gravelly Range wolf activity, which included information about FWS flying to the area in a helicopter, landing, and viewing the wolves and wolf tracks. "These people are the defendants in this case," I said. "It is the defendants that are saying that there is no evidence of any wolf packs or that wolves persisted in the Yellowstone area. This memo, by itself, disputes that, that their assertion is not supported by the facts in the administrative record."

Then, I reviewed the record of dead wolves with the court — the Chico wolf in 1988 and the Teton wolf in 1992. I reviewed more reports of pack activity made by agency personnel and pointed out that even wolf researcher John Weaver had heard a wolf howl, even though he recommended "restoring this native predator by introducing wolves to Yellowstone."

"A wolf population exists in Yellowstone National Park," I said. "They howl, they leave their tracks, they kill prey and they've reproduced."

Honnold was up next, giving short closing remarks, then it was Downes's turn once again. He said: "Counsel and parties, we did not get to this day overnight. Congress has had a longer time to sort all of this out, and several secretaries and their staffs have toiled over this for, as has already been pointed out to me, many times, for two decades. I won't have as much time. But it is time to move this thing on and to come down with a decision that allows parties to move forward, obviously to a room where there's more than one judge. Obviously, someone is not going to be happy with my decision. With every pun intended, there will be howls of indignation from one table or another . . . I see it as one of the — ironically, at the outset of my career, it may be one of the most important things I ever put my hands on, as a federal judge."

Downes pledged to try to issue his decision within sixty days "because I think this is an important public policy issue, and I think you've waited long enough for a decision."

His decision, however, came nearly two years later.

⌐

On February 10, 1996, two days after the hearing, an adult male Yellowstone wolf, 12M, was seen in northern Sublette County along the Green River near Daniel, Wyoming.[2] He had crossed the Wind River Range and, on February 11, was found dead along a road near Daniel. The Rose Creek female's subadult female pup was seen with a young male wolf.[3]

At 9:30 A.M. on Wednesday, February 21, I received a telephone call from Merna-area rancher Louis Roberts, saying he had found tracks of a wolf that had crossed his pasture just hours before — this only a few miles from where the Yellowstone male wolf had been found dead two weeks earlier. Roberts was concerned about a wolf being where he was pasturing and feeding his horses and cows, and where the cows would begin calving in six weeks. The snow was about four feet deep and this had caused the elk and moose to leave the area, so the one remaining source of large prey for the wolf happened to be Roberts's livestock. By early afternoon, Bernie Holz of WGF was on the ranch, trailing the wolf. Over a foot of new snow had fallen during the preceding few days and the county had plowed the road the afternoon before. Holz and Roberts discovered that the wolf had waited out the storm under an overhang in an old ditch three-quarters of a mile from the county road. After the snow stopped, the wolf had come out of its cover, circled the pasture full of livestock, eaten a porcupine, and headed north toward the Merna Road, where its tracks disappeared in the hard-packed snow.

Roberts and Holz collected samples of gray hair the animal had left as it rubbed on the willows and the overhang. The tracks of the wolf were 5 inches long by 3 inches wide, and Roberts noted that the animal was over-reaching badly with its hind feet — a sign that it was running full bore. Holz, upon returning to his office in Pinedale, called FWS to inquire if any of the released Canadian wolves were missing from the park. The answer was "No" — all were accounted for.[4] There was only one explanation for the origin of the wolf on the Roberts place — it was a native wolf.

FWS remained mum on the death of 12M. Although it was found dead alongside the Merna Road, information about the cause of death was not released. Some suspected that it had been shot, and within two weeks FWS, still not releasing the cause of death and only stating that it had been killed illegally, offered a $1,500 reward for information leading to the identification and conviction of the person or persons responsible for its death.[5] By mid-March, 1996, the reward was increased to $2,000. The responsible party was never found.

Meanwhile, Judge Downes held a hearing to review the Montana stockgrowers request for an injunction prohibiting the release of the seventeen wolves being held in the pens in Yellowstone. Unwilling to make a decision on the injunction too quickly, Downes granted a temporary restraining order against the release of the wolves. On March 29, 1996, he let the restraining order expire and denied the stockmen's injunction, clearing the way for the release of the penned wolves.

In June, 1996, FWS Director Mollie Beattie lost her battle with cancer. A wolf pack was later named in her honor.

On June 23, 1996, a radio-collared wolf, B-21, was found dead in a leg-hold trap in a stream in Idaho. This was the wolf that supposedly had been euthanized six months earlier after biting biologist John Weaver while in its shipping crate.[6] FWS found itself in another uncomfortable situation, having to explain how a dead wolf in a shipping crate wound up dead again, six months later, in a trap in the wilds of Idaho. FWS declared that the awkward circumstance due to a "clerical error."[7] We promptly filed a brief in Judge Downes's court, requesting that FWS be required to explain to the court how the discovery of B-21 as a free-ranging individual did not violate the court's order to monitor all released wolves, since B-21 had roamed the mountains of Idaho and had attacked livestock in the Cascade area without FWS knowing it, until its existence was proven at its death.

NPS and FWS, due to criticism that they were not keeping the public informed on the whereabouts and movements of the wolves released into Yellowstone, established a telephone number that people could call to hear recorded updates about wolf movements. By late July, 1996, the agencies reported that there were thirty-four free-ranging wolves in the Yellowstone area, including nine pups born to three litters. In addition, nine wolves were being held in pens in the park, awaiting release, while another was being held in captivity pending shipment to a facility in Minnesota. Twenty-nine of the free-ranging wolves were members of five packs, while another five animals were loners.

Vern Keller, the Montana rancher who filed the lawsuit attempting to stop the release of wolves into Yellowstone in 1996, had eight sheep killed by the released wolves by the end of July.[8] No relief was in sight. FWS knew that it was a Yellowstone female wolf accompanied by her three pups that was doing the damage, and tried without success for several weeks to capture the group and place them back into the park.

In August, 1996, FWS took four gray wolf pups from the northwestern Montana population and placed them in pens in YNP. FWS took this action after killing the pups' mother because she had been killing livestock. The pups were to be kept in the pen until they were old enough to be released and survive on their own.

Chapter 14

Killing Wild Wolves

By March, 1997, more than one year had passed since Downes heard oral arguments on the lawsuits and two years had passed since the wolf reintroduction experiment was launched. YNP officials reported that fifty-one Canadian wolves were in the Yellowstone area and eight pairs were expected to produce young in the following months. Of the fifty-one wolves, thirteen remained in captivity, awaiting release in April and June.[1] The wolf-information telephone message stated that there were thirty-four free-ranging wolves officials could monitor and "four that we cannot."

Jim and I decided to file a "show cause" motion with the court, trying to convince the judge to have FWS explain why it should not have an injunction slapped against it for the agency's treatment and management of native wolves in the Yellowstone area.

⌣

Deep snows and severe weather conditions in western Wyoming during the winter of 1996–1997 had driven big game animals to lower elevations, often onto private property where conflicts can occur. Not surprisingly, the wolves followed, and two in particular started making news.

In November, 1996, a female wolf had been discovered living along the East Fork of the Wind River on Fred Finley's ranch near Dubois, Wyoming. Finley had seen wolves a few times over the years. Hunters had reported seeing wolf tracks and had photographed an uncollared wolf in the area that fall, but officials discounted the reports until a pair of radio-collared Canadian wolves moved into a nearby area.[2]

By December, 1996, the existence of the uncollared wolf near Dubois had become known to the public. While state and federal officials debated whether to capture the animal, FWS decided she was prob ably a wolf-dog hybrid or a pet wolf. FWS biologist Joe Fontaine was quoted as saying, "It's up to local authorities what to do with that animal."[3]

FWS did not attempt to provide any protection for the animal, and instead, through Fontaine's statement, made it clear that it should not be protected. Fortunately, the animal was not destroyed before the agency, a month later, changed its position and stated it was indeed a wild wolf. The wolf reportedly had killed three deer in ten days.[4] FWS also said the wolf without a collar seemed to be "co-habitating" with the radio-collared pair, just as the breeding season had started.

By early February, 1997, the uncollared female disappeared from the East Fork and a pair of uncollared wolves was reported to be on a ranch along the South Fork of Shoshone River near Cody. FWS speculated that the East Fork wolf had moved into the South Fork. The agency finally decided to capture one of the South Fork wolves and fit it with a radio collar. FWS also declared only one wolf was in the area; a second one, from their perspective, did not exist.

Ed Bangs, acting in his official capacity as an employee of FWS, issued the order for the free-ranging wolf in the South Fork to be shot and killed. He claimed that this wolf was a released captive, an opinion seemingly based on the fact that the wolf was not a member of the released wolf population and, Bangs said, it had an inappropriate lack of fear of humans. This animal had been in the South Fork for a month, surviving on its own, and had not been involved in livestock depredations.[5] Nonetheless, it was shot on March 4, 1997. The whereabouts of the second wolf, which FWS refused to acknowledge, was never resolved.

Fred Finley, the rancher who first discovered the wolf, called the killing "a dastardly act."[6]

Bangs noted the wolf's abnormal behavior of remaining in one area (while at the same time putting forth the opposite claim that it had traveled from Dubois to the South Fork) as a reason for considering it to be a captive-raised animal. "It was absolutely clear-cut. There's no question whatsoever."[7]

Finley flat disagreed, insisting the animal was a wild wolf. "I'm just positive it was a real wolf. There's no doubt about that. I would swear to that. It makes me feel bad to think somebody shot it . . . I have lived here on the East Fork since the summer of 1937 and have seen wolves every so often in these mountains and valleys ever since I came here. Just because the government brought in some wolves from Canada doesn't mean that they are the only wolves in this area. There have always been wolves around here."[8]

Riverton Ranger publisher Steven Peck editorialized on the matter. "Federal wildlife managers are looking at least a little foolish for their handling of a couple of cases of wolf sightings in Wyoming that can't be explained through the federal wolf reintroduction program. A memorable phrase in the recent discussion of one wolf-like animal came when it was decided not to trap the critter for tests and study so as not to 'stress the animal.' So what did the wildlife managers do instead? They shot the wolf. Yea, we sure don't want to 'stress the animal,' would we?"[9]

Late in February, 1997, a wolf visited the Mayo Ranch near Boulder, Wyoming, for four consecutive nights during which time it killed seven of his sheep and wounded another. On Friday morning, February 21, 1997, Bill Mayo roped the wolf from his snowmachine and locked the animal in a horse trailer until FWS arrived on the scene to take possession of it. The wolf was a female, estimated to weigh about eighty-five pounds, and was neither marked nor wearing a radio collar.[10] Several other area residents had reported seeing the wolf and wolf tracks in the week prior to her capture.

On Thursday night, February 20, Phyllis Mayo had called WGF game warden Dennis Almquist to report that a wolf had been killing sheep on their ranch. She requested WGF provide "some help or relief" from the situation, Almquist said in an interview at the time.

Almquist, who had received a report of wolf tracks in the Silver Creek and Muddy Creek areas nearby just a few days before, attempted to contact the WGF large-carnivore staff members for advice and assistance, but was unable to reach them. He then contacted FWS Special Agent Roy Brown of Lander and made arrangements to meet at the Mayo Ranch the next day to investigate.

Almquist said he and Brown arrived on the scene Friday afternoon. Mayo was not home at the time, but investigators looked at and measured "very large canine tracks" and the sheep kills. The dead sheep had bite marks on the head and hocks, as well as on the throat and neck. Almquist said the investigators felt "a big dog or a small wolf" could have left the evidence on the scene.

USDA ADC Supervisor Merrill Nelson arrived on the scene and had followed the tracks for some distance when Mayo arrived home. Mayo then told the investigators he had locked the animal in a horse trailer. Mayo said that he was sick of the killing of his sheep and had waited for the animal to return to the sheep flock in order to capture it. Mayo told Almquist that he "didn't want to kill it, but he wanted it out of there."

Almquist then radioed WGF warden Duke Early and requested that Early bring immobilization drugs and equipment to the Mayo Ranch. Almquist administered an injection to the wolf as she cowered in the corner of the trailer. The Mayos provided medicine and bandages for officials to treat a wound on the wolf's leg. Almquist described the wolf as "light colored, with dark guard hairs. It basically looked like a big coyote" (Figure 23).

Brown took possession of the animal and transported her to a secure location in Lander. The wolf was treated by a veterinarian for what Brown called "a minor injury."[11] He reported that "the animal is alive and well. He didn't attempt to kill it. Under the regulations, he can harass it all he wants to, as long as he doesn't kill it or inflict any permanent injuries."

Before FWS officials examined the animal, they began to put a "spin" on the incident, with Bangs saying the animal could be a hybrid or a transient from the northwestern Montana population, but the chances that it was a native "are about zero." Bangs admitted the animal was not one of the released Canadian wolves or one of their offspring.[12] Bangs said his agency would move the wolf into a holding pen in YNP to observe her behavior[13] and that DNA samples would be taken in an attempt to learn the genetic identity of the animal.

Figure 23. After Wyoming rancher Bill Mayo roped and captured a wild wolf that was not supposed to exist, state and federal officials arrived on the scene to sedate and remove the animal to captivity. (Photo courtesy Dennis Almquist/Wyoming Game and Fish Department)

Suddenly FWS had several wolves it could not make sense of — the Boulder wolf, the female wolf spotted near Dubois, and a pair of wolves seen on the South Fork of the Shoshone River near Cody.

According to Bangs, "None of these animals appear to be any we released or their offspring." He voiced suspicion about two female wolves appearing within one hundred miles of each other over a short time period, suggesting the animals might have been captives. Bangs said if DNA tests indicated the Boulder wolf was related to the recently killed wolf from the East Fork, she would also be killed.

Bangs did all he could to discredit Jim's and my concern about either of these animals being native wolves. He said: "That would be my 99th guess. Yeah, it's one that stayed invisible over the last fifty years,"[14] and told a reporter "I think the odds are probably better that Martians put it there than that wolves existed for sixty years undetected."[15]

One letter to the editor of the *Casper Star-Tribune* took FWS to task over its too-casual statements about how easy it must have been for Mayo to have roped the wolf. Mayo's neighbor, Joel Bousman, wrote: "Do you have first-hand knowledge of his proficiency with the lariat? Neither did I get to see the wolf lassoed, (and I would give my eye teeth to have seen it), but I have seen Bill Mayo rope. He is a master. If it can be roped, Good Neighbor Bill can rope it . . . In any roping contest, my money is on Bill."[16]

Bousman pointed out that: "In exercising his responsibility to defend the lives of his sheep, Bill Mayo could have chosen to be judge, jury and executioner. Instead, he arrested and detained this criminal wolf for the federal authorities, at no charge to taxpayers."

Mayo himself explained a few things to Bangs in a letter.[17] He wrote:

"One of the sheep which was killed was a bum lamb that was nursed back to life in a box in our house for its first week. This process involves feeding every two hours (including all night). This lamb was bottle-fed until weaning. In her adult life, she always would call to me as I headed across the field with a horse, and she always had her head in the grain bucket as I fed corn daily — she was a pet. Another ewe that was bitten, even though she was in the barn and medicated with antibiotics and topical medications, lived in pain and suffering for four days before she died.

"We did everything in our power to do things right." His assertion was reinforced by a restricted internal FWS law enforcement memo that stated Mayo's action "seems to confirm his intent to put an end to his livestock losses, while saving the wolf. His actions averted what could have been the immediate death of the wolf and allowed Service biologists to observe the wolf firsthand, to determine the origin of the animal."[18]

On March 21, 1997, we sent a letter to David D. Freudenthal, US Attorney in Cheyenne, requesting that Bangs be prosecuted for killing the wolf on the ranch on the South Fork near Cody. Our letter reviewed the details leading to the incident, as outlined in briefs filed in the pending litigation over the wolf reintroduction program:[19]

• On March 4, 1997, Ed Bangs ordered the shooting of a free-ranging wolf near the South Fork of the Shoshone River. Bangs said the animal was a wolf.

• FWS admitted the animal was a wolf.

• The ESA prohibits the taking of threatened and endangered species.

• The experimental population rules established for the reintroduction program state that "All wolves found in the wild within the boundaries of [the experimental population area] after the first release will be considered nonessential experimental animals."[20]

• FWS admitted that killing the Cody wolf was illegal by noting in a brief to the court that the provision of the rules which provide it with authority to destroy wolves only applies to situations outside the experimental population area; in this case, outside Wyoming. "Through oversight, this provision of the rule as drafted only applies outside the boundaries of the experimental population area: the Service is currently taking steps to amend the regulation to extend this provision to

animals found within the boundaries of the experimental population area."[21]

• Thus, while FWS termed this intentional destruction of a
Wyoming wolf an oversight, it was, in fact, a violation of the
ESA and its implementing regulations.

In our letter to Freudenthal, we wrote: "Ed Bangs, FWS Wolf
Recovery Coordinator, should be prosecuted by the United States Attorney General, as other Montana and Wyoming citizens have been
prosecuted for similar actions." One example of this was Chad
McKittrick of Red Lodge, Montana, who had been sentenced in February, 1996, to six months in prison and one year of supervised release for killing a wolf. McKittrick claimed he thought the animal
was a dog.

A similar case even closer to home, and which Freudenthal's
office prosecuted, was decided in April, 1996. Jay York, a Meeteetse
ranch hand, pled guilty to killing a wolf. York believed he was shooting a coyote in the calving pasture. York was fined $500 by US Mag-
istrate William Beaman. A statement released by Freudenthal's office
at the time of York's sentencing quoted the attorney as saying, "This
is an appropriate disposition of the case, in light of the specific facts
and circumstances."

Both McKittrick and York were charged with violations of the
ESA for killing wolves they believed were members of another species. But Bangs knowingly and intentionally ordered the killing of an
animal he knew to be a wolf. He did not claim the animal was a member of another species; he claimed it was a wolf and had it shot. Our
request for prosecution merely asked that federal officials, including
Ed Bangs, be held to the same legal standard as are all other citizens.
When interviewed about our request for prosecution, Freudenthal said:
"It's a legitimate issue that they raised. We'll take a look at it."[22]

A month after we filed the request for Bangs's prosecution,
Freudenthal sent us a letter stating: "An investigation has been initiated. However, this office has been recused from the investigation of
the shooting incident. This office will continue to be involved in the

civil litigation. Responsibility for the shooting incident has been transferred to the United States Attorney's office for North Dakota, and I am forwarding your letter to that office. Please also understand that Department of Justice policy prevents me from commenting on pending matters."[23]

While we sought Bangs's prosecution with the US Attorney's Office, federal attorneys had to respond to our show-cause filings in the federal court as well. It was humorous to note that some of the arguments made by those attorneys actually supported our claims that a remnant wolf population had survived in the Yellowstone area. But we also had arrived at the point where any wolf found in the wild in northwestern Wyoming that was not genetically a member of the introduced subspecies was to be destroyed or placed in permanent captivity.

In a memo attached to its notice to the court, Bangs noted that the Boulder wolf and the wolf killed near Cody were not members of the reintroduced wolf population. Both were female wolves in estrus.

Bangs listed several reasons why he concluded that the Boulder female was not a wild wolf. The first was that the animal "attacked livestock and stayed in the area of depredations for several days, while other lone wolves tend to travel widely."

It was not clear what lone wolves Bangs was referring to, but a wild radio-collared wolf had recently started killing sheep in Sublette County on the Bridger-Teton National Forest. This animal was trapped and transported back to YNP and released, after which it returned to Bridger-Teton and resumed killing sheep, showing no inclination "to travel more widely."·

Bangs's second reason for reaching his conclusion was that "the only known wolves in the Greater Yellowstone Area are marked, this one was not, or accounted for while being monitored."

But federal officials had already admitted that there were a few lone wolves in the Yellowstone area prior to the reintroduction. What was disputed is whether these wolves were lone dispersers from the Canadian wolf population or if they represented a remnant population of the native wolf.

Bangs also noted that the Boulder wolf's DNA "did not match any known wolves from the western US or Canada." We considered this clear support for Nowak's theory that *C. l. irremotus* is not closely related to *C. l. occidentalis*.

Bangs also found other reasons for doubting that it was a wild wolf, including its overall appearance, its hair banding and hair shedding patterns, and the fact that it was found farther south than any monitored wolf of which FWS was aware. We found that all of these reasons supported our claim that this animal was a member of the native population.

Bangs also noted that "its behavior while in captivity was different than observed in other wild wolves." The atypical wolf behavior to which Bangs eluded apparently included avoiding people while in a small kennel and snapping as its muzzle was removed.

Bangs concluded, "While, individually, these conditions do not rule out the possibility of it being a wolf, together they overwhelmingly indicate the animal is not part of the reintroduction and recovery program in the western US and in all likelihood is a wolf-dog hybrid released from captivity by unknown persons."

We never believed that the Boulder wolf was part of the reintroduced wolf population and knew that there was no evidence supporting Bangs's assertion that the animal was a hybrid released from captivity. In fact, it was a wolf that was captured in the wild in Wyoming.

Bangs asserted that the DNA tests indicated the Cody wolf was not related to the Boulder wolf. Actually, however, the DNA report concluded that the Cody wolf and the Boulder wolf were not siblings, but it made no further claim as to the relationship of these animals. In reality, the animals were similar in appearance, they were determined not to be from the same litter, and they most certainly might have represented *C. l. irremotus*.

The serology lab report on the Cody wolf stated, "Although it was most similar to the mtDNA of gray wolves, it was not represented among the western gray wolf reference standards in our data base."[24]

As for the Boulder wolf, Bangs asserted that it probably had been a captive, probably was a hybrid, and had been released by persons unknown. However, since this wolf was surviving in the wild, it was not likely a released captive, and there was no evidence that it was a hybrid. Further, the DNA results indicated that the wolf was neither a long-range disperser from Montana nor an offspring of the reintroduced wolves.

As a last possibility, Bangs suggested that "it is a member of a remnant wolf population that survived in the Yellowstone area since the 1930s."

We argued in a brief to the court that, according to the experimental population rules, "All wolves found in the wild within the [Yellowstone Nonessential Experimental Population Area] after the first releases will be considered nonessential experimental animals."[25] The Boulder wolf was found in the wild in the Yellowstone experimental area, thus FWS had no legal authority to remove this animal from the wild.

While FWS relied on the claim that the animal was a hybrid in order to allow its removal, this action was not allowed under the experimental population rules either. The parts of the rules that allow such action only applied to such animals as they occur "outside an experimental area."[26]

FWS could only respond by attempting to change the rules. Although the agency was at that time attempting to change the rules to allow such action within the experimental areas, the rule change had not been completed.

On June 9, 1997, US Attorney for the District of North Dakota John Schneider issued his letter declining to prosecute Ed Bangs.[27] "This determination rests upon an analysis of whether the killed animal was a gray wolf (canis lupus) or a wolf-dog hybrid." Schneider said Bangs believed that the animal was either a hybrid or a wolf and that pursuant to USDI policy, hybrids are not protected. To prosecute, the evidence would have to be conclusive that the animal was a wolf and not a hybrid.

Schneider stated: "It is our position that we would have to prove, beyond a reasonable doubt, that the animal was not a hybrid but, rather, a species protected under the Endangered Species Act. The DNA results are not helpful in this regard." The DNA results placed the animal within *Canis lupus*, which includes both wolves and dogs. Morphological examination concluded that the animal was within the range of variation found in gray wolves and known wolf-dog hybrids. "Without expert evidence that the animal is a gray wolf, as opposed to a hybrid," Schneider's letter read, "the government's case is greatly weakened and, in this writer's opinion, has no chance of prevailing."

"In hindsight, would it have been better policy for Bangs to have attempted to capture the animal and brought it into humane services where it may or may not have ultimately been euthanized or destroy it with a rifle as was done in this instance? It certainly would have been the better exercise of judgment to capture the animal," Schneider wrote.

"I emphasize again that the shooting of the animal was not a rash, impetuous act," Schneider said, since Bangs had discussed the issue with other wolf experts, law enforcement agents, and affected families.

"I believe that the Service was justified in 'taking' the wolf as the Service was allowed to protect human life and safety," Schneider wrote.

"I recognize that there has been a certain amount of discussion that has arisen over this issue as to whether agents of the Service are held to a different standard than individuals would be," Schneider wrote. "The answer simply is that they are held to a different standard."

Bangs had admitted that he did not consider the Cody wolf a likely threat to humans, but added, "However, since captive wolves and wolf-dog hybrids have been documented to attack people but wild wolves have not, there was some discussion that the animal should not be left in the wild for human safety and liability reasons."

Schneider wrote, "Everyone acknowledges that the animal presented no immediate danger or safety hazard to livestock or human life." Such an immediate threat would have authorized killing the animal.

"In conclusion, I deem it extremely difficult to prove beyond a reasonable doubt, based upon DNA evidence, that the government would be able to prove that the animal was a gray wolf and not a hybrid . . . What an individual is allowed to do under immediate threat for his or her safety, the Service is allowed to do upon deliberation and discussion that there is a threat to human life or safety as was done in this instance."

Schneider wrote that his declination to prosecute "is, in no way, meant to condone the judgment exercised by Mr. Bangs when he ordered the animal to be killed in the field. It was regrettable that this animal had to be killed in the fashion it was done."

～

On November 10, 1997, we sent a motion to Judge Downes requesting "expedited consideration" of the lawsuit. Simply put, it was a respectful way of asking Downes to hurry up and make a decision. We reminded Downes that when we had requested a preliminary injunction, which he had denied, FWS assured the court it would be able to terminate the experimental release of wolves within a period of one or two years after the experiment was initiated.

Bangs had written in a declaration opposing the injunction: "The experiment could be terminated with an extremely high degree of confidence within the first year or two. Since all reintroduced wolves will be radio-collared, likely all, and certainly most, could be recaptured or if necessary, killed once released. Modern radio-telemetry collars normally last at least two years and are highly reliable."

But the first two years of the experiment now had passed. The radio collars were expiring, and it was doubtful that FWS would be able to capture all the released animals and their offspring. In addition, many of the offspring of the released wolves were not wearing radio collars. In fact, only sixty of the 160 wolves in Yellowstone and central Idaho were actually wearing collars.

FWS continued to refuse to consider evidence that a native population of wolves survived in the Yellowstone area. Instead, the agency was actively implementing a policy that resulted in the removal of any wolves from the wild in Wyoming if their presence could not be attributed to the experimental release of Canadian wolves.

The Cody wolf was killed before any biological evidence was examined, and only months after she was killed did we learn that she possessed "abnormalities" linking her to the native wolf population. FWS did not even consider that she might have been a native wolf, desperately in danger of extinction by the agency's own actions.

The same held true for the Boulder wolf. Instead of releasing the animal back into the wild, FWS sent her to a private facility in Texas, where the policy was to spay or neuter the captive animals.[28] In doing so, FWS ensured the young female wolf could never be used for future recovery efforts.

Bangs wrote to the FWS Regional Director in September, 1997, "I am directing that the wolf-like canid being held in a pen in Yellowstone National Park be permanently placed in captivity." This female wolf was transported to the captive facility in Texas, only to die a few months later.

"I believe that the canid is not a wild wolf and is likely a wolf hybrid," Bangs wrote, adding that the DNA test results "indicated it was not related to any known wolf sampled in the western US."

We responded by writing to the court: "It would have been far more useful to science, and to recovery efforts, if the agency refused to release this female wolf back into the wild, to kill her and examine her skull. Instead, defendants took a course of action that guaranteed the animal could not jeopardize the experimental reintroduction effort."

We asked for a final ruling in the wolf lawsuit, noting that "further delay in disposition of this litigation will moot the issues in dispute, allowing the final and complete extinction of the irremotus subspecies." Downes declined to act on our motion.

Chapter 15

Downes's Decision

Finally, on December 12, 1997, Judge Downes issued his decision on our suit. Downes determined that the final rules establishing the non-essential experimental population of gray wolves in central Idaho, Wyoming, and southwestern Montana "are hereby found unlawful and set aside" and "by virtue of the plan being set aside, Defendants must remove reintroduced non-native wolves and their offspring from the Yellowstone and central Idaho experimental population areas."

⌒

Our claims that FWS violated NEPA by failing to address the impacts of reintroduction on naturally occurring wolves, the maintenance of wolf subspecies, and the need for more research on naturally occurring wolves was quickly rejected by Downes in his decision. He wrote that in reviewing a challenge to the adequacy of an environmental impact statement, the court's job is not to "second-guess the experts" in policy matters, but rather to determine whether the "statement contains sufficient discussion of the relevant issues and opposing viewpoints to enable the decision-maker to take a 'hard look' at environmental factors, and to make a reasoned decision."

"The Urbigkits argue that the Endangered Species Act, which was intended to provide a program for the conservation of endangered and threatened species, requires the consideration of wolf subspecies. In particular, they argue that, because the ESA provides that the listing of a given taxon includes all lower taxonomic units, the ESA makes subspecies relevant to recovery efforts . . . The Urbigkits also rely on a letter from Dr. Ron M. Nowak, commenting on the draft EIS with regard to taxonomic issues, wherein Dr. Nowak states, '[T]here is the misleading suggestion that the original Yellowstone wolf has affinity with the wolves that would be reintroduced, when in fact there is a pronounced subspecific distinction. It also is wrong to state that the 1978 listing made subspecies irrelevant . . . A big part of the conservation of a full species is to insure that its component sub-species and populations remain intact and in place, and that over-all diversity and evolutionary potential are maintained.'

"Thus, Urbigkits argue, the gray wolf subspecies indigenous to the Yellowstone area, *Canis lupus irremotus*, which was listed as en-dangered in 1973, deserves full protection under the ESA. Urbigkits further argue that because the wolves from Canada are of a distinct subspecies from the indigenous wolves, Defendants' reintroduction plan will have an adverse impact on the conservation of the irremotus subspecies existing in the Yellowstone area, an impact which Urbigkits allege Defendants failed to adequately analyze. Finally, Urbigkits ar-gue that Defendants failed to adequately address the need for more research on the naturally occurring wolves to determine the potential impacts of the reintroduction plan on them.

"In response to such concerns, the FEIS explains the reasons why these issues/impacts were 'not chosen for detailed analysis.' With respect to the alleged impacts on naturally occurring wolves in the Yellowstone area and on the maintenance of wolf subspecies, the FWS reported that '[n]o evidence exists that wolf populations persisted in the northern Rocky Mountains of the US [since their extirpation in the 1930s] to the present time or that the lone wild wolves occasion-ally reported in these areas are other than dispersing wolves from Canadian populations.'

"The record shows that the FWS investigated the alleged exist-ence of wolves in the subject areas and studied the taxonomy issues. After the conclusion of such research, the FWS exercised its discre-tion in choosing from admittedly conflicting opinions and results. The fact that, in developing the wolf reintroduction plan, the FWS fol-lowed opinions and conclusions contrary to that held by the Urbigkits does not undermine the validity of the plan. The Court cannot say that the FWS' determination regarding the insignificance of the issues and alleged impacts raised by the Urbigkits (to the decision being made) was unsupported by evidence in the record or that the FWS made a clear error of judgment."

We were appalled at Downes's logic. It was apparent that he had relied on the FWS statements without looking at their sources to confirm their accuracy, a violation of the court's standard. Downes's order was full of inaccurate citations. Regardless of which set of citations were used, there was no factual support, or citations for factual support, to be found in the administrative record, on the pages cited by either Downes or FWS. The district court did not conduct the review of the facts in the record, as simply laid out in federal court standards, but rather based the entire review on unsupported claims made by the agency in defense of the agency decision.

From reading Downes's decision, and attempting to follow his citations to find facts supporting his statements, it became apparent that the district court did not itself examine the administrative record, and did not itself find and identify facts to support the agency's action. Downes's order made statements such as "FWS reported," and "Defendants assert," or "Defendants argue," but did not ever state that the court itself made any factual findings.

Where did the district court identify the facts? It simply did not. Instead, the court improperly relied on statements made by counsel and relied on claims made in the FEIS that were not supported by the facts in the record. The district court had failed to fulfill its affirmative duty to "define specifically, those facts which it deemed supportive of the agency decision."

Downes also ruled on our contention that the reintroduction of Canadian wolves into the Yellowstone area would jeopardize the continued existence of the wolf subspecies indigenous to the area, noting, "However, this claim also fails given the Court's finding herein that the FWS' determination that any existing wolves in the Yellowstone area will not be significantly impacted by the plan was not arbitrary and capricious."

The district court obviously did not review the record to learn if the provided citations supported the assertions made, or if the assertions were contradicted by the record itself. Had the court conducted an in-depth review of the administrative record, it would have been unable to discover substantial evidence to support the decision.

Representative differences between citations used by the court and what the record actually substantiated include the following:

1. "No evidence exists that wolf populations persisted in the Northern Rocky Mountains of the US to the present time or that lone wild wolves occasionally reported in these areas are other than dispersing wolves from Canadian populations (Brewster & Fritts 1992, Nowak 1993)."[1]

What the record substantiated: The FEIS mischaracterized the work cited, and the federal court apparently relied on this presentation as fact. Brewster and Fritts did not claim that "no evidence exists that wolf populations persisted," but in fact cited Glen Cole's 1971 work that stated, "There were small numbers present since the 1930s. He further concluded that based on observations from 1969 to 1971 that one and possibly two pairs of wolves produced young."

Brewster and Fritts actually discussed the evidence that wolves had persisted and finally concluded that the reports of wolf presence "would be consistent with very low wolf numbers."

The administrative record did not support the FWS allegation that "no evidence exists that wolf populations persisted" which was relied on by the district court as fact. The record was replete with records of wolf presence from the 1930s to the present. When the native subspecies was listed in the 1970s, NPS estimated the Yellowstone population to be ten–fifteen animals, with several breeding pairs of wolves present.

The district court cited FWS's wolf monitoring program as negating the need for FWS to examine the issue of the need for additional research on naturally occurring wolves in the FEIS. The FWS monitoring program relied on by FWS and the district court is summarized in the FEIS, but the statements in the FEIS regarding the monitoring program were actually contradicted by evidence in the administrative record.

2. "The Wyoming Game and Fish Department summarized 9 reports of wolves from 1978 to 1985. Reports were sporadic (never a

cluster of similar reports within the same year), were of single animals, and did not show concentrated activity or indicate the presence of wolf pack activity in northwestern Wyoming."[2]

What the record substantiated: A document in the administrative record before the court included a WGF memo which summarized the information referred to in the FEIS statement above. It revealed that all but two of the reports were from the Green River Lakes area near Pinedale. A 1978 report described a pair of gray wolves, while the next summer a dark wolf accompanied by a smaller gray wolf which traveled with a limp was reported. The observer reported hearing what he thought were pups in the area. Two years later, a pack of five wolves were reported to be in the same area, led by a dark wolf, and trailed by a gray colored wolf which appeared to be limping. WGP employees reported tracks of a wolf three times in the area over the next winter (1982–1983). The FWS characterization of the information in the FEIS is false.

3. "In 1989, the FWS instituted a more aggressive wolf reporting system and established a network of state and federal agency contacts to record reports of wolf sightings. The FWS also encouraged the public to report wolf sightings to appropriate authorities."[3]

What the record substantiated: A document in the administrative record showed that, in 1990, a reporter was asked to leave an interagency meeting where the wolf reports were being reviewed because "we were very concerned about publicity about wolves generating sightings."

4. "In 1991, the FWS received reports of wolves in the Dubois area, southeast of YNP. Fish and Wildlife Service conducted interviews with people and surveys of the area in March 1991 but did not find wolf presence."[4]

What the record substantiated: A document in the administrative record noted that snow conditions precluded a search at that time.

5. The FEIS at 6-90 reported "National Park Service and WYGF personnel conducted additional field surveys in the Donor area in August 1991 but wolf presence was not detected."

What the record substantiated: A document in the administrative record described this search, noting that the investigators heard low-pitched wolf-like howls on four occasions in two days, and they were confident the animal was not a coyote. They also found a 3 ½-inch by 4 ½-inch canid track in the area, and received reports of wolf howls from two different observers in the area at the same time.

6. "Fish and Wildlife Service, USDA Forest Service, and WYGF personnel conducted an additional survey later in August 1991 in the Dubois area and did not find convincing or conclusive evidence of wolves or wolf presence in the area."[5]

What the record substantiated: A document in the administrative record demonstrated that this group that went back into the area did not hear any howls, but found what FWS determined were three to four possible wolf scats.

7. "In late spring, a Forest Service employee reported hearing wolves howling south of the park . . . Additionally, US Fish and Wildlife Service and Forest Service personnel visited this backcountry location searching for wolf sign for several days and found none. No wolf howling was heard. No further reports of multiple wolves were received from the area."[6]

What the record substantiated: According to the wolf reports in the administrative record, the next month, in August, 1993, observers stationed at both the Thorofare Ranger Station and the Trail Creek Cabin both reported wolf howls from multiple animals. These cabins are within five miles of Hawks Rest, where the earlier search was conducted, and about fifteen miles east of where the wolf was shot in the Teton Wilderness the previous fall. Facts in the record demonstrated that FWS claims regarding evidence of wolf presence were false.

Had the district court examined the record and attempted to find substantial evidence to support the claims made by FWS, it would have learned that the FWS claims were assertions that were overwhelmed by evidence to the contrary. The blatant assertion by FWS that "no evidence exists that wolf populations persisted" was discounted by evidence appearing throughout the record, a quick review of which will show convincingly the continuity of wolf sightings in the area from the last days of the predator control era to just prior to the release of Canadian wolves into the park. The available record indicated that a few wolves had survived in the area, and that both NPS and FWS had confirmed the presence of wolves during this time.

So why was this issue discounted in the FEIS? There could only be one answer — to allow the wolf reintroduction to take place. It is no secret that NPS had pushed for a wolf reintroduction program since the late 1960s. In fact, at the First Interagency Meeting for the Management of the Northern Rocky Mountain Wolf, held in the park in 1971, FWS and NPS discussed doing just that.

At that meeting, Glen Cole had mentioned that he was concerned about the limited gene pool of Yellowstone's wolves and wanted to strengthen it by bringing in more wolves. The overpopulation of elk in the park was a management problem, as was noted in the record of the meeting. "Now the park needs an unknown number of wolf packs to control these ungulates. Possibly 30 to 40 wolves in the northern Yellowstone area could be accommodated. Cole indicated that the park would accept live trapped wolves even though they might disrupt some of the existing packs."

Regardless of the reason, the fact remained — FWS unfairly discounted this issue in the FEIS. FWS stated "no evidence exists" that wolves had persisted, when in fact, the evidence was overwhelming, and Downes let the agency get away with it.

Later, in his decision on our suit, Downes tackled the ESA language that allowed the release of experimental populations of endangered or threatened species that are "introduced into areas outside their current range, but only when and at such time as, the population is wholly separate geographically from nonexperimental populations of the same species."

FWS contended that it had determined that the experimental population areas were outside the current range of the gray wolf, and that such a determination was based on the conclusion that there were no known "populations," as defined by FWS. FWS claimed that the "wholly separate geographic" requirement applied only to "populations" and not individual animals.

Downes decided that the FWS definition of population "is based on a permissible construction of the ESA . . . which seeks to secure the recovery of listed species."

"While the court must defer to the FWS's definition of population, a more thorough analysis of the reintroduction plan's compliance with the requirements of § 10(j) is necessary." Downes noted that 10(j) only allows an experimental population to be maintained "when, and at such time as, the [experimental] population is wholly separate geographically from nonexperimental populations of the same species."

"Erroneously focusing only on the definition of 'population,' Defendants argue that no geographic overlap exists, given their conclusion that no 'populations' of wolves exist in the experimental areas. However, Defendants' own statements contained in the administrative record establish that members (or part) of the natural wolf populations in Montana and/or Canada exist, and will continue to exist, in the experimental population areas."

Downes noted that the Teton wolf was "from one of the packs in the Montana population." Then, he continued:

"Further, the mere fact that Defendants have drawn a line which purports to ensure no geographic overlap between the existing wolf population in Montana and either of the proposed experimental population areas is insufficient and contrary to law. The legislative history and Defendants' own regulations require that an experimental population may be maintained only when the times of geographic separation from nonexperimental (non-introduced) specimens are reasonably predictable as a result of fixed migration patterns or natural or man-made barriers."

"Defendants resolve this problem by treating all wolves found within the boundaries of the designated experimental population areas as nonessential experimental animals," Downes noted. "However, such treatment is contrary to law as provided in the Defendants' own regulations."

In a footnote to the decision, Downes added:

"The Farm Bureaus and Urbigkits also contend that the experimental population of Canadian wolves was not introduced within that species' 'probable historic range' in violation of 50 C.F.R. § 17.81(a). They argue that the wolf indigenous to the Yellowstone and central Idaho areas was once recognized as a distinct subspecies, Canis lupus irremotus, different from the Canadian wolves, and that this subspecific distinction is still relevant in light of the opinion of Dr. Nowak. However, Plaintiffs' contention on this issue cannot be sustained in light of this Court's previous finding herein that the Defendants' determination regarding the insignificance of subspecific distinctions is not arbitrary and capricious.

"The same problems exist with Defendants' arguments concerning the Farm Bureaus' and Urbigkits' claims that the experimental population areas are not outside the current range of the gray wolf. In attempting to refute such claims, Defendants ignore the plain language of the statute and attempt to turn the current range of such species into the current range or territory of naturally occurring packs or populations of such species. Because they contend that no pack or populations of wolves presently exist in the experimental population areas, Defendants argue that their determination that the experimental population areas are outside the current range of the gray wolf is rationally based and supported in the record. However, the plain language of [the act] speaks to the range of the species without specific reference to a population.

"Such an interpretation is consistent with the Court's previous analysis regarding the wholly separate requirement. To further prevent the occurrence of overlap between experimental and nonexperimental populations, Congress required that an experimental population could only be introduced to the extent it was outside the current range of such species . . . Congress clearly intended to guard against the overlap of introduced and non-introduced individuals or specimens of a particular species. The requirement that an experimental population only be authorized if it is outside the current range of the species is a reflection of that intent. Given Congress' intent, and the Defendants' acknowledgment that naturally occurring wolves exist in and will likely migrate to the experimental population areas, Defendants' determination that the designated areas are outside the current range of the species is arbitrary and capricious.

"The National Audubon Plaintiffs contend that the central Idaho reintroduction plan illegally withdraws and denies full ESA protections from wolves naturally migrating to central Idaho in violation of the ESA. In support of this argument, these Plaintiffs assert that the experimental population rules operate as a de facto delisting of the naturally occurring wolves.

"The introduction of an experimental population cannot operate as a de facto delisting of naturally occurring wolves . . . Therefore, Defendants' blanket treatment of all wolves found within the designated experimental population areas as experimental animals is contrary to law."

Downes concluded his judgment with: "Mindful of the dedication, talents and money which have been expended in the development and implementation of the wolf recovery program, the Court reaches this decision with the utmost reluctance. The Court is especially mindful of the concerted efforts of the Government and wolf recovery advocates to accommodate the interests of stockgrowers and others who may be adversely affected by the wolf recovery program. The fact that the program has been responsibly implemented, however, cannot obviate the limitations Congress has imposed upon the application of § 10(j). The laudable ends aspired to by the wolf recovery plan cannot justify the Secretary's impermissible means."

In yet another footnote, Downes added: "It is ironic that as a result of the inability to implement an experimental population in these areas, no flexibility in ESA protections will be available to those individuals economically effected by natural wolf recovery. As the adage goes, 'Be careful what you wish for, you might just get it.'"

Downes ordered the reintroduced wolves to be removed from the area — but he put a stay on his removal order, pending the outcome of the appeals he was confident would be filed.

Chapter 16

The Appeal

On January 16, 1998, Judge Downes clarified his removal order. He wrote:

"The evidence before this court revealed that defendants could remove non-native wolves from the experimental population areas and transplant them elsewhere within the territory of the United States. The record suggests that if the non-native wolves can be humanely captured and transferred to the experimental population areas, they can also be humanely captured and removed. The order to remove the wolves is not intended to serve as a license to euthanize wolves and any interpretation that it does so is misplaced."[1]

Downes's original decision had caused some hysteria from the reintroduction advocates, some of whom were blaming ranchers for what might have amounted to a wolf slaughter. Some news accounts also reported that we, the Urbigkits, were ranchers at the time. Neither was accurate.

In an editorial to the *Casper Star-Tribune*, Jim and I wrote:

"The blame for the forthcoming wolf slaughter and the past waste of millions of taxpayer dollars belongs firmly on the reintroduction supporters and the agency who undertook this program: the US Fish and Wildlife Service.[2]

"The public should not forget that three lawsuits challenging the legality of the reintroduction program were filed — only one was from ranching interests. One case was filed by environmental groups, while we filed the third — Wyoming citizens fighting to protect Wyoming's naturally occurring wolf population. The plaintiffs in all three cases argued the same legal point and we all won. We were right, the program was illegal.

"This was not something that happened overnight. The plaintiffs in all three cases have been belaboring this point to FWS long before the wolves were ever captured in Canada. We filed a lawsuit in 1991 trying to get FWS to realize the illegality of its effort, but the case was dismissed so the agency could move forward with preparing an environmental impact statement for an illegal action.

"As soon as the official decision to reintroduce wolves was made, the three lawsuits were filed. FWS moved ahead with the program, while the cases made their way through the court, until the decision was issued last month.

"We consider ourselves the most radical wolf recovery proponents involved in the whole debate. The whole purpose for our efforts over the last 12 years has been to fight for legal protection for Wyoming's naturally occurring wolf population. Wolf reintroduction supporters, not comfortable with our position, doubt our motives. It's unfortunate.

"During our legal arguments before Judge Downes, we presented documents from the administrative record that naturally occurring wolves were present in the Yellowstone area. These included National Park Service estimates of the native wolf population in the early 1970s and reports confirming the presence of wolves and packs in areas outside the park boundaries.

"As a technical point, we were not trying to prove to the Court that wolves existed. In fact, even FWS agreed at least some wolves were present.

"We were arguing a point of law based on the National Environmental Policy Act and an earlier precedent-setting decision which requires federal agency decisions to be based on the facts in the record. The 'Olenhouse' decision requires that agency action must be supported by substantial evidence in the administrative record used by the agency to make its decision. So from the record, we cited substantial evidence showing wolves lived in the proposed release areas. We demonstrated that FWS claims to the contrary were not supported by substantial evidence.

"Unfortunately, it doesn't seem Judge Downes had a very keen interest in the NEPA violations. Or perhaps we just failed to argue the point well enough. Downes did not hold FWS to the substantial evidence test, so our NEPA claims were dismissed.

"But what really floored us about the decision was that Judge Downes did not rule on our primary Endangered Species Act complaint which charged FWS with violating the law by failing to protect and conserve Wyoming's naturally occurring wolves. We believe these wolves are remnants of the native wolf population, a subspecies distinctly different from the reintroduced Canadian wolf subspecies.

"Judge Downes did not rule on that portion of our ESA complaint, but instead apparently dismissed this disputed issue by stating in the background portion of his decision that wolves were extirpated from the western portion of the United States by the early 1900s. This, in spite of the fact that Wyoming's native wolf (known to exist in low numbers) was placed on the list of endangered species in 1973.

"O. Fred Finley, who has lived on the East Fork of the Wind River since the summer of 1937, has seen wolves every so often since he moved into the area. He says wolves were always there.

"But Ed Bangs, the team leader for the reintroduction project, says wolves were eradicated by the 1930s. Mr. Bangs has never lived in Wyoming and has never searched for wolves in Wyoming. What on earth would make us believe him over Fred Finley? Or over Reid Jackson, George Gruell and Al Boss, who worked on the Bridger-Teton National Forest and said wolves still survived in the 1970s?

"It is this issue, and the NEPA claims, which we now plan to appeal.

"Here in Sublette County where we live, it is generally accepted as common knowledge that there was a small breeding population of wolves here before the reintroduction. We do occasionally meet people that don't agree, but they are a small minority, and they surprise us as much as though they believe the world is flat.

"So, even though we received a notice from Judge Downes in the mail notifying us that we had judgment in our favor (and it felt good), we are still no closer to saving our native wolf than before, so we will appeal the decision.

"We've maintained that the greatest single threat to the continued existence of the native wolf is the reintroduction of another subspecies.

The removal of the Canadian wolves is one part of Judge Downes' decision we will continue to support.

"We continue to be chagrined that people who claim to support the protection of endangered species, such as the Wildlife Federation and Defenders of Wildlife, continue to fight so doggedly for the extinction of Wyoming's native wolf.

"We continue to be saddened that the people charged with protecting our wildlife, the Wyoming Game and Fish Department and the Wyoming Game and Fish Commission, continue to sit and silently watch as our native wolf is pushed to extinction."

∽

NWF commissioned a public opinion poll to learn that the majority of those polled opposed the removal of the reintroduced wolves and would support congressional action to keep the wolves in place.[3]

GYC suggested that, if the appeals court were to uphold Downes's decision, three options were available, ranging from removing the wolves through congressional action to reclassifying all wolves as endangered with full protections under the ESA.[4] "Given these three options as a scenario for wolves, GYC supports reclassifying all wolves as endangered," GYC noted, while also suggesting that supporters write to the American Farm Bureau Federation to tell the organization "to let the wolves stay on the ground."

DW put the blame for the possible removal of the wolves squarely at the feet of the Farm Bureaus as well. Defenders President Rodger Schlickeisen said, "If it refuses to do so, the American public will know that the blood of Yellowstone's wolves is on the hands of the Farm Bureau and its members."[5]

The Sierra Club of Montana called on Interior Secretary Bruce Babbitt to suspend the rules allowing the wolf transplant.[6] "We call on ... Babbitt to immediately take steps necessary to protect the wolves of Yellowstone by granting them the full protection of the Endangered Species Act," said spokeswoman Betsy Buffington.

Babbitt did not act on the request, but did pledge "no wolves will be removed from Yellowstone on my watch."[7]

Doug Honnold of Earthjustice wrote: "What is not in doubt is that despite all the mudslinging, conservationists on all sides want the same thing — to save wolves. And what is equally clear is that the Farm Bureau does not. They are the enemy to the wolves here and will continue to be their biggest threat."[8]

In Jim's and my view, Downes's ruling was sloppy and convoluted at best. We did appeal his decision to a higher court, the Tenth Circuit Court of Appeals in Denver. In our opening brief before the appeals court, we argued that the district court incorrectly treated the conservation of subspecies and naturally occurring wolves as a matter of discretion rather than a legal mandate. In addition, the district court, in its review, did not itself examine the administrative record and did not itself identify facts to support the agency's action. Instead, the court improperly relied on conclusory statements made by FWS that either were not supported by substantial evidence in the administrative record, or were actually contradicted by the facts in the administrative record.

We sided with the district court and the Farm Bureaus that the court had correctly ruled that FWS violated Section 10 (j) of the ESA when it established the "experimental populations" of wolves where wolves already existed, because experimental populations must be wholly separate geographically from nonexperimental populations of the same species, and because the releases of experimental populations may be conducted only outside the current range of such species.

We argued that because the experimental population designation illegally reduced protection for naturally occurring wolves, the district court's order regarding the removal of the reintroduced wolves should be upheld. The removal of the reintroduced animals would aid in the conservation of the naturally occurring wolf subspecies, an action mandated by the ESA. We asked the appeals court, in addition to upholding the district court order as it pertains to the use of Section 10 (j) and the subsequent removal of the reintroduced wolves, to order that the naturally occurring wolves finally be subject to a conservation program thus far illegally withheld by FWS. We gave example after example of how the statements in the EIS were contradictory to the evidence in the record before the court.

Ironically, the twenty-seven pages of the FWS reply brief dedicated to rebutting our arguments were the most extensive discussion of the issues we had attempted in vain to have discussed in the EIS. Rather than twenty-seven pages, however, the EIS dismissed the issues in a few paragraphs.

Many of the statements and assertions made in the FWS reply brief were misleading, skewed, exaggerated, or just simply wrong. Appallingly, at least one of the arguments being posed by FWS counsel was the exact opposite of statements made by the agency in the FEIS.

FWS counsel, in its reply brief, stated that the EIS determined no subspecies of gray wolf remained extant in Yellowstone, no wolf populations existed in Yellowstone, and that: "Of the multiple reported sightings of wolves, none could be definitively confirmed as being a wolf. Even the 1992 canid which the Service's biologist indicated at trial was probably a wolf dispersing from Montana, was never confirmed as such . . . Thus, even this canid, which the Wolf Recovery Coordinator speculated might come from the northwest Montana population, was never actually confirmed to be a wolf."

In the FEIS, however, FWS had claimed exactly the opposite: "On September 30, 1992 a male wolf was shot . . . This was the first wolf killed close to the park . . . Genetic investigations verified this animal was genetically related to wolves in northwestern Montana." Nowhere in the FEIS did FWS cast any doubt that this animal was anything other than a wild wolf.

Other FWS statements attempting to rebut our arguments were false. FWS argued that reports of wolf sightings in the Yellowstone area persisted from the late 1920s, but "no report indicated the presence of a pack of wolves, however, and no dens were ever reported or found; as a result, no reproduction was ever reported, much less documented." This was precisely the kind of statement that had landed us in a federal court against FWS. This was not a "full and fair discussion" as required by NEPA, but an outright falsehood, as was documented in the administrative record.

FWS, in its reply brief, placed the court on a merry-go-round of words, attempting to draw the court into the position of having us prove that a population of wolves, as defined by the agency, existed in each recovery area at the time of reintroduction, entirely missing the point of our arguments about process.

Federal law and judicial process require that the agency's action be supported by evidence in the administrative record, and that a full and fair discussion of significant issues be provided in the EIS.

FWS had yet to explain why it acknowledged the presence of wolves in the reintroduction areas in the past, but attempted to deny wolf presence in the FEIS. FWS claimed to the court that the only timeframe for which wolf sightings could be relevant were the ten years prior to the reintroduction, because wolves only live ten years and there was "no evidence of pack formation."

We were once again on the word merry-go-round. FWS, through-out its filings in the court, continued to use words such as "lone wolves, strays, stragglers and dispersers," pretending that groups of wolves and reproduction had not been reported, and that any wolves that appeared in the reintroduction areas must be lone, dispersing animals. Evidence of pack formation within this so-called relevant time period could easily be found in the administrative record. FWS did not provide any analysis of the issue within the EIS, and instead deliberately claimed the evidence did not exist.

FWS made other misstatements of the facts in its reply brief. We did not attempt to address them all, but we did address a few of the most significant in terms of demonstrating how the record did not support FWS claims. One such example involved the filming of a wolf in YNP in 1992. In court, FWS now claimed "its presence was never again documented," but a memo from the Northern Rocky Mountain Wolf Recovery Coordinator dated October 19, 1992, noted that, "An apparent wolf was filmed in Hayden Valley of Yellowstone Park in August 1992 and has been observed in that general area about six times since; we are confident that this animal is not the one that was shot, based on its distinctive markings."

FWS also claimed that John Weaver's 1978 report "showed that there were no wolves in Yellowstone and that the wolf specific to

Yellowstone had been exterminated in the 1930s." According to Weaver's report, what he actually found were "two separate sets of tracks and heard one series of howls which may have been a wolf . . . The howls were not recorded, but I am confident the animal was not a coyote." Weaver noted the reports "do not indicate a viable wolf population in the park." He concluded: "A departure from natural conditions exists in Yellowstone National Park because fewer pure wolves, if any, occur now than in the past. Control by humans — both within and outside the park — has brought the Yellowstone wolf to the edge of extinction." Weaver did not determine that no wolves existed, as FWS now claimed.

Our arguments proved that the statements in the FEIS cited by FWS, and by the district court in dismissing our claims, were not supported by the evidence in the administrative record. FWS did not fairly examine, address, and dispel this evidence, but denied its existence altogether. For this reason the statements in the FEIS were not supported by the record — as a result, it was flawed, thus so were its conclusions.

The Farm Bureaus had to appear in appeals court to defend the district court decision. The Farm Bureaus called the reintroduction scheme an "ill-conceived and ill-fated program."[9]

Farm Bureaus' arguments were quite similar to our own and pointed out in the appeal that the district court was correct in ruling that the establishment of experimental populations was illegal in areas where wolves already existed. The organization also argued that the court was correct in ordering FWS to remove all the Canadian wolves and their progeny, calling the removal "the only appropriate remedy."[10]

The Farm Bureaus pointed out that if the district court had not ordered the wolves to be removed, "FWS would have had no legal authority under which to manage the wolves as experimental. Thus, in effect the wolves' status would change to endangered by default."[11]

The Farm Bureaus pointed out that this was the remedy FWS had set forth in the final rules when it provided that "All reintroduced wolves designated as nonessential experimental will be removed from the wild and the experimental population status and regulations revoked when . . . legal actions or lawsuits change the wolves' status to endangered under the Act."[12]

FWS, through USDJ, filed an appellant brief with the appeals court on May 12. The FWS brief essentially argued the case all over again, alleging that the court was required to give deference to an agency's interpretation of the statute under which it operates.[13]

FWS argued that since the agency did not find a "population" of wolves in either reintroduction area, the occasional presence of a few wolves should not invalidate the reintroduction program. The agency further defined a wolf population as "at least two breeding pairs of gray wolves that each successfully raise at least two young" yearly for two consecutive years.

FWS cited a recent Ninth Circuit Court of Appeals ruling in Chad McKittrick's case. McKittrick had shot, killed, skinned, and decapitated a wolf and, as a defense, claimed that because the reintroduced wolves were not "wholly separate geographically" from wolves already present in Yellowstone, the experimental population designation was invalid and the wolves not protected.

The appeals court disagreed, stating that the FWS regulations establishing the experimental population met the geographical separation requirement. The Ninth Circuit is based in California and had no jurisdiction over the wolf reintroduction lawsuit ongoing in the Tenth Circuit.

The Ninth Circuit ruling said: "Although McKittrick points to sporadic sightings of isolated indigenous wolves in the release area, lone wolves or dispersers, do not constitute a population . . . We do not agree with the Wyoming District Court's analysis that (the ESA) must be read to apply to individual specimens as well as populations . . . A single straggler does not a population make."

The FWS brief in the Tenth Circuit claimed that Downes misinterpreted the ESA. It stated that, "In sum, the district court erred by imagining a congressional concern for individual, stray wolves, and by translating this concern into an intent to bar introduction of experimental populations under the circumstances here."

FWS also argued that since Congress authorized the development of the EIS on the wolf reintroduction proposal, and was periodically updated on the proposal, it had "an imputed knowledge that the re-introduction program would probably result in the intermingling of a few dispersing wolves from the naturally occurring wolf populations with the introduced wolf populations" implying that Congress repeatedly endorsed the FWS proposal.

In a later brief, the federal government wrote: "The Service agrees with Dr. Nowak's basic concept — that if a surviving population of a distinctive type of wolf were found in Yellowstone, then recovery efforts should and would give the strongest consideration to promoting the recovery and conservation of those animals. However, research indicated that there were no wolves left in the Yellowstone area."[14]

FWS closed its arguments with statements as to how important the wolf reintroduction project has been to the nation. In this regard, the agency said:

"Wolf recovery is so compelling a public value that Congress passed (amendments to the ESA) with that purpose specifically in mind, and subsequently allocated additional resources specifically to further the gray wolf experimental population regulations . . . The district court has acknowledged that the FWS has 'responsibly implemented' the recovery program, with 'dedication, talents and money.'

"As a result, reintroduction has been a tremendous ecological and economic benefit to both Yellowstone and Idaho, as anticipated by Congress. The district court's misconceptions as to the underlying biology and the statutory requirements should not be allowed to interrupt this program of national significance."

The FWS brief requested that Judge Downes's order be overturned so the program could proceed as FWS originally envisioned.

Chapter 17

Friends of the Court

Several environmental organizations not involved in the original wolf litigation in Downes's court joined together to file "friend of the court," or "amici curiae," briefs with the Tenth Circuit.

One such brief was filed by the Environmental Defense Fund (EDF), World Wildlife Fund, Wildlife Conservation Society, Izaak Walton League of America, Idaho Conservation League, Wolf Recovery Foundation, and the Center for Marine Conservation.[1]

The amici brief of this group argued that:

"The return of the wolf has meant more than entertainment for park visitors. It has also begun to counter some of the ecological perturbations that occurred as a result of the earlier elimination of this keystone predator. In the absence of significant predation or legal hunting, numbers of elk and other park ungulates soared. Their heavy browsing reduced the regeneration of alders, willows and other plants.[2]

"Like the ripples from a pebble cast into a pond, the elimination of the wolf set off a chain of ecological events that transformed the very nature of Yellowstone. In only a few years, the wolf's return has again begun to work dramatic changes in the relationships among the park's plants and animals."[3]

The main point of the EDF et al. argument was that, "The fatal flaw that the district court purported to find in the program to reintroduce wolves experimentally into the two areas was the fact that one or more individual wolves might already occur in, or subsequently move into, those areas, and thereby lose some of the protection they formerly had."[4]

EDF et al. maintained that "the court erred, however, in giving this fact pivotal significance," because individual animals routinely lose and gain protection simply by moving about the landscape through areas of different protective designations.[5] "The court misconstrued the requirements of the statute and improperly subordinated the law's overriding concern with the well-being of a species to its clearly lesser concern for the extent of legal protection afforded individual animals of that species."[6]

The EDF et al. brief also sought a reversal of Downes's order to allow the FWS reintroduction program to continue according to the FWS plan.

Although the National Parks and Conservation Association (NPCA) was not involved in the litigation in Downes's court, it also filed an amici brief with the appeals court. Like the groups involved in the EDF et al. brief, NPCA argued that removing the reintroduced wolves "would upset the much-restored ecological balance in the park."[7]

The NPCA brief sought to overturn Downes's decision, stating that the removal "of scores of wolves now thriving in Yellowstone National Park and central Idaho is improper . . . and wholly contrary to the language and purposes of the ESA."[8]

The major difference between this brief and the other briefs supporting the reintroduction plan was that NPCA requested if the court agreed with Downes, it wanted the appeals court to remand the case back to FWS "to correct its own error as it deems best" rather than order the removal of the wolves.[9]

NPCA then made several suggestions as to what FWS could do to correct the error. First, the wolves could be reclassified to fully endangered status. "The most logical result of the lower court's decision would be to alter the classification of the affected wolves, not to hunt them down and remove them." A second alternative would be to re-draw the boundaries of the reintroduction areas "to ensure that they are situated outside the current range of all naturally occurring wolves."[10] Thirdly, FWS could implement a plan "to capture and relocate any naturally occurring wolf that strays into the experimental areas."[11] And lastly, NPCA suggested that if a removal plan were necessary, that it only be performed outside of YNP, since NPS "has both a mandate and management capability to oversee wolf activity within the Park."[12]

NPCA also stated: "Finally, even if the court were to conclude that [FWS] misinterpreted [the ESA] and further, that removal would be a logical consequence of the error, the court has the power, in deciding whether to impose an equitable remedy, to decline to impose a solution that is far worse than the problem — and simply leave the wolves in place as an experimental population." NPCA alleged that other courts have conducted similar actions "when retroactive application of a remedy would be worse than the triggering violation of law."[13]

"There is no equitable justification for destroying wolves in order to save them," the brief stated.[14]

James Hill, a private citizen living in Washington, DC, filed a friend of the court brief in support of upholding Downes's decision. Hill argued that the private environmental organizations involved in the wolf reintroduction project "have been bootstrapped into an advantageous position" by the government's proceeding with the reintroduction program while the litigation was pending.[15]

Hill argued that the intervenors in the original litigation (DW, NWF, and others) "have no justifiable interest in this matter because the administrative rule which has been appealed from involved a future rather than a present environmental condition."[16]

In essence, Hill claimed that once the wolves were released, the environmental groups "acquired claims to standing which they otherwise would not have had."[17] Had the litigation been decided before the reintroduction took place, a decision to not reintroduce the animals would not have injured the environmental groups, giving the groups no basis on which to sue.

Hill also argued that "the intimate involvement of a lobbying campaign in the promotion and implementation of the wolf project coupled with a private financial investment in the project in the form of an indemnity fund created a conflict of interest and a compromise of the public trust."[18]

Hill's perspective on the wolf case was unique in that his concerns arose from dealings with FWS with another species entirely — mute swans in the Chesapeake Bay area. The local population of mute swans, determined to be a non-native species, was eradicated so that trumpeter swans, a native species, could be reintroduced.

In September, 1998, the wolf case took an interesting turn. National Audubon switched sides in the case and this thereby put Audubon in support of a program it originally claimed was illegal.

In a motion before the appeals court, NAS asked that it be allowed to drop its partnership with other conservation groups seeking protection for naturally occurring wolves in Idaho and instead realign itself with the federal government in support of the wolf reintroduction program.

Audubon had joined with Predator Project, Sinapu, and the Gray Wolf Committee in appealing the FWS program for the reintroduction of an experimental population of wolves in central Idaho. Audubon successfully argued that FWS was illegally lessening protection for naturally occurring wolves.

Although Audubon actually won the lawsuit, the group was not happy with Judge Downes's remedy — removal of all the reintroduced wolves. So, after three years of one argument and eight months after filing the appeal, Audubon joined the organization against which it had originally filed the lawsuit.

The Audubon motion stated, "After reappraising the law and the facts in this case, National Audubon has concluded that the Secretary of the Interior's implementation of the wolf reintroduction program in Central Idaho fully complies with (the ESA)."[19]

Audubon also wrote that the "continued sound administration of the program will fulfill the goals of the statute. Interior's careful design and administration of the program holds real promise for successful recovery of the species."

NAS said it "no longer has a controversy with the Secretary with respect to the wolf reintroduction program." Instead, "we strongly disagree with the District Court's order to remove all introduced wolves and their offspring from Yellowstone and Central Idaho (a result Audubon never sought or in any way endorsed below)." Audubon called Downes's removal order "ill-conceived" and claimed it would reverse all the progress made toward wolf recovery, "lead to the death of many or all of those wolves, and deal a devastating blow to the cause of wolf conservation."

The Farm Bureaus offered harsh criticism, saying that Audubon's move was "dishonest and amounts to a fraud upon the judicial system."[20]

Audubon countered:

"As this extended litigation stretched out further and further, it became clear that the Secretary's administration of the wolf program was truly well-balanced and increasingly successful. In this context, Audubon's original complaint that Interior did not go far enough to maintain full protections for naturally occurring animals or their off-spring seemed injudicious in retrospect.[21]

"Having carefully reweighed the implications of a stance which now appears mistaken, Audubon's only honest and good-faith course was to file the instant motion."

The court granted Audubon's motion, allowing it to join the alliance supporting the wolf reintroduction program along with the federal government, DW, NWF, EDF, NPCA, and the Nez Perce Tribe.

Audubon's history in the wolf reintroduction issue had its twists and turns, extending as far back as the 1980s. For example, NAS's Wilderness Research Team provided a report to natural resource agencies about its wolf encounter near Dubois, Wyoming, on June 28, 1988.

The report noted that as the team ascended Three Waters Mountain they startled a cow elk that then became separated from the herd of forty elk. "A large wolf was then spotted approximately 400–500 yards southwest of the team. This animal had no apparent red coloration and loped with its tail held straight out behind it. Its muzzle appeared to be short and stalky and the ears short and round." The wolf was positioned between the cow and the rest of the herd. The cow retreated farther, stopped and bugled — a piercing one-syllable bark. Eventually all of the animals disappeared over the horizon, out of view. The wolf was observed for approximately five minutes, with each of the three team members having a chance to view it with binoculars.

There was no doubt that Audubon's researchers had seen a wolf in the wilderness of Wyoming. It was four years later that the Audubon

Council of Wyoming invited me to its annual meeting at Trail Lake, near the wolf encounter, to give a presentation about Jim's and my wolf research.[22] Afterward, National Audubon's wolf expert, Brian Peck, told me that while he was not convinced about the presence of a distinct wolf population, he was convinced enough to pressure FWS to conduct research and census efforts. It is unknown — actually doubtful — if Peck ever followed through with this pledge.

National Audubon's Bob Turner had a more interesting response. He avoided me for a while after my presentation, then told me he felt like he was "being slapped back and forth" as he listened. He questioned how long wolf recovery should wait while we tried to determine if the wolves represented the native subspecies.

Back in the federal court, the Farm Bureaus' reply brief noted that it had "feared that environmental groups would wait until the Canadian wolves were introduced and then sue to have all the wolves (introduced and naturally occurring) declared endangered."[23]

In order to allay this fear, FWS had put in the self-executing remedy to remove the wolves if their experimental status was lost. The Farm Bureaus' fears had become a reality when various environmental groups filed suit. Their real motive was to have all the wolves — both reintroduced and naturally occurring — declared fully endangered.

With Audubon jumping ship, Predator Project and its allies argued that FWS "properly determined that the extensive travels of individual wolves that leave their natal packs and no longer take part in pack social life do not determine the 'current range' of the species for ESA purposes."[24]

The brief argued that the district court was correct in ruling that any wolves naturally occurring in Idaho and their offspring could not be treated as experimental wolves. The brief said:

"Because such wolves were neither translocated and 'authorized by the Secretary for release' nor 'offspring arising solely therefrom,' they cannot be treated as part of an experimental population under the clear, unequitable language of the statute.[25]

"Predator Project did not challenge in the court below, and does not challenge here, FWS's ability to translocate Canadian wolves and designate those wolves as members of an experimental population. The Predator Project claims speak only to the legal status of naturally occurring gray wolves in the Idaho reintroduction area. Predator Project did not seek the removal of any wolves or any alteration in the legal status of the translocated Canadian wolves."

Instead, the groups argued, naturally occurring wolves must be able to retain their fully endangered status. The Predator Project brief stated: "Casting its net far and wide, FWS declared that all wolves in the Idaho reintroduction area — regardless whether they were transported to the region by FWS or whether they migrated to the area naturally — would be treated as members of the nonessential, experimental population. This approach deprived Idaho's naturally occurring wolves of their status as an endangered species and instead treated them as a species that merely had been proposed for listing under the ESA."

The groups continued to oppose any wolf removal and sought to have the case remanded back to FWS to "modify its Idaho gray wolf reintroduction program so as to afford Idaho's naturally occurring wolves their proper legal status as endangered."

The groups maintained that when naturally occurring wolves intermingle with reintroduced wolves, the reintroduced wolves should lose their experimental status and be treated as fully endangered animals.

Predator Project sought to have naturally occurring wolves given endangered status. This group argued that the remedy for any legal improprieties in the experimental population program for wolves would be to remand it to FWS for correction.

"FWS may respond by amending the wolf reintroduction plan to conform with the law or it may decide to remove the wolves altogether," Predator Project noted. "That decision, however, is within FWS's discretion and it would be an improper trespass on the separation of powers for this court to take that decision out of FWS's hands by failing to remand."[26]

The outcome sought by Predator Project would be for all the wolves to be declared endangered, whether naturally occurring or reintroduced. The group concluded, "This court should uphold the gray wolf experimental population rule except for its inclusion of Idaho's naturally occurring wolves and their offspring within its ambit and remand the matter to FWS so that it may conform its conduct to the dictates of ESA."[27]

More briefs were filed, including one written by lawyers for two of the nation's largest environmental groups. The brief, filed on behalf of DW and NWF, as well as the Wyoming and Idaho wildlife federations and the Wolf Education and Research Center, put forth arguments in support of the wolf reintroduction program.[28]

Ironically, the Wyoming Wildlife Federation had joined its national counterparts in supporting the wolf reintroduction lawsuit. In 1986, the Wyoming Wildlife Federation was extremely concerned with conservation of Wyoming's existing wolves. The organization had been so concerned, in fact, that it fought the Bridger-Teton National Forest's efforts to conduct a timber sale in western Wyoming that year because of the presence of the wolves.[29]

In the forty-nine-page brief, the environmental groups first provided a history of the extirpation of wolves from the northern Rockies. Both this brief and the reply brief by the same organizations contained numerous exaggerations and inaccuracies, while also straying far outside the administrative record being reviewed.

According to the brief, western hunters and settlers decimated native ungulate herds, the wolves' natural prey, and replaced them with livestock. "Predictably, some wolves turned to livestock as an alternative food source, and thereby fed general fear and hatred of all wolves," the brief stated.[30] "Today, however, the factual and legal bases supporting gray wolf extirpation from western ecosystems are no longer present."

The brief said the legal environment now mandated wolf recovery, and native ungulate populations had rebounded. "There is once again room — and indeed an ecological need — for wolves in the American west."[31]

The environmental groups' brief claimed that the US Congress supported the wolf reintroduction program, despite the fact that a vote on the program never took place. In support of this claim, the groups noted that since 1988, Congress requested and received several reports discussing the impacts of a proposal to conduct the reintroductions. Thus, the brief concluded, "Congress has actively monitored and encouraged the development of a wolf reintroduction program. Wolf reintroduction has occurred with legislative support."[32]

After conducting exhaustive research, the brief claimed, FWS chose to conduct the reintroductions using the more flexible management provision of the "non-essential experimental population" designation of the ESA.

But this designation could only be used for reintroduction programs "outside the current range of the species" and only when the reintroduced populations can be kept "wholly separate geographically" from non-experimental populations of the same species.

The brief claimed that one issue FWS confronted was how to ascertain the presence of naturally occurring wolves in the reintroduction areas. "Faced with numerous unconfirmed and unreliable reports, and the presence of an unknown number of wolf-dog hybrids,"[33] FWS then, the groups claimed, rightfully defined a minimal wolf "population" to be used to determine whether either reintroduction area supported natural wolf populations that would preclude the "experimental" reintroduction program.

"Yet despite a conservative definition and years of extensive searching, FWS found no evidence that either experimental population area was even close to supporting a minimum population of wolves,"[34] the brief stated.

And FWS provided far greater management flexibility by drawing the experimental areas to include all of the state of Wyoming, the groups claimed. Because experimental wolves are not treated as a threatened species, "the broadly drawn boundaries of [the reintroduction areas] provided a benefit to stockgrowers who were nowhere near Yellowstone and Central Idaho. As instituted, the program grants livestock owners far more flexibility than FWS is obligated to provide."[35]

The brief claimed "the wolf reintroductions were successful beyond all expectations,"[36] citing a November, 1995, FWS memo stating that all the wolves reintroduced into Yellowstone had remained in packs, and that there were no conflicts with livestock. The brief did not mention or tally the number of livestock lost to wolves in

Wyoming after the date of the memo. The brief then stated, "The gray wolf is well on its way to recovery."[37]

The groups noted that the federal government had a wolf control program in place for depredation wolves "despite strong evidence that wolves account for an insignificant portion of livestock losses."[38]

The brief also argued that, because DW had established a wolf compensation fund to pay for livestock losses, "livestock producers need not bear even the minimal costs imposed by wolf reintroduction."[39]

The brief stated flatly that Downes erred when he decided that FWS unlawfully introduced the wolves. "Even if this court finds that [FWS] have not fully complied with [the ESA], the proper remedy is not to compel FWS to remove, and most likely kill, experimental gray wolves that are currently aiding the recovery of the species. This court should instead remand the matter back to FWS so that it may address any regulatory shortcomings in an otherwise lawful program."[40]

The groups argued that FWS, using the best scientific evidence, determined that no wolf population existed in either reintroduction area, so the reintroduction as conducted was legal. "Further, FWS's methodology provided a predictable, verifiable boundary that did not subject gray wolf recovery to the vagaries of unconfirmed sightings and isolated dispersers scattered throughout the immense experimental areas . . .[41]

"[Downes's decision] also subjects reintroduction programs to the bad-faith acts of those who oppose recovery. A maliciously released captive wolf, or maliciously reported sightings could be used willy-nilly to disrupt the statutorily encouraged, and scientifically supported, recovery program."[42]

The groups then argued against Downes's conclusion that an erroneous designation of a reintroduced population as experimental calls for the removal of the reintroduced animals. Their brief stated: "If and when facts on the ground change, FWS may determine to modify the experimental designation or the experimental area. But neither the ESA nor its legislative history supports the removal of the reintroduced wolves."

The groups stated that because the FWS reintroduction program was deemed illegal, Downes concluded that the wolf reintroduction program must be terminated and the wolves removed, but the groups argued that if FWS did err, "This error cannot invalidate the entire reintroduction program."[43]

The order requiring removal of the wolves "was legally errone-ous . . . and an abuse of discretion," the environmental groups asserted, as well as being "unsupported" and "unreasoned."[44] The brief argued:

"To the extent that this court finds any defects in the wolf rein-troduction program, the proper administrative law remedy is to re-mand those defects to FWS so that the agency may conform the pro-gram to federal law. The court should provide to the agency . . . the opportunity to correct any errors of law in its program, and thereafter proceed as corrected.

"An unreasoned or unlawful treatment of naturally occurring wolves in the experimental population areas does not warrant an or-der to remove wolves that Congress otherwise authorized and encour-aged FWS to release. Such a remedy is contrary to the congression-ally imposed obligation to recover the gray wolf."[45]

The groups requested that the appeals court overturn Downes's decision. "Removing these wolves will destroy a program that public policy and public opinion has sanctioned. Finally, the balance of the equities tips in favor if the wolves . . . The Endangered Species Act cannot be used to extirpate members of a species that are entitled to the Act's protection."[46]

On the same day the environmental groups filed their brief, rep-resentatives of Idaho's Nez Perce Tribe also filed a short brief in sup-port of the reintroduction program.[47]

Although the tribe had not been involved in any of the litigation over the wolf reintroduction program, it requested permission to file a "friend of the court" brief in the pending litigation.

In 1995, the tribe signed an agreement with FWS to conduct the monitoring and management of the wolves reintroduced into central Idaho — the first time that an Indian tribe had been responsible for managing a species under the ESA.

The Nez Perce brief stated that wolves are central to the tribe's culture and beliefs. Nez Perce Elder Horace Axtell was quoted as saying:

"For a long while, wolves have been missing. Now they're back. The circle of life is stronger."[48] Jaime Pinkham, a member of the tribe, stated that: "The return of the gray wolf to Nez Perce country is a kind of mirror for Indian people. When the non-Indian settled the West, there were obstacles. The Nez Perce people were one of them: They got in the way — and they were removed. The gray wolf suffered a similar fate. Now, man and animal are each struggling to regain their rightful place."[49]

The Nez Perce Tribe supported continuing the federal reintroduction program and claimed that Downes erred when he issued a remedy that would remove all reintroduced wolves from the recovery area. "Such relief is inconsistent with fundamental principles of administrative law and is certainly unfair to the wolves. If a reviewing court determines that an agency has committed an error of law, the appropriate remedy is to remand the issue to the agency for it to correct,"[50] the brief stated. It also requested that the court reverse Downes's ruling and uphold the gray wolf recovery program.

Three conservation groups joined together in filing a brief against the removal of the reintroduced wolves. Predator Project, Sinapu, and the Gray Wolf Committee joined together in the brief.[51]

The animal rights group Friends of Animals filed a friend of the court brief as well, with its main claim being that no legal authority existed for the killing of an endangered species such as the wolf, even if the animal had been determined to have been involved in livestock depredations.[52]

Chapter 18

Legal Maneuvers

In October, 1998, Jim and I filed a motion for an emergency injunction with the appeals court "to prevent further killing of naturally occurring wolves of unknown origin."[1] We noted that while the legal arguments continued, the very subject of our concern was being exterminated by the federal agency in charge of wolf recovery.

We requested that FWS be prohibited from killing any wolf discovered in the wild in the recovery areas whose presence was not the result of the reintroduction program until the final disposition of the litigation. "Rather than killing any wild wolf whose origin cannot be attributed to the reintroduction program that has been determined to be a problem wolf, FWS should be ordered to capture these animals and hold them in the safety of the wolf pens in Yellowstone National Park until the appeals are decided," we argued.

Our motion detailed the circumstances involving the Cody wolf, which had been discovered in November, 1996, and killed March 4, 1997; the Boulder wolf, which had been discovered in February, 1997, and placed in a captive facility in October, 1997; and the Kemmerer wolf, which had been discovered in August, 1998, and killed October 5, 1998 (Table 9).

WGF officials had been notified by a local rancher on August 20, 1998, that there was a black wolf in the Pomeroy Basin area north of Kemmerer. A WGF biologist watched the animal for nearly half an hour, determining the animal was most likely a wolf, even though it was not wearing a radio collar.[2] The animal was seen infrequently during the next days and weeks until the night of September 24, when it killed a donkey. The male wolf began preying on sheep in the area on October 5. USDA Wildlife Services, the agency handling depredation problems for FWS, had been called in to verify the kills and consult

Table 9. Significant Wolf Mortalities (1943-1998)

1943	Sheepherder kills wolf on Wind River Indian Reservation
1949	Federal control agent kills white wolf with poison set near Lander
1950	Cora, Wyoming, man traps wolf in Gros Ventre
1969	Wolf shot in Snake River Canyon
1988	Chico wolf ran over and killed 30 miles north of Yellowstone park
1992	Teton wolf was shot in the Teton Wilderness by an elk hunter
1996	Cody wolf ordered killed by federal officials
1997	Boulder wolf roped by rancher dies in captivity
1998	Kemmerer wolf killed after preying on livestock

with FWS. Flying over the area the morning of October 7, a USDA Wildlife Services employee shot and killed the male wolf of unknown origin.[3] Similar to the description of the wolf killed near Cody, officials said the Kemmerer wolf seemed to have shorter legs and smaller feet than those of the reintroduced Canadian wolves.

This wolf was killed less than ten miles south of Commissary Ridge, which has a long history of wolf sightings.[4] Agency professionals had attested to wolf presence in the area in the past.[5]

Interviews with wildlife officials about the killing of the Kemmerer wolf brought to light the presence of yet another wolf of unknown origin in Wyoming. Wildlife Services confirmed that a wolf had killed sheep near the North Fork of Horse Creek, west of Daniel, Wyoming, in mid-September of that year. Sheepherders in the area observed the black wolf several times and wildlife officials found canid hair and tracks. Because the sheep were removed from the area the day after the kills were verified, no control action — no attempt to kill the animal — was initiated.[6] But the wolf was confirmed to be in the area, with one strike against it for killing livestock. This wolf was now in jeopardy, we told the appeals court.

During the past year, FWS had "removed" — killed or placed into captivity — three wolves of unknown origin that were surviving

227

in the wild of northwestern Wyoming. The last such event occurred with the killing of the Kemmerer wolf.

On October 16, 1998, after Jim and I learned the details of the Kemmerer wolf and that another wolf of unknown origin and known to kill livestock was confirmed within the Wyoming experimental area, Jim contacted Alice Thurston, counsel for the government in the appeals. He requested that she consider entering into a stipulation declaring that there would be no further killing of wolves of unknown origin discovered in the wild until the appeals had been decided. Thurston told Jim she would consider the request, but doubted such an agreement would occur.

Later that day, I contacted Ellen Rich Reiter of the Tenth Circuit Clerk's office and inquired about filing a motion for an emergency injunction, in the event the government refused to enter into the stipulation.

At approximately 1 P.M., Jim telephoned Thurston and left a message explaining that since we had not heard back from her, we would probably be filing an emergency motion for an injunction dealing with this issue.

I then contacted Rick Krause, counsel for the American Farm Bureau Federation, notifying him that such a motion would be forthcoming.

On the morning of October 19, 1998, Jim left another message for Thurston, letting her know the motion would be forthcoming.

We filed the motion for an emergency injunction, arguing that FWS was killing the very animals we had sued to protect. That FWS would continue the killing was a given. Thurston declined to enter into an agreement, stating that such killing would not happen in the future and thereby demonstrating that FWS had no intention of straying from current policy.

We requested, "Rather than killing any wild wolf whose origin cannot be attributed to the reintroduction program that has been determined to be a problem wolf, FWS should be ordered to capture these animals and hold them in the safety of the wolf pens in Yellowstone National Park until the appeals are decided."

Stunningly, the coalition of national environmental groups filed a statement of opposition to our motion. The statement filed with the court read, in its entirety, "National Wildlife Federation, Defenders of Wildlife, Wyoming Wildlife Federation, Idaho Wildlife Federation, Wolf Education and Research Center and the National Audubon Society support the Federal Appellants'/Cross-Appellees' opposition to the Urbigkits' emergency motion for an injunction pending appeal. The Urbigkits' emergency motion should be denied."[7]

The court declined to grant our motion.

~

By November, 1998, FWS reported that the wolf population in northwestern Montana had declined from eighty-eight wolves in seven packs in 1993 to sixty-five wolves in six packs.[8]

A total of thirty-five wolves had been reintroduced into central Idaho in 1995 and 1996, and by the fall of 1998, that population was estimated to contain 120 wolves, including ten packs that had produced pups.

As a result of a control action in Montana in 1997, FWS placed four four-month-old pups in a pen in central Idaho to prepare them for release, only to have two of the pups be killed by adult wolves in the same pen. Another pup died from handling. The remaining survivor was released into the wild that spring.

Forty-nine of the wolves in central Idaho were wearing radio collars. Although researchers stated that no wolf packs or lone wolves existed in central Idaho at the time of the first reintroduction in 1995, some wolves of unknown origin were discovered.

While one female wolf released into Idaho in 1995 was found with two different mates from the Montana wolf population, another released female found a mate of unknown origin in the Frank Church Wilderness in 1997, and produced pups in 1998. At the same time, another male of unknown origin mated with another released female south of Stanley, Idaho, and produced a litter of pups in that area.

Thirty-one wolves were reintroduced into YNP in 1995 and 1996, and in 1996, ten five-month-old pups from Montana were placed in pens in the park for later release. In the spring of 1998, researchers estimated the Yellowstone population to be at 116 wolves in seven packs which produced ten litters of pups.

Wildlife officials noted that by winter, some of the pups born to the reintroduced wolves in Yellowstone — nine in 1995, twenty-five in 1996, and ninety-nine in 1997 — would be sexually mature and would begin to disperse from their natal packs. The researchers wrote:

"Because dispersing wolves typically travel extensively and settle in areas without resident packs, we anticipate that these wolves will initiate significant expansion in the number and distribution of wolf packs in the northern Rocky Mountains. Dispersal was expected to increase management costs and controversy, because many of these wolves will not be radio-collared and will attempt to colonize areas of private land used for livestock production. Wolves that disperse southward in central Idaho and (the Yellowstone area) will increasingly encounter sheep, which are more susceptible to predation than cattle.

"We believe because of high elevation and rugged terrain, (Central Idaho and Yellowstone National Park) have sufficient space for only a few more packs and that extensive colonization outside (those areas) is imminent."

A wolf was killed by an M-44 coyote-getter fifteen miles west of Powell, Wyoming, in December, 1998.[9] Since the set, aimed at killing coyotes, not wolves, had been put in place by an animal control agent working for USDA Wildlife Services, DW sent a letter to US Attorney Dave Freudenthal asking for prosecution. Freudenthal declined.[10]

As we all awaited the outcome of our lawsuit, the political situation became volatile, as detailed in an editorial written by American Farm Bureau Federation President Dean Kleckner in January, 1999. That editorial, published in the organization's national newsletter and in numerous newspapers around the country, is reprinted here in its entirety.

"As early as 1991, legal advisors told the Interior Department that their plan to stock portions of Idaho, Montana and Wyoming with Canadian wolves could be illegal. Their words supported Farm Bureaus' contentions. Interior Secretary Bruce Babbitt pursued his plan, despite two pending lawsuits and with the knowledge of the probable illegality of his actions.

"In December 1997, a federal judge agreed with the Farm Bureaus, ruling the Canadian wolves imported under the federal program would have to be removed. And that's when some supporters of the wolf program decided the rule of law did not apply to them.

"Defenders of Wildlife launched a nationwide campaign against Farm Bureau in the press, television, radio, and Internet, falsely describing our organization and our lawsuit.

"Wolf stocking program advocates, incited by Defenders of Wildlife, organized a campaign of harassment and intimidation against Farm Bureau with the aim of forcing us to ignore our farmer-written policies and to drop our lawsuit.

"We have since received several bomb threats and threats against the lives of Farm Bureau officers and their families. Even a federal judge's life was threatened. Hostile callers appear to be motivated by lies spread by Defenders of Wildlife. Working Assets Long Distance, a self-proclaimed 'activist' telephone company, created a toll-free complaint line to our headquarters. The hot line barrage was designed to interrupt our daily work and prevent us from pursuing continued legal actions against the wolf-stocking program.

"The big lie is that Farm Bureau seeks to have imported Canadian wolves killed. That is not true, never was true, and never will be true. Remember, we notified the government of the illegality of their program before a single wolf had been trapped in Canada. Yet Defenders of Wildlife continues to make their claim that Farm Bureau seeks to destroy wolves. They know full well that the federal judge ruled that 'removing' the wolves need not and should not result in killing them, but should rely on their humane relocation. They also know that he specifically ordered that the wolves could remain where they were while his ruling was appealed. Finally, federal agents assured the judge that the wolves could be captured humanely and removed to Canada without loss of life.

"Still the lies continue about killing wolves. Working Assets brags of sending us 34,000 letters and calls. Defenders of Wildlife had to have spent tens of thousands of dollars on advertising in big city media to achieve this result.

"We think their campaign is more about fund raising than wolf saving. Farm Bureau and the federal judge are eager to avoid harming wolves. Yet Defenders of Wildlife talks incessantly about killing wolves.

"We respect and support our opponents' right to have and promote a different view on wolf relocation. While those viewpoints diverged widely, they were resolved in a court of law. Defenders of Wildlife and Working Assets crossed a line when they intended to shut down our phone system and encouraged callers to harass us into dropping our case against the Interior Department's illegal program. Because of their campaign's announced purpose, Farm Bureau filed a complaint with the Federal Communications Commission to hold them accountable for their actions. And we are cooperating with the Federal Bureau of Investigation in their efforts to track down those who have threatened us.

"Concern for wildlife should not overshadow concern for people. So to the Defenders of Wildlife, we admit that your distorted ads, messages and threats are disconcerting. But we are not intimidated. We'll see you in court."

In February, 1999, a federal judge in Idaho ordered a man convicted of killing a reintroduced gray wolf to pay nearly $16,000 for the offense. Daniel Thomas Kloskowski of Eden Prairie, Minnesota, was ordered by Idaho federal judge Edward Lodge to pay a $25 court assessment, as well as $10,000 fine and $5,477 in restitution.[11] The $10,000 fine is the maximum fine that could be imposed for Kloskowski's one count of taking a federally protected species the previous September in central Idaho. Kloskowski was also ordered into an intensive supervised release program in lieu of federal prison time, was subject to home detention with electronic monitoring for one month of his one-year supervised release, was denied all hunting privileges for one year, was not allowed to possess a firearm during that one-year period, and was required to submit to the search of his home, vehicle, and/or person upon demand of his probation officer, without need for a warrant. In addition, according to his sentencing report, Kloskowski was required to "request information from the

Department of Fish and Game or the Nez Perce Tribe regarding endangered species, in particular the gray wolf. The defendant shall write a report to the court within 60 days stating his findings and feelings regarding the Endangered Species Act and the gray wolf." Kloskowski was ordered to pay his restitution of $5,477 to the Nez Perce Tribe, which had a contract with FWS to monitor the wolves reintroduced into Idaho.

By the spring of 1999, several federal lawsuits had been heard for the illegal taking of reintroduced gray wolves while the legality of the reintroduction itself was pending before the higher court. In April, 1999, YNP officials estimated that the wolf reintroduction program in the park had resulted in a population of 110 wolves in eleven packs in and around the park.[12] Nine of the packs inhabited the park itself or areas adjacent to the park, while others established their ranges in areas more distant from the park.

Chapter 19

The Canadians Can Stay

When all the briefs and motions had been filed, it was time to appear before the appeals court panel for oral arguments. Our July, 1999, trip to the appeals court in Denver was uneventful. It quickly became apparent that the appeals court justices had not even bothered to read our briefs. We were given a full five minutes to make our oral arguments and we left the courtroom knowing the case for Wyoming's native wolves had been lost. At least we had been given ninety minutes to make our case before Downes.

Judge Wade Brorby opened the questioning by asking federal government attorney Alice Thurston what the record before the court showed for the existence of wolves, to which she replied "there were no wolves extant in the area," and any wolves found there were lone dispersers from Montana.

Judge Robert Henry latched onto that, in all his comments referring to "lone wolves" and "single wolves." Although the Farm Bureaus' attorney Timothy Bishop talked about Idaho's Kelly Creek wolf, a naturally occurring wolf in Idaho that bred with a released Canadian wolf, later in the discussion Henry referred to this as a "hypothetical wolf." That was appalling because this was a well-documented animal that FWS had named "the Kelly Creek wolf." That comment, and Brorby's asking about the presence of wolves, demonstrated to us that the judges were unfamiliar with the briefs filed in the case. Judge William Holloway questioned whether the court could even focus at all on NEPA, indicating the court had no interest in procedural issues raised under the law.

I did enjoy watching the Farm Bureaus' attorney argue that the offspring of the Kelly Creek wolf and the Canadian wolf are endangered, and his arguing that naturally occurring wolves must be treated as endangered. It was ironic to hear the Farm Bureaus and a group like the Predator Project agree that these animals should have full protections under the ESA.

Brian O'Neill, attorney for the environmental groups siding with the government, told the court that the statute "is for wolves" and not against them. DW brought a wolf to Denver and paraded the animal for the media on the courthouse steps.[1]

Once the courtroom part of the appeals process was over, we loaded up our files and headed back to Wyoming.

On January 13, 2000, the Tenth Circuit Court of Appeals issued its decision, which stated: "The district court ordered the reintroduced non-native wolves and their offspring removed from the identified experimental population areas, but stayed its own judgment pending this appeal. Discerning no conflict between the challenged experimental population rules and the Endangered Species Act, we reverse."

The decision addressed the geographic separation issue:

"The agencies do not dispute individual wolves may leave (and, from time to time, have left) Canada and Montana and enter the experimental population areas in central Idaho and Yellowstone. The Farm Bureaus and the Urbigkits argue, and the district court agreed, that this possibility establishes an overlap of wolf populations, or the overlap of the experimental areas and the current range of naturally occurring wolf populations in contravention of the requirement in section 10(j)(1) that experimental populations of an endangered species must be wholly separate geographically from nonexperimental populations of the same species. We do not accept that contention.

"As the district court recognized, the Endangered Species Act does not define the relevant terms or otherwise address the precise question at issue — whether the phrase wholly separate geographically from nonexperimental populations means that a reintroduced population of animals must be separate from every naturally occurring individual animal. Instead, as the statutory language and legislative history make clear, Congress deliberately left the resolution of this type management/conservation issue to the Department. Thus, each experimental population has its own set of special rules so that the Secretary has more managerial discretion. This flexibility allows the Secretary to better conserve and recover endangered species.

"We therefore defer to the Department's interpretation of the phrase wholly separate geographically from nonexperimental populations, so long as its interpretation does not conflict with the plain language of the Endangered Species Act. We perceive no conflict.

"[With respect to the population issue and FWS's definitions] . . . These definitions preclude the possibility of population overlap as a result of the presence of individual dispersing wolves — by definition lone dispersers do not constitute a population or even part of a population, since they are not in common spatial arrangement sufficient to interbreed with other members of a population. Moreover, since it is highly unlikely a lone wolf will encounter another solitary wolf of the opposite sex and reproduce for two years running, the populations left behind by the lone wolves do not expand simply because they travel away.

"[Congress used various terms in the ESA, and] . . . This reference to species vis à vis populations or population segments, as opposed to individual specimens, is repeated throughout the text of section 10(j), thus reflecting the paramount objective of the Endangered Species Act to conserve and recover species, not just individual animals. This broader objective is further evidenced by the well-established fact individual animals can and do lose Endangered Species Act protection simply by moving about the landscape.

"Moreover, we find nothing in the Endangered Species Act that precludes steps to conserve a species in order to protect isolated individuals. Nor are we convinced the challenged rules present complicated law enforcement obstacles. The Department specifically determined the experimental population area does not currently support any reproducing pairs of wolves; thus, the legal protection afforded any particular wolf is clearly known, depending entirely on where the wolf is, not where it might once have been. For these reasons, we hold the Department's interpretation of the geographic separation provision reflects the goals of the Endangered Species Act to protect natural populations and to avoid potentially complicated problems of law enforcement, and is well within the scope of agency discretion granted by Congress and licensed by the Supreme Court.

"Plaintiffs' argument the agencies failed to release the Canadian wolves outside the current range of naturally occurring wolves is similarly flawed since Plaintiffs rigidly define current range as it is used in section 10(j) to be that territory occupied by an individual wolf. The plain language of the statute does not support their interpretation . . . By definition, then, an individual animal does not a species, population or population segment make. Therefore, the Department, exercising its discretion under section 10(j), reasonably interpreted the phrase current range to be the combined scope of territories defended by the breeding pairs of an identifiable wolf pack or population."

The court did not see the need to protect naturally occurring wolves either. Although the district court held the final reintroduction rules constituted a "de facto delisting" of naturally occurring wolves and illegally denied full ESA protections to offspring of naturally dispersing wolves, the appeals court did not agree. The court decision stated:

"We believe this holding unnecessarily limits the administrative discretion and flexibility Congress intentionally incorporated into section 10(j), ignores biological reality, and misconstrues the larger purpose of the Endangered Species Act.

"The Secretary intentionally identified the experimental population as all wolves found within the experimental areas, including imported wolves and any lone dispersers and their offspring. The Department determined it could best manage the wolf reintroduction program to achieve species recovery in this manner. We find nothing in the Act that invalidates this approach by requiring the protection of individuals to the exclusion or detriment of overall species recovery, or otherwise limiting the Department's flexibility and discretion to define and manage an experimental population pursuant to section 10(j).

"[W]e interpret the plain language of section 10(j)(1) as an expression of Congress' intent to protect the Secretary's authority to designate when and where an experimental population may be established, not as a limitation on the Secretary's flexibility.

"[A more restrictive interpretation] . . . could actually undermine the Department's ability to address biological reality (i.e., wolves can and do roam for hundreds of miles and cannot be precluded from intermingling with the released experimental population), and thus handicap its ability to effectuate species recovery. The Endangered Species Act simply does not countenance that result. To the contrary, Congress' overriding goal in enacting the Endangered Species Act is to promote the protection and, ultimately, the recovery of endangered and threatened species. While the protection of individual animals is one obvious means of achieving that goal, it is not the only means."

The appeals court dismissed outright our concern for a unique subspecies. The relevant part of the decision read:

"After careful analysis, we conclude these claims lack both factual and legal support.

"The agencies decided to reintroduce gray wolves from Canada without reference to subspecific differences. They based this decision on (1) the lack of evidence any wolf population existed in the reintroduction areas at the time of reintroduction; (2) scientific evidence that most of the historically recognized subspecies of Canis lupus (including irremotus) do not warrant recognition under modern taxonomic classification methods; and (3) the likelihood that even if there had been a distinct subspecies found in the middle to northern United States, as wolves are known to disperse and interbreed over hundreds of miles, its range would have overlapped with a more northern subspecies in southwestern Canada and the border states.

"Because this is a scientific matter within the agencies' expertise, and because there is ample evidence in the administrative record to support the Defendants' position, we uphold their subspecies conclusions.

"The Urbigkits further argue on cross-appeal the district court erred in rejecting their claim the Defendants violated the National Environmental Policy Act by failing to adequately analyze the impacts of wolf reintroduction on naturally occurring wolf populations, including distinct subspecies, or to investigate the need for additional research. Having studied the arguments and administrative record, we agree with the district court the Urbigkits' National Environmental Policy Act claims boil down to a disagreement over scientific opinions and conclusions. The fact the Urbigkits disagree with the Defendants concerning the existence of a distinct subspecies of wolf in Yellowstone National Park and the impacts of the reintroduction program on that subspecies and other naturally occurring wolves, and cite evidence in the record they believe supports their position, simply does not constitute a National Environmental Policy Act violation.

"The administrative record establishes that the agencies analyzed the alleged existence of naturally occurring wolves in the experimental population areas, studied the arguments pertaining to subspecies identification and recognition, and catalogued the research studies and scientific sources on which they relied. Because of the lack of evidence of wolf populations (pack activity) in Yellowstone or central Idaho, and the scientific evidence supporting a reduction in the number of recognized subspecies, the agencies determined to forego additional analysis of these specific issues in the Draft Environmental Impact Statement or Final Environmental Impact Statement.

"We appreciate that the Urbigkits patently disagree with the agencies' conclusions concerning the existence of naturally occurring wolf populations, the existence of an alleged subspecies of wolf unique to Yellowstone National Park, and the significance of any impact the wolf reintroduction program would have on naturally occurring wolves. We also recognize the Urbigkits cite evidence in the administrative record they believe supports their position. However, the mere presence of contradictory evidence does not invalidate the agencies' actions or decisions. The Urbigkits fail to show a lack of substantial evidence in the administrative record to support the agencies' conclusions, or that the Final Environmental Impact Statement was otherwise inadequate to foster informed public participation or informed decision-making. Consequently, we hold the agencies did not violate the National Environmental Policy Act.

"[In conclusion,] . . . Because we uphold the challenged wolf reintroduction rules as lawful under the Endangered Species Act and the National Environmental Policy Act, we need not address the propriety of the district court's remedy. We reverse the order and judgment of the district court, vacate the district court's stay order, and remand with instructions to the district court to enter an order upholding the challenged wolf reintroduction rules."

The federal government won it all. The Canadian wolves could stay.

Chapter 20

Indian Dogs

Starting in 1997, the Diamond G Ranch near Dubois was subject to repeated predation by reintroduced wolves. Depredations occurred every year thereafter with prey ranging from the family's dogs to colts and cattle. After several years of problems, the owner of the ranch, Steven Gordon, filed a lawsuit calling for removal of the Yellowstone wolves from his ranch. The suit was not successful, although federal wildlife officials killed numerous stock-killing wolves on the ranch over the years both before and after the litigation.[1]

Wolves began killing sheep and cattle in the Upper Green River region of western Wyoming in the summer of 2000. That year marked the start of an educational process for livestock producers, some of whom were stunned to learn that FWS would not initiate control actions against gray wolves that preyed on domestic dogs on public lands, even if the dogs were important elements of livestock operations on federal grazing allotments.

While federal regulations called for wolves to be relocated to another area after they had preyed on dogs or other pets on two occasions on private lands, no such regulation existed for controlling wolves that killed dogs on public lands. This gap in the regulation soon became cause for heartburn to some livestock producers who used dogs for herding or guarding purposes. What these livestock producers learned is that their dogs just did not stand much of a chance when they encountered a wolf pack.

Ingalls and Sons of Riverton raised Angus cattle as well as Catahoula cow dogs as part of their agricultural operation. Catahoulas "are tough, will outwork any man or horse, are smart and friendly, and are good at staying out of trouble," Dan Ingalls said in an interview. "They're just like people."[2]

Famous for its light-blue eyes and known as "the Indian dogs the cowboys adopted," the Catahoula breed originated with Indians in Louisiana, and historically has been used for hunting, companionship, and in war. Ingalls started to use Catahoulas in his cattle operation on the Bridger-Teton National Forest in response to the increasing numbers of grizzly bears and wolves. When bears would enter camp, the Catahoulas convinced the bears to retreat. Primarily, however, Ingalls used his dogs to go into deep dark timber to help gather his cattle.

"They'll go places you can't go with a horse," Ingalls said, "and will bring the cattle back. My dogs are my livestock, besides being our friends and hard-working partners."

But three of Ingalls's dogs were killed by wolves. The Gros Ventre wolf pack had killed a heifer calf and seriously injured a bull calf by biting its tail off and ripping its side open. When the wolves later returned, Ingalls said that Callie and Tex, two of the Catahoulas, ran the wolves away, only to then be turned on once they were away from camp. The dogs did not stand a chance.

The next night, the wolves returned to kill Sally.

"Sally was our first one," Ingalls said. "That's why it was so hard to lose her." Callie was a pup, less than a year old. Tex was a stud dog purchased out of Texas, with world champions on both sides of his pedigree."

When the Gros Ventre wolf pack attacked the Ingalls dogs, the wolf pack consisted of ten animals — three adults, two yearlings, and five sixty- to seventy-pound pups. In contrast, the Ingalls dogs varied in weight from forty to nearly ninety pounds.

Since the Gros Ventre wolves had by that time been involved in multiple livestock depredations, control actions were initiated. Merrill Nelson of USDA Wildlife Services set padded-jaw traps in the area and caught three female wolves. Two of the wolves were euthanized, while the other was fitted with a radio collar and released. The released wolf was the alpha female, mother of the five pups born early that spring.

Ingalls said that even after the three wolves were trapped, the pack returned to his camp the next two nights, looking to kill more dogs.

Nelson was authorized by FWS to kill the wolves to disrupt the pack structure in hopes of stopping the livestock depredations. The dog killings were not a factor.

"That's why we have so many dogs," Ingalls said. "They're used to running bears off."

Ingalls said that, in a normal year, he may have fifteen to twenty-five dogs on the mountain. He said while that is a lot of dogs, when up to eight riders take off from camp in different directions, four dogs go with each rider to help.

"One thing I worry about with these grizzly bears," Ingalls said, "is a lot of my boys are young."

All six of Ingalls's sons had helped work the outfit, but his three youngest sons, ages eighteen, sixteen, and fourteen, rode horseback, moving and checking cattle on the mountain.

"When they go, I don't want to have to worry," Ingalls said. "The dogs will take a bear and take it away from you." Ingalls likened the dogs to a bull-fighting clown, controlling whatever it is herding from the head — face-on.

"They are not fierce, but just have this uncommon ability to handle anything," Ingalls said.

The killing of Sally, Tex, and Callie was a personal loss to Ingalls. "They were very loyal, hardworking friends and I'm not ashamed to say I bawled my head off burying them" high on the mountainside where they had served him well (Figure 24). "The rules need changed on these dogs. They need to take the wolves out on the first offense."

While Ingalls had lost three dogs to wolves, Dubois rancher Jon Robinett had seven dogs killed by wolves in three years. Other attacks and dog killings occurred in Idaho, Montana, and Wyoming following the release of the Canadian gray wolves.

But the FWS EIS for the wolf reintroduction program had little to say about wolves preying on dogs, other than: "Although a remote

Figure 24. Dan Ingalls buried his beloved cattle dogs on a mountain near Jackson Hole after they were killed by Canadian wolves. Here, Dan's horse stands at the gravesite. (Photo courtesy Dan Ingalls)

possibility, wolves that repeatedly (two times in a calendar year) attacked pets, working animals, or other types of domestic animals (fowl, hogs, goats, etc.) on private land would be moved by management agencies. Chronic problem wolves (depredating once after relocation) would be removed from the wild."

Wolves preying on dogs was said in the EIS to be "a fairly uncommon event" and occurrences were expected to be "very infrequent."

Chapter 21

Protected Predator

Joe Sampson was one of the first private landowners in Wyoming to learn what it is like to live with federally protected wolves.[1] Joe is a private but friendly man who, with wife Melanie, runs a small herd of sheep in the Upper Green River region north of Pinedale. Theirs is a small place, nestled against the Wind River Mountains. Joe serves as the president of the county wool growers association.

In the fall of 2000, a lone black wolf was seen repeatedly roaming from the Upper Green River region downriver toward the town of Pinedale.

"At first it wasn't bothering anything," Joe said, but the wolf eventually befriended Joe's guard dog, which began running with the wolf on occasion.

"Then the wolf had free liberty to come into the corrals," Joe explained, because it was accompanied by the guard dog. The wolf was a young male, and the guard dog was a young spayed female Akbash, a Turkish guardian breed. With the wolf befriending the guard dog, Joe believed his sheep did not fear the new canine.

"He'd become habituated to humans and my sheep became habituated to him," Joe said.

Joe saw the wolf up close on numerous occasions, once walking into his sheep pen to find the wolf already there. Joe also saw the wolf marking its territory in the Sampsons' yard. Joe took action on occasion to scare the wolf away, but the wolf only returned under the cover of darkness.

Joe said the wolf would come in every four or five days, sometimes staying around for a night, other times for two or three days.

"We don't know how many times he's been in our corral," he said.

One night, the wolf entered the pen and attacked a pregnant Columbia-Targhee ewe. Surviving the attack with injury to her throat, the ewe seemed to be recovering. But about six days later, the wolf returned, attacking the same ewe, in addition to attacking a pregnant Suffolk ewe, again biting the neck. Sampson said that the ewe that had been attacked twice again appeared to be recovering, but the Suffolk did not survive. It had trouble eating, and coughed while she ate, leaving Joe to believe there was a great deal of damage inflicted on her trachea.

"They were quite traumatized," he said. Using guard dogs, the Sampsons had not had any coyote attacks, or other predation, on their herd for several years. The ewes were in the corral on the nights of the wolf attacks.

"It does take a toll on the sheep, especially when they're pregnant," Joe said.

The Sampsons began locking their sheep in the barn at night, with the guard dog sleeping at its door. Maximum protection for the herd was critically important since the herd was slated to begin lambing two months later.

"And I sleep better at night," Joe added.

Joe was not surprised the wolf just attacked the sheep and did not even begin to feed on them. "I don't think he's hungry," Joe said, since the wolf had been seen feeding on road-killed deer in the area. In addition, the Green River Lakes elk feedground was nearby and provided adequate prey.

Joe said when the wolf first started visiting his place, "it was like a novelty," but quickly became somewhat nerve-wracking.

The wolf was finally trapped and euthanized by federal officials. But the wolf's impact would not be fully known until months later. The Sampsons ended up losing one-third of their lamb crop because the stressed pregnant ewes resorbed their fetuses. It is not an unheard of occurrence in animal husbandry, although it is usually associated with starvation or other severe stress. This time, it was brought on by a wolf.

Joe's frustration with the ordeal was based in part on the fact that by law, there was little he could do about the situation. Joe pointed

out that when a federally-protected wolf appears on private property, the property owner has few rights.

"The wolf comes in, he's been in my corral and wouldn't leave. He has tracked me. I've walked down the road and backtracked him and looked behind me and the wolf was walking behind me. And there is nothing you can do," Joe said. "My sheep are my property and I should be able to protect them."

Joe's options for dealing with wolves were severely restricted under federal rules. Even though this wolf had become habituated to people, and was highly visible for a period of three months, it took repeated livestock depredations for the animal to be destroyed. It would not be much longer before I would understand the Sampsons' frustrations, based on my own experiences.

Chapter 22

Night of the Wolves

In January, 2003, some eight years after we had sued to prevent the release of Canadian wolves in Yellowstone, one legacy of our failed legal effort literally came home to us. We lived near Big Piney, Wyoming, and we were raising domestic sheep. We had started with orphan lambs, which I bottle-fed, then continued to expand our herd (Figure 25). It was about 5 P.M. Monday, January 6, when I got the call from a friend, letting me know he had seen a pair of wolves basking in the sunshine on the hill across the draw from my house, just outside our fenceline. He wanted to be sure I knew so that our Anatolian guardian dog would not go out patrolling, be outnumbered, and never make it back home.

Figure 25. Cat Urbigkit kissing one of her sheep. (Photo by Jim Urbigkit)

Unfortunately, I had shipped our Anatolian guard dog earlier in the day, having traded her for a young female Great Pyrenees with ten suckling pups. My new four-legged family was tucked away in a warm home in the corner of my front yard. Just outside the yard fence in the sheep pen were our eighty head of Rambouillet ewes and their rams, ready to bed down for the night.

We live in the sagebrush rangelands of western Wyoming, a few hundred miles south of where the federally protected gray wolves had been reintroduced into YNP in 1995. Our rangeland is just that — it is the northern edge of the Little Colorado Desert, not the mountainous country most people envision when they think of Wyoming wolves.

I was glad to have been told the wolves were in the area so that we could prepare. Jim began calling neighbors up and down the river, letting them know to get their dogs in for the night because wolves are notorious for killing dogs. Around 5:30 that evening, we stepped outside into the dark to see the sheep all standing in the pen, not willing to lie down. We could hear the wolves howling from the hill behind the house. I decided to call the feds and let them know we had a problem.

No, the sound of those howls did not send chills up my neck and no, it was not eerie or cool or anything else, except maddening — it made me madder than hell because Jim and I knew the wolves had been camped out waiting for the opportunity to come in to our sheep. I caught Mike Jimenez of FWS on his cell phone in his hometown 150 miles away. Jimenez, who I called as often as once a week for information for articles I was writing for the local newspaper, was not at all surprised to hear from me, but he was surprised when I told him "I have a herd of sheep and a pair of wolves."

At this point, the wolves had not moved in on us, but were just making themselves known with the howling. Jimenez told me that I knew as much about the rules as anybody, so I was welcome to chase them off. But the wolves could not be killed unless they were documented to have attacked livestock, with freshly wounded or dead stock as the standard of proof. I reminded him that a rancher had a cow killed by wolves four days ago and twenty miles away, which is not much of a jaunt for a wolf.

Jimenez told me he would call USDA Wildlife Services and have them fly our place the next day to see if they could find any radio-collared wolves. Word had already spread in the ranching community, and I received a call about there being wolf tracks down our county road. As soon as it was said, I knew it was true, because I had seen them myself on the way home, but had already forgotten about it.

By 7:30 P.M., a black wolf approached near our back yard, flushing our two horses from in front of the old wooden boxcar near the house and chasing them around the side of the corrals into the meadow. Jim chased the wolf in the truck, using a spotlight and firing his 12-gauge shotgun into the air, around the yard, around the corrals, and away.

The sheep fled the pen — I could hear them quietly running through the snow even though I could not see them because it was too dark.

I got back on the telephone and relayed information to the Wildlife Services pilot in Rock Springs, one hundred miles away, who had called to get directions on where to fly in the morning. After hanging up the phone, I went to help Jim get the sheep back into their pen. I drove the truck, shining the spotlight for the herd to see their way, while Jim walked them back. They were scared and did not want to go, but we got them in and Jim locked the gate. They had been perfectly silent throughout the entire ordeal.

By 8:30 P.M., I was exhausted. Jim was still patrolling with the truck while I tended the telephone and tried — and failed — to convince my son Cass to go to sleep so he could get up for school the next morning.

Just before 9 P.M., Wildlife Services Wyoming Director Rod Krischke called, wanting to know if Jimenez had talked to me about a kill permit, which he had not. Rod wanted to know if we were interested, but I was unsure. While we would have liked permission to kill the wolves, we preferred that killing wolves be the agency's responsibility. I reminded Rod we were the people who had filed the lawsuit against the wolf reintroduction, so increased scrutiny of our actions in killing a wolf would be expected. Rod said he had already recalled that fact.

At 9:30 P.M., we were in the house taking a needed break. We had known that the wolves were in the area for only four hours but already it seemed like we had had such a very long night.

The night dragged on as we tried to sleep, but we heard every sound. And, we took spins in the truck with the spotlight — looking, looking, looking for the wolves. We never saw them, but the next day we learned that the wolf had indeed been at our house and in our yard several times that night between Jim's laps in the truck with the spotlight.

Early the next morning, through the fog, we heard the Wildlife Services airplane as it made a pass over our place. Jim and I both had stayed home from our jobs in town, twenty-five miles away, to keep the dogs and the sheep near the house where we could monitor events more closely. We both imagined the carnage we would have faced that morning if we had not been forewarned and stayed up, and out, most of the night.

Just over an hour after we had seen the plane, Wildlife Services shot and killed one of the two black wolves it spotted just north of our house. It was a large male. I was glad to see it, but wished it had not been alone in the back of that truck when Wildlife Services came by the house to give us an update. FWS had instructed Wildlife Services to leave the other radio-collared black wolf alone.

Later in the morning, Wildlife Services killed a second black wolf a few more miles down the river. It was a female and was accompanied by yet another wolf, this one wearing a radio collar. But they did not find the silver-colored wolf we knew was out there. When I pointed out that we had made progress since we had two dead wolves, Jim pointed out that we still had at least two live wolves, just like we had the day before.

After our sleepless night, we learned that the wolves that terrorized our place were former members of the Teton wolf pack, which had twenty-three members until nine two-year olds dispersed from the pack the week prior to our event. These wolves had scattered from their mountainous territory one hundred miles to the north, winding up throughout Sublette County.[1] Even though two wolves were killed at our place, we found out there were seven more out there. We just hoped that when our ewes began giving birth to their beautiful snow-white lambs in the meadow below the house in a few short months that the wolves would be many, many miles away.

Chapter 23

Terrorist Attack

After our night of the wolves, which was well publicized, other people began to speak out, telling of their own wolf encounters.

Big Piney's Holly Davis, one petite but tough cowgirl, and one of Wyoming's first female brand inspectors, said she was lucky to have been forewarned on December 28, 2002, that a pack of three wolves was headed her way from the Bench Corral elk feedground.[1]

"On the 30th, they came," Holly said. "At nine in the morning, they headed for the heifers, two to the front and the black to the back." The one hundred head of heifers circled up tight, Holly said. "They got in a tight circle. Horses snorting and whistling . . . dogs paranoid."

"It was a terrorist attack," she said. "When you have wolves circling your livestock, it feels like a terrorist attack. We scared them off. We shot in the air" and then they followed the wolves out with a snowmachine.

Ranchers were getting nervous about lambing and calving season, which was quickly approaching. Holly never relaxed her guard. She continued feeding the heifers close to her house as a protective measure, even knowing that when the snow melted, her ranch yard would be a muddy manure hole.

And her house stayed chilly at night, since she continued to sleep with her bedroom window open so she could hear the sounds of the night. To understand how extreme this measure is, understand that Big Piney is known as "the icebox of the nation," with winter temperatures often dropping 20–30 degrees below zero overnight. Holly was not the only one with a cold house at night. We came to learn later on that many ranchers throughout western Wyoming who had experienced wolf visits were doing the same thing.

Kelly Hake of Pinedale said she was just flat tired of the wolf in her residential neighborhood.[2] "It has hung around for a month now, right in Pinedale, right behind the clinic. It comes out at dusk and goes away at sunup."

"It's not a nice thing," Kelly said, adding that the gray wolf was seen chasing horses and playing with neighborhood dogs. "We've got kids," Kelly said, but the wolf comes "right outside the house and runs all over the place. It's about the same size as our black lab." Therein was part of Kelly's concern; the wolf was trying to breed her female lab. If pups are produced, then what? FWS's Jimenez said such instances are fairly rare, but he has learned to "never say never."[3] "It would be very unusual," he said, but wolves had been seen playing with dogs and breeding them on occasion in the past.

Sometimes the damage caused by wolves is not what you would expect, as became apparent on Jon Malinski's High Lonesome Ranch at the head of South Cottonwood Creek.

Ranch worker Lyman Clark told a story of the ranch losing four calves in two incidents. The third time the wolves returned, Lyman said he was just finishing feeding, and saw the pack.

"They had a bunch of calves in the willows," Lyman said. "They had the calves in a circle. They were working them, playing that game, getting ready to kill."

Lyman jumped on his snowmachine and raced to the scene.

"I ran them off," he said, with two gray wolves jumping the fence to escape, while he chased a third gray animal through the meadow and off the property. He chased the wolves over the next hill.

There was little left of the calves, with the exception of one carcass. In that case, the mother cow had apparently circled over the top of the calf as the wolves attacked, stomping the calf to death in the process. Lyman said while the wolves had not actually left a tooth mark in that calf, they were certainly responsible for its death. "You could see the whole story in the snow," he said. After that, Lyman moved the cow herd closer to the house, fully expecting the wolves to return. "I'm sure they will," he said.

It was just a few months later when federal wildlife officials confirmed that a pack of sixteen wolves had been "discovered" in the area. This super pack included ten grays and six black-colored wolves.

The Wyoming Range went from officially not having a pack of wolves to having at least sixteen wolves running in one pack.[4]

Jimenez explained that when federal officials responded to a report of a dead yearling heifer, trapping efforts were initiated and four wolf pups had been caught in two days. The pups were all fitted with radio collars and released unharmed. The five-month-old pups each weighed about sixty pounds, and their adult teeth were just coming in. But in the process of capturing the pups, a total of sixteen wolves were seen by the federal trappers.

"It's probably two litters," Jimenez said, because there appeared to be a lot of pups in the pack.

While some locals suspected that at least two separate groups of wolves may have joined together to create this "super" pack, Jimenez said he thought a double litter of pups was responsible. Regardless of how the pack became so large, this previously undiscovered pack had become the largest in the region outside of YNP.

A similar situation occurred with the Teton pack several hundred miles to the north, as a result of it having two litters of pups two years in a row, Jimenez said. The pack grew from three wolves, to twelve, then to twenty-three. Then one female died, a litter died, and a bunch of the wolves dispersed. It was some of these dispersers that repeatedly preyed on livestock in the Upper Green River region of the Bridger-Teton National Forest earlier that summer.

"A lot of the wolves we've taken out were those wolves," Jimenez said. When the Daniel pack was discovered, the Teton pack had about twelve to fourteen wolves in it, including pups.

By late 2003, federal officials had killed seven wolves in Sublette County, including two in January near our house, three in the Upper Green River region during the summer, and two in the fall in the Wyoming Range.

Merrill Dana of the Antelope Run Ranch confirmed that he had seen six wolves feeding on a dead yearling heifer on the ranch, the one that Wildlife Services had confirmed as a wolf kill.

Merrill and his wife had seen wolves in the area on numerous occasions (Figure 26), and had a pack of three wolves inhabiting their

Figure 26. Merrill Dana's son Mike took this photograph of a released Canadian wolf on the Dana's Sublette County ranch in 2001. This area is within the home range of the famous Daniel pack. (Photo courtesy Mike Dana)

area for the two years prior to this larger pack being documented, as well as one adult with five pups. Merrill said the pups were not especially shy, adding that it was not difficult to get within a few hundred yards of the pups. Since the dead heifer was right next to the county road, a number of people saw the wolves as they fed on the carcass.

"It's a bad deal now, since we got so many so quick," Merrill said. "It's gonna get nasty. It's coming too fast."

Neighboring rancher Jim Greenwood said while he had not had any problem with the wolves in his cattle, "what's spooked are the antelope, and it's not because of hunters."

"There are more in and around the cattle than out where they usually are," Jim said. "I think the Wyoming Game and Fish Department employees should be worried about having a job with as many dead wild game animals as there are." Jim said that he had seen quite a few dead antelope in the area, while there were few moose to be found.

Greenwood predicted that if the large wolf pack stayed intact when winter set in, "There is no way they're going to hold those elk on those feedgrounds, not with that big of a pack. They were blowing them off with three wolves chasing them last year."

"It's only a matter of time before they want to play with the cows because the elk are too hard to find," Greenwood said. "There is no way the elk are going to stay on the feedgrounds."

Jimenez said he had heard concerns both for livestock and wildlife in the area of such a large wolf pack. "That's a lot of wolves, all the sudden," Jimenez agreed. "That was a surprise. Double litters are always a surprise."

Reports of wolf sightings from the public indicated that sometimes the wolves were seen together, but at other times, the wolves seemed to be in two different groups, which is actually typical for wolf behavior, Jimenez said. "It's not sixteen adult wolves, and how many pups survive into the winter is something else." While there is higher pup survivorship inside protected areas such as YNP, that survival rate drops outside that boundary to about an eighty-percent survival rate from the time they are first seen outside of their dens to when they enter their first winter.

"If they start killing livestock in a repetitive way, we'll start taking some out," Jimenez said. When it was pointed out that the wolves had already been involved in livestock depredations, he responded that "We've already taken two out. We've killed two adults."

Jimenez was referring to the deaths of two adult wolves in the Wyoming Range. After wolves had become involved in killing domestic sheep in the area, efforts to capture and collar the wolves were made, but the two wolves initially captured died from apparent heat-related stress from the capture effort.

Wildlife Services also confirmed that the wolves killed several domestic sheep in the area in September, and were probably responsible for the death of another beef calf. But since the sheep and cattle were soon slated to begin moving off grazing allotments in the Bridger-Teton National Forest, FWS reported that no control actions would be initiated on this pack.

Although wolves had preyed upon domestic sheep in the Wyoming Range several times during summer, those depredations were minor compared to incidents occurring at the same time in Idaho.[5] Over the weekend of September 12–14, 2003, a previously unknown pack of four or five wolves attacked domestic sheep herds about thirty miles north of McCall, Idaho.

Federal officials confirmed that more than fifty head of sheep from multiple herds were killed in the attack. FWS reported "The total number of dead sheep is in the 70s and 4–5 bands that are protected by dogs and herders have been hit. This group of wolves is likely the same bunch that has been killing sheep about 7–8 miles away. Wildlife Services was authorized to kill this pack of 4–5 wolves."

Wolves had been busy killing livestock in other areas of Wyoming as well. Among other incidents, a beef calf was reportedly killed half-way across the state in the Big Horn Mountains early in September.

According to FWS, multiple wolves were in the area where a USDA Wildlife Services specialist shot a depredating wolf off a sheep carcass a few days after the initial attack.

With all these problems, it seemed that wolves were everywhere. But FWS said the rate of growth in the wolf population was slowing in 2003.[6] The agency reported:

"While these estimates are admittedly very rough and could change significantly once fall-winter aerial tracking with snow cover has been conducted, we have currently documented an estimated wolf population of: By recovery area: northwestern Montana, 90 wolves and 3 breeding pairs; central Idaho, 362 wolves and 21 breeding pairs; Greater Yellowstone Area, 295 wolves and 22 breeding pairs.

"By state these estimates are: Montana, 161 wolves and 8 breeding pairs; Idaho, 346 wolves and 21 breeding pairs; Wyoming, 240 wolves and 17 breeding pairs. The total wolf population estimate for 2003 is 747 wolves and 46 breeding pairs compared to 663 wolves and 43 breeding pairs in 2002."

In January, 2004, wolves were confirmed to have attacked cattle near the Colorado border at Wamsutter.[7] It appeared that one or two wolves were involved in the cattle killing and Wildlife Services animal damage control specialists were granted authorization to remove up to two wolves from the area, but the culprits were never found.

Rancher Charlie Juare said when he began gathering cattle on the checkerboard area of the Red Desert north of Wamsutter right after Christmas, two severely crippled cows were found, as well as other stiff and sore cattle. Injuries to the cattle included having their tails chewed off near the backbone and severely infected wounds to their front legs at the elbow. All of the affected cattle were bred yearling heifers weighing about 900 pounds. One of the cows could not get up and subsequently died. Federal wildlife officials skinned her carcass and discovered the trauma associated with wolf predation. A second cow was killed as well.

"We had two that wouldn't get up anymore," Juare said. "About 10 or so had no tails, and we've still got a few more in the barn that are hobbling along." Trying to gather cattle that have been subject to predation had proven to be difficult as well, since spooked cattle do not want to be handled. "They're pretty rank," Juare said.

Shane Christian of Pavillion, who runs cattle with Juare, said "They're scattered all over creation down there. They don't really want to herd back up."

Juare said having wolf depredation at any time of year is a new experience, but he was dreading calving, which was set to begin in April. Juare said ranch workers had not seen nor heard of any wolves in the area prior to the attacks on the cattle.

Six months later, members of the public began reporting seeing a wolf further south, about thirty miles west of Denver, Colorado. The public was proven right when a two-year old female wolf was killed by a vehicle along I-70 in June, 2004. This wolf had traveled more than four hundred miles from her original home range in Yellowstone.[8]

Chapter 24

Watching Wolves

In hot, dry weather, our sheep herd leaves its bedground at a run by about 6:30 most mornings. The sheep graze for a few hours on the dew-covered vegetation, then bed down again to get through the heat of the day before leisurely grazing away the evening.

One August morning in 2003 started out this way as well, and I sent my twelve-year-old son Cass out to push the sheep away from the mesa fence and down toward the draw (Figure 27). A few minutes later I looked out the back window of our house and saw an animal watching Cass and the sheep, which by this time were just out of my sight. I looked through the binoculars at the light-colored canid, which had positioned itself on high ground, trying to figure out if it was one

Figure 27. A young Cass Urbigkit checking new lambs. A few years later, when he was twelve years old, a pack of three wolves watched Cass while he was herding sheep. (Photo by Cat Urbigkit)

of our three young guard dogs or a coyote. I only briefly considered it being something else.

The animal was behaving cautiously and secretively, and I could not get a clear view of its silhouette, although I looked at it off and on for the next forty-five minutes. It retreated into the shadows as the sheep and dogs passed below it.

Cass returned to the house, and then it was my turn to push the sheep, this time away from the industrial traffic on Paradise Road. I spent about half an hour out with the herd, played with the guard dogs near the eastern property boundary, and then headed back to the house.

Doing my morning chores drew me to look out the back window again. I did, and I nearly fainted when I saw two extremely large canids walking where their lighter-colored counterpart had been earlier. These two dark wolves had their heads down when they moved and their shoulders were massive.

It was at that instant that I realized the animal that had been lying on the hillside watching my son herding sheep had been one member of a pack of at least three wolves. I was enraged. I ran for the gun case, but in my panic, could not find the right shells to go with the guns I was grabbing. Cass, who was outside, heard my screeches for help and came at a run. Being a mannerly young man, he ran through the front door, stopping on a dime to begin taking off his shoes so he would not get the floors dirty. He quickly abandoned that idea and continued to the gun cabinet.

By that time, I had guns and shells scattered all over the room, but Cass shoved the 20-gauge shells into my hand and I was out the door. By some miracle, and the help of that twelve-year-old, I made it to the car with a 20-gauge shotgun, matching shells, a cell phone, and a set of binoculars.

I began shooting into the air when I reached the top of the hill overlooking the draw, and could hear the echoes of Cass's .243 rifle fire as well. Not familiar with the break-open shotgun I was firing, I pulled back to cock the gun when I had meant to push the break-open lever. My hands were shaking and my brain had definitely kicked out.

The wolves were gone, having slipped away into the folds and dips of the mesa. We made a lot of noise in their wake anyway.

While I walked the draws, hillsides, and fencelines looking for tracks, I called the FWS office in Lander on my cell phone and left a message about the wolves, requesting a return call. That call came a few hours later.

Cass pushed the sheep toward their mid-morning bedground near the corrals, and they settled in. I left Cass, a twelve-year-old man with a rifle, to guard the herd while I headed to town for more shells and other supplies in case we needed to pen the sheep and feed them for a few days while the wolf situation got sorted out.

FWS returned my call, sounding sympathetic, but noting that no action would be taken because the wolves had not really done anything like actually attacking my sheep. No blood had been shed. Our action to scare the wolves away was the appropriate response, I was told, but if problems did occur, please call again.

It was later that evening that I learned from a friend that wolves had killed a calf near Cora sometime during the night. I will bet, just a few hours later, those cattle killers were on a hill, near my home, watching my son herd sheep.

Chapter 25

Testimony

They came from all corners of the state, driving for many miles to have their say. Many of the stories were similar and all were heart-felt. They filled the Cheyenne meeting room, nervously waiting their turn to testify.

The February, 2003, meeting of the Joint Travel, Recreation, Wildlife and Cultural Resources Committee of the Wyoming Legislature had been convened to accept public input on wolf management in Wyoming (Figure 28). It would be the first step in an attempt to show FWS that Wyoming was ready for wolves to be delisted and fall under state management.[1]

Figure 28. Senator Delaine Roberts held the line on wolves in the Wyoming Legislature. (Photo by Cat Urbigkit)

Co-Chairmen Senator Delaine Roberts of Etna and Representative Mike Baker of Thermopolis presented opening remarks and comments about the bills they were sponsoring.

Baker's House Bill 229 proposed a dual classification for wolves, meaning that in some portions of the state, wolves would be trophy game in which regulated hunting could take place, but in other areas, wolves would be classified as predators, with unregulated take. The bill's seventeen-pages of details, including a requirement for at least fifteen packs of wolves in the state outside of YNP, generated a great deal of concern for those who attended to testify.

"House Bill 229 is not perfect," Baker said, but pledged to work with the public on improving it. He said one way to improve the bill would be to insert a provision that would allow the state to withhold the names of any person or persons who legally killed a wolf.

Baker said this provision was necessary because he knew that there might be threats against anybody who killed a wolf, adding, "I have had some vague ones tossed at me."

More than fifty Wyoming residents testified, from Chuck Sandberg, who owns game processing plants in Jackson Hole, to Crook County rancher J. W. Nuckolls.

Moran rancher Alan Rosenbaum said he had been on the front line of the wolf issue for the past three years, with the Teton wolf pack denning in his area and recently coming less than twenty yards from his house. In addition, he said, there was a second wolf pack in the area that FWS had yet to acknowledge, and reminded that the Teton pack had recently killed a two-year-old, 1,100-pound pregnant heifer, He added:

"I need help . . . I need protection for my family, for myself and for the property I'm entrusted to take care of.

"Since the wolves moved in, I've slept every night from fall to spring with the window open, so I can hear what's going on. This spring, in nine days, I had three stampedes of 200 head of cattle and their calves. If any of you have ever heard a cowherd frightened to death, you'll be awake, I don't care how sound a sleeper you are . . . I've developed a lot of gray hair in the last few years from having to deal with these circumstances."

The stampedes stopped when federal officials trapped a 123-pound lone female wolf that had been coming into the pasture and chasing the cattle herd.

"Wolves are here to stay, in my opinion," Rosenbaum said, but citizens "need to be able to protect our livestock, ourselves and our families."

Lander's Jim Allen, president of the Wyoming Dude Ranchers Association and a board member of the Wyoming Outfitters Association, told legislators of the impact of wolves on big game.

"We're killing the golden goose and we can't do that," Allen said. He also said he feared for his family's safety "They better stay safe or . . . I'm going to shoot a wolf."

Lincoln County Commissioner Alan Linford reminded the legislators that his county's official position is that wolves are not welcome within its boundaries because of the threat the animals posed to the economy, health, and safety of its citizens.

Dubois rancher and former state legislator Budd Betts testified that wolves had killed three dogs on his ranch, including a precious family pet, "shredded to bits, literally . . . twenty steps from the house."

"I do not believe wolves don't present a threat to human safety," Betts said, despite claims to the contrary by wolf advocates.

Fremont County Commissioner Crosby Allen advocated that wolves should retain their predator classification outside YNP, an idea FWS despised. Allen noted that there would be litigation over removing wolves from federal protections and urged the state to go it alone, basing its decisions on its jurisdiction of wildlife within state borders. Allen questioned the legislators, "Do we want to go into that court handcuffed to the US Fish and Wildlife Service?"

Farmer Glen French of Powell said that he joined others in enjoying area wildlife, but said herd numbers were dropping as the wolf population increased. "The economic impact is tremendous," French said. "When the elk are gone, the ranchers are next." French noted that wolves were pushing the elk out of the mountains and down onto farmlands in the Powell area.

Phil Cross said of his Dubois-area ranch: "I think we're the leading beef-feeders to the wolves at this stage of the game — in fact, I know we are. We need to be rid of them." Cross added that he does not begrudge the wolves, but does "have a grudge against the people who put them in here."

Crowheart cattleman Joe Baine said he summers cattle on the Cross ranch and "We never get all of them back."

Big Horn County Commissioner Keith Grant was firm in his stance. "We don't have any wolves and we're not going to have any wolves . . . We're just not going to allow it."

Big Piney elk feeder Mike Schaffer testified about his experience with wolves on the North Piney elk feedground. By the time of his testimony, the wolves had run the elk away and eliminated his feeding job.

Dunoir rancher Jon Robinett recounted the history of depredations on the Diamond G, which persisted even after the ranch had sold off a great many of its cattle. Wolves also had killed dogs on the ranch on five occasions, and had come onto the ranch house's front and back porches. In one case, Robinett's wife was walking the dog to the barn to lock it up when the wolves appeared and killed the dog instead. In addition to cattle and dogs, wolves had killed two adult horses and a colt on the ranch. Now, Robinett testified, when his wife takes her Jack Russell terrier outside at night, it requires a leash, a pistol, and a spotlight. "I blame the United States Congress for this," he said. "We can't go on with these kind of losses."

Representative Randall Luthi of Freedom noted that there is an expanding front line of people dealing with wolves, adding that officials in Utah recently had confirmed the presence of wolves in that state.

"Utah was so excited about it, they sent it back to Wyoming," Luthi said, urging the legislators to remain firm in dealings with federal officials on the wolf issue. Local governments need to help decide where a species like wolves are allowed to live, Luthi said.

Afton outfitter Maury Jones told the legislative committee that he supported wolves outside YNP being classified as a predator. "If he steps foot outside that park, he's a coyote," Jones said.

B. J. Hill, a Jackson Hole outfitter, said he had watched wolves run cattle on federal grazing allotments. "Between the grizzly bear and the wolves, the cowman in western Wyoming has no chance," Hill said. Hill referred to environmentalists, with their "anti-elk feeding agenda . . . This Canadian killer is their guarantee to get rid of sport hunting." Hill said the nonessential, experimental wolf reintroduction conducted by the federal government was a failure. "The experiment failed because it was too successful."

Lincoln County Commissioner Kathy Davison said her county commission stood in opposition to the wolf reintroduction. She said there used to be thirteen domestic sheep outfits in her county, but that number had dropped to about two. Davison said she feared "this industry will be completely lost" without controls being placed on the wolf population.

Wyoming Game and Fish Commissioner Linda Fleming of Baggs advocated a dual classification for wolves. "We need to have dual classification . . . as quickly as possible to minimize the damage and danger to the people of this state."

"A week ago today, my life was changed," said Darlene Vaughan, when wolves moved onto her ranch just three miles outside of Lander. "These wolves will eat us out of house and home," she said, noting that calving season would begin in two short weeks.

Dave Vaughan, Darlene's husband, testified that he was the most recent graduate of the "rubber-bullet, bean-bag shooting school" sponsored by FWS. "I feel like a hostage," he said, in reference to the limits imposed on livestock producers in protecting their herds.

Big Piney cattleman Bill Barney was in the same situation (Figure 29). He told the committee that calving on his ranch would start soon. "We're going to have the only calves on the ground for about a month. We're not looking forward to that." He urged the committee to modify its legislation so it would work for the people of Wyoming. "If we can't do that . . . delay delisting."

Bill Barney's son, Colin Barney, testified as well, noting he had the difficult realization of establishing new rules for his five-year-old daughter and three-year-old son because wolves had moved into the

Figure 29. Big Piney rancher Bill Barney became concerned for the safety of his grandchildren once wolves showed up on his cattle ranch south of town. (Photo by Cat Urbigkit)

area near their home, just south of Big Piney. No more walking to the school bus alone in what had become wolf country.

Daniel rancher Charles Price said HB 229 needed some changes and cautioned the committee, "Don't buy anything we can't live with."

Price's neighbor Albert Sommers (Figure 30) told of livestock losses in the Upper Green River region. "I can't sustain a seven-percent calf loss on my summer range . . . I simply will run out of business,"

Figure 30. Rancher Albert Sommers has had his family's cattle herds hit hard, year after year, by depredating wolves. (Photo by Cat Urbigkit)

Sommers said. He urged changes to HB 229 as well, adding, "I do not want 'delistment' to feed me to the wolves."

Fontenelle sheep rancher Mary Thoman (Figure 31) told a harrowing story of wolves preying on her sheep herd, located 150 miles south of Yellowstone, and scattering injured sheep for miles. "It was a massive massacre . . . We're running in the red because of these losses." She also urged the legislators to not "compromise our industry or our way of life."

Angela Denney of Cheyenne and her husband Scott owned an outfitting business in Wyoming and Idaho. "I've seen the devastation in Idaho . . . It's only a matter of time," she said, before a similar situation develops here in Wyoming.

E. K. Bostick of Cody said: "We have dogs in our yard to keep the grizzlies away. With the wolves, I can no longer turn my dogs out. The dual classification everyone talks about is a death knell." He said the committee must insist that there be "no wolves nowhere outside of Yellowstone National Park."

Larry Bourett of Laramie, a long-time opponent of wolf reintroduction, asked the legislators to consider that "not all stakeholders have the same stake . . . You need to remember that," suggesting that people in northwest Wyoming have the greatest stake in the outcome of the proceedings.

In the end, legislation and a state management plan were adopted that called for a dual-status classification of wolves. FWS

Figure 31. Dick and Mary Thoman's family had wolves preying on their domestic sheep flocks, first while the sheep grazed in the mountains in the summer and fall, but eventually on the lower-elevation lambing grounds near Farson. (Photo by Cat Urbigkit)

then rejected the plan as inadequate to protect wolves and refused to delist the wolves in the tri-state Yellowstone region. That prompted state officials to contest the rejection of the wolf plan, citing the fact that FWS was playing politics, not biology.

Chapter 26

Elk Woes

It was not just the ranchers who were in such a terrible position. In March, 2003, a month after the Cheyenne meeting, Montana wildlife officials announced their count of the Northern Yellowstone elk herd. The count was 8,335, half the size of the herd in 1994, the year prior to wolf reintroduction.

By early 2003, WGF officials had come to realize that wolves had created management problems on several of western Wyoming's twenty-two state-administered elk feedgrounds, where thousands of elk were being fed hay to sustain them through the winter months (Figure 32). As the wolf population expanded, wolves too arrived on several of these feedgrounds, hundreds of miles from Yellowstone.

Mike Schaffer was a WGF elk feeder on the North Piney elk feedground located on the eastern flank of the Wyoming Range Mountains. During the winter of 2002–2003, federally protected gray wolves eliminated his job.[1] "It's been an all-winter battle and I finally lost."

Schaffer said he had started feeding early in November and was caring for 388 head of elk on the feedground. "Everything was going good," Schaffer said, "but the wolves started hitting us in December and it's been problems ever since." Although there were at least five wolves running in two groups in the area, the problems on the feedground involved a pack of three.

Schaffer said because the wolves would chase the elk up into the trees, leaving only the blood trail out in the open, he had not found wolf-killed elk on the feedground itself. The wolves would run into the elk herd, "get two or three wounded and bleeding like hell," and then ease off. It appeared the wolves "let them bleed until they get good and weak," before moving back in on them and continuing the chase. Schaffer said when the wolves would harass the herd, "It took

Figure 32. The Wyoming Game and Fish Department manages numerous elk feedgrounds in western Wyoming and it did not take long for the reintroduced Canadian wolves to become aware of these sources of seemingly limitless prey. (Photo by Cat Urbigkit)

three days to get them back to the feedground and get them settled." Settled they were, Schaffer said, with the animals calming down and coming right up to the sled for their daily ration of hay.

On one occasion, when Schaffer went to feed, he followed wolf tracks up the snowmobile trail to the feedground. "You couldn't imagine the blood . . . up and down the feedground," he said. The blood trail went right to the feed row and continued up into the trees. Some of the elk came back, but "the wolves hit them that night from above."

This time, "they wreaked havoc up and down that creek bottom. God, I just hate this." This time the blood trail started a full three miles from the feedground. "The elk just left," he said, and did not come back to the North Piney feedground. "They just can't take that much pressure . . . They've got to get out of there." The herd eventually moved to a lower-elevation feedground, Bench Corral, located closer to Big Piney, but the wolves followed.[2]

The pack of three wolves that hunted the North Piney and Bench Corral feedgrounds had been documented killing and chasing elk in those areas for the past two winters by the elk feeders. These wolves, because they had not been documented to have successfully raised pups, were not included among the ten packs that were categorized as assisting in achieving wolf recovery in the Yellowstone region.

Less than two weeks after the wolves chased the elk from the North Piney feedground, three other wolves chased all the elk off of the Black Butte feedground, north of Pinedale, fifty miles away, wildlife officials confirmed.[3]

WGF feedground manager Scott Werbelow said that there had been 485 elk on Black Butte and two wolves were reportedly in the area for most of the 2002–2003 winter. Werbelow said that early in December, three wolves had been reported in the Black Butte area, but eventually that number dwindled to two.

Wolves had killed two elk on Black Butte during the winter, then started killing elk every day. By the third day, the elk herd had fled the feedground. "The three wolves are probably what made them leave the feedground," Werbelow said.

Black Butte elk feeder John Fandek said when he went to feed one morning, he found "the elk had beat a trail out of there." Wolves had used the feedground for the last three years with no adverse reaction from the elk herd. "They have accepted the presence of those wolves," Fandek said. "They never reacted like this." But this time, with so little snow and some of the herd knowing the route to the Soda Lake feedground, "They just trailed on out . . . They got harassed enough that they decided to pull out" and traveled east to the Soda Lake feedground.

Werbelow confirmed that while wolves had not been documented to have killed many elk on the state's feedgrounds, the big lesson he had learned was the unpredictability that wolves brought into feedground management. He said the problem was in trying to estimate the number of elk that would use any given feedground in any given year — the challenge of anticipating elk movements and planning for the appropriate amount of hay in each location. "It complicates things."

It also apparently became a complicated tradition, with wolves hitting the feedgrounds early the next winter, in December, 2003, after severe storms had left deep snows, accompanied by freezing temperatures.[4] After two attacks at the North Piney elk feedground, the elk fled the site and headed seven miles downcountry to the Bench Corral feedground — but that did not mean they were safe from predation. A few days later, wolves hit Bench Corral, after which some elk headed to the southwest and Billy Canyon while others headed to private ranchlands along Cottonwood Creek. The same day, wolves hit the Jewett elk feedground and forced about three hundred head to leave. They returned the next day.

Wolves also hit the Franz feedground for three days in a row and scattered 100–150 elk onto neighboring ranchlands. A few days later, WGF herded the elk back onto the feedground using snowmachines. At about this same time, Werbelow said, at least four wolves were seen moving between the Black Butte and Soda Lake elk feedgrounds.

With a lot of snow on the ground, there were more elk than usual on feedgrounds during the winter of 2003–2004. Some elk had traditionally tended to winter away from the feedgrounds, but it appeared that some of these animals had moved onto the feedgrounds as well, Werbelow said, reacting to their need for increased security in the face of pressure from prowling wolves.

Each winter, the wolves had developed a predation pattern on the elk feedgrounds that caused the elk to vacate the feeding sites and scatter widely. By late December, 2004, the North Piney elk feedground had already shut down for the winter. According to WGF feedground manager Gary Hornberger, "The wolves ran the elk off to Bench Corral, like they typically do."[5] That year, the feeder at Bench Corral had upwards to eight hundred head of elk to feed, far above the feedground objective of 250 head.

That winter the wolves also harassed elk on the Black Butte feedground, scattering the elk onto the highway and along the river before they returned to the feedground. A pack of nine wolves hit the Finnegan feedground for the first time ever, chasing the elk off the site for a few days until they calmed down and returned. Federal wildlife officials killed two of the wolves as a result of livestock depredations, but seven members of the pack remained. A total of fifteen wolves were killed in response to livestock depredations in Sublette County in 2004, but many more were left in the area.

It is impossible for wildlife officials to plan for the impact that wolves might have on elk feeding operations, Hornberger said, even though his agency tried to plan for the worst-case scenario in terms of feed and winter severity. "So much for planning, when the wolves move another 400 to 500 elk to another feedground," Hornberger said. In 2003, the road into the Bench Corral feedground had to be plowed to allow for more hay to be hauled in to feed the unexpectedly large number of elk that had moved to the site in response to wolf activity elsewhere.

Confirming the fears of many Montana hunters, Montana Fish, Wildlife and Parks officials announced in December, 2003, that it would cut the number of late-winter cow elk permits in the northern range Yellowstone elk herd from about 1,400 to 100. FWS reported, "With the full compliment of large predators preying on them — bears, lions, wolves and humans — this herd may not rebound from the deliberate high hunter harvest of cows as quickly as it has in the past."

Chapter 27

Compensation Fraud

In order to try to gain support for the wolf reintroduction efforts, DW began a program to compensate livestock producers for losses caused by federally protected gray wolves. This program paralleled one already in place by which WGF paid for losses of livestock caused by grizzly bears. It quickly became apparent that the DW compensation program appeared to generate good publicity for the environmental group writing the check, but did little in terms of compensating livestock producers for their actual losses, according to those experiencing livestock depredations in western Wyoming's Upper Green River Basin.[1]

Pinedale rancher Stan Murdock sustained four confirmed wolf kills and seven confirmed grizzly bear kills during the 2003 grazing season in the Upper Green River region. "What we're after is adequate compensation for what we are actually losing," Murdock said. DW's program would pay for kills confirmed by federal wildlife officials as having been caused by wolves, while also setting the price that would be paid for the lost animal(s). "They decided this year that a calf is worth exactly $500," Murdock said. In contrast, WGF agreed with stockmen that a calf was worth $556.71, based on market statistics.

The major difference between the state's and environmental group's programs was that the state recognized that not all calves killed by bears could be located, so adjustment for missing calves had been implemented. That compensation factor was up to 3.5, meaning that for every confirmed bear kill, when other animals were missing, the livestock producer would be paid for the confirmed kill plus up to another two- and -one-half animals. This compensation factor of 3.5 only applied to missing calves; it did not apply to yearling or adult cattle. It is important to note that this compensation factor was based on specific research aimed at determining how many grizzly bear kills are actually discovered on western Wyoming's forested grazing allotments.

So for Murdock's seven confirmed grizzly kills, he would receive compensation for up to 24.5 missing calves. That may seem like a lot, but it still did not compensate for all of the animals unaccounted for over and above the normal death loss of about two percent, which was subtracted before the claimed losses were submitted for compensation. Murdock's actual losses totaled more than forty head. That means ten percent of his cows came off the forest without the calves they had at their sides when they were placed on the range in the summer.

In contrast, DW would only pay for cattle killed by wolves when the kills had been found, inspected by federal officials, and confirmed. The organization would not pay for missing livestock, even though federal wildlife officials acknowledged that direct evidence of only a small percentage of wolf kills is ever actually found.

"We're not finding these wolf kills," Murdock said. "It is understandable there is no evidence left because wolves hunt in packs and when they are hungry they leave nothing to confirm."

The DW program required confirmation, based on direct evidence of each wolf kill, and would pay the producer only about $500 for each such confirmed kill. Consequently, the producer was shorted $56.71 because the animal was not valued at market price. More importantly, research in Idaho had found direct evidence of only one of every eight wolf kills. Based on these figures, the $500 check received by a livestock producer should have been written for $4,453.68 if the intention was to provide compensation for the total market value of predation losses.

The one-in-eight ratio held true for Big Piney rancher Bill Murdock. In the 2003 grazing season, he had one confirmed wolf kill, but ended up with a total of eight calves unaccounted for at the end of the season. Murdock refused to file for compensation from Defenders. "You kind of hate not to [file]," Murdock said, but "for principle's sake," he declined. "It would just give them ammunition to make the public feel that people are being compensated for their losses when they're not."

Upper Green River Cattle Association members had a total of ten head of cattle confirmed as killed by wolves in the 2003 grazing season on the Bridger-Teton National Forest. It might not sound like a lot, one here and one there, but that does not take into consideration the number of cattle killed by wolves that are not found. That ten head confirmed represents only a small part of the eighty head actually lost to wolf predation. Although Defenders might end up paying a few thousand dollars in compensation for the confirmed kills, the value of the animals actually killed by wolves is closer to $50,261.44. When losses to grizzlies are added in, the value of the livestock losses rises to more than $100,000 for that year's grazing season. Bears and wolves kill differently and animal damage experts can differentiate between the kills of each species.

Daniel rancher Charles Price had six calves and one yearling confirmed as killed by grizzlies in 2003, in addition to having one calf killed by a wolf. Price received compensation from the state for his bear losses, but did not file for compensation from Defenders for his wolf kills because he did not want the group to get any more good publicity.

"Basically the program is a publicity ploy. It's cheap advertising for them," Price said. Using a more conservative rate of five calves killed for every one wolf kill found, Defenders was, in reality, getting away with paying less than twenty cents for every dollar or more lost by the livestock producer. In doing so, Defenders can claim they have compensated the rancher, "and the rancher shouldn't squawk."

Another problem with the compensation program was that it did not even begin to acknowledge the numerous problems caused by wolf predation on livestock, Price said. "They chase the cattle and get them all stirred up." The animals are then unsettled, hard to handle, and fail to continue to gain weight. Management can be impacted negatively by cattle refusing to use certain parts of their allotments or pastures in response to pressure from predators, and that affects allotment utilization rates. And, predation can cause groups of cattle to scatter in all directions, including through fences.

"The predators are doing the distribution and moving of the cattle," Big Piney rancher Eddie Wardell described. "The bears and the wolves will decide where you are going to go and when you are going to go."

"They like to run them," Price agreed. "They enjoy chasing them as much as they do killing them. It's not just the direct losses . . . but the fact that you have additional costs from them running the animals."

Wardell added that finding the kills often seems to be a matter of luck, despite intensive efforts to locate the kills and get them confirmed. Within a matter of hours, all that is left of a calf kill is a blood spot on the ground, leaving nothing to confirm, Wardell described.

In the past, Stan Murdock did not file for compensation, even though he had substantial losses. His view was that the compensation was not adequate and good publicity should not result from a flawed program. But when that meant forfeiting tens of thousands of dollars, he was forced to change his mind. He has since submitted the claim for compensation, but stipulated that it is only "partial" compensation. "They are not paying their fair share," Murdock said of Defenders. "They advertise their program, but in actuality, are only making token payments which fall far short of compensation for actual predation losses."

Chapter 28

Dead Wolf

Wednesday mornings were chaotic at the *Sublette Examiner*, the newspaper office where I worked in Pinedale, since that was the day we actually produced the paper and, early in the afternoon, sent it to Jackson for printing. October 1, 2003, fell on a Wednesday, and I had agreed to cover an important meeting in Daniel at 10 A.M., write my story during the meeting, then race back to the office at lunch so it could be flowed into the front page of that week's edition.

I had booted up the computer and just started to retrieve the e-mail a little before 8 A.M. when the office telephone rang. It was a friend letting me know that there was a dead wolf in the Wyoming Range and offering me the opportunity to see it. My editor, Rhonda Swain, had just arrived, and I put her on the spot for an immediate decision as to whether I could go. She gave her approval, so I was out the door within about two minutes, driving hell-bent for the mountain. It was in the same area where a pack of sixteen to nineteen wolves had recently been discovered by FWS and where wolves had been confirmed to have killed cattle and sheep. Although FWS had pledged to kill wolves that preyed on livestock, the agency had finally decided that since the cattle and sheep soon would be leaving their Forest Service grazing allotments for the year, no control action would be initiated.

When I arrived at the scene, I saw a dead brown-colored wolf, without a radio collar, lying in the thick sagebrush, and I did not see signs of a wound or any criminal activity. While I was photographing the animal, I watched an airplane as it flew into the area, crossed above me, and then concentrated its flight on the sagebrush-covered hillside about half a mile away. I realized then that this was a wolf-monitoring flight. It continued to work back and forth across the area while I photographed the dead wolf and left the scene, driving in a hurry so as to make it to the Daniel meeting and be organized when I got there.

I was fairly certain that FWS had not yet found the carcass, which I believed to be at least about four days old. I mentally debated whether I should report the carcass to FWS and whether the *Examiner* should publish the photographs.

I considered that FWS's reaction would be to want all the information I had about the carcass and how I came to know about it, which I felt was none of their business. Then, I thought of my tight timeline for the newspaper article, and the time I anticipated FWS would want from me in locating the carcass. I also thought of the less-than-honest response that the public had received from the agency over the years, as well as the fact that I had not seen any criminal activity. I decided against notifying the federal agency at that time, but decided to advise Rhonda that we should print one of the photos. That meant FWS would find out about the wolf when the public did.

I arrived at the Daniel schoolhouse about 9:30, so I had a little time before the meeting. I called Mike Jimenez of FWS on my cell phone, but the reception was bad and we agreed that I would call him at noon for a wolf update.

I sat through the meeting, wrote my article, drove back to town, and then contacted Mike a little after noon. He told me about what was going on with wolves in the Upper Green — and noted that he also had just flown the Wyoming Range wolves but could not give me a count on the number of individuals because they were in the trees where an accurate count could not be made. That was not where I saw the flight concentrating its efforts, but our's was a short conversation and I did not provide any information about my morning's activities.

The *Sublette Examiner* went to print with a short article on page eleven about the Green River Lakes wolves and a photo of the dead wolf (Figure 33) accompanied by the wording, "A dead wolf was discovered earlier this week in the vast sagebrush along the Wyoming Range Front near where a pack of at least 16 wolves are known to roam."[1]

I enjoyed the rest of my afternoon, figuring it to be a lull before the storm that was about to hit.

Figure 33. This photograph of a dead wolf discovered in the Wyoming Range was printed in the *Sublette Examiner*, causing an explosive reaction from the US Fish and Wildlife Service. (Photo by Cat Urbigkit)

I was at home the next morning about 11 A.M. when the phone rang. It was Jimenez, pointing out that there was a photo of a dead wolf in my newspaper and insistently questioning, "Who was it reported to?" He asked this over and over. I told him I had no idea, that I had no idea if it had been reported. He was hollering, saying, "Cat, Cat, why didn't you call me? You know better, citizens have a responsibility to report . . . It's a federally protected species."

I told him it just appeared to be a dead wolf, not any big deal, not a crime scene. If it was not a big deal, he asked, why was a photograph of it in my newspaper?

"Because people are curious about wolves," I responded.

He continued his hollering tirade, to which I interjected and said, "Okay Mike, what do you want to know?"

He responded: "No, I can't help you now. This is going to law enforcement. They'll be contacting you."

He hung up, so I called my husband and let him know what was going on, and then called to line up an attorney. She told me to take a deep breath, have a cup of coffee, and if anyone called, those calls should be referred to her.

An hour later, FWS Special Agent Roy Brown called, telling me his phone had been ringing off the wall in regard to my dead wolf photo. He asked where the carcass was. I gave him a fairly detailed description of how to find it. We reviewed the instructions and he asked if I had seen any gunshot wounds or anything, to which I said I had not. I asked if we were finished and he confirmed that we were.

I spent a few hours cleaning house, then drove into town for a short meeting with my attorney. We were on the same page, especially with regard to the fact that I had gathered the photos as a legitimate news-gathering activity so any confidential sources I used for that activity should be protected from discovery.

On my way home, at about 5:15 P.M., my cell phone rang. It was Jimenez. He said he and Special Agent Roy Brown were on the scene and could not find the carcass. I went over the instructions again, noting that the sagebrush was thick and tall in the area, so the carcass was hard to find. Jimenez hung up to continue the search. I pondered the quick response to see a dead wolf, unlike the response I had received two months earlier when a pack of wolves had been watching my son herd sheep. No one had driven over the mountain to look at those wolves.

I was not contacted again, and later learned that the carcass had been found and loaded into the back of a federal government pickup truck, but not before the private landowner caught the federal officials on his land without permission. It is my understanding that he was pretty angry about the whole thing, but I have not talked to him about the matter. I had not obtained permission to be on his land either.

Chapter 29

Federal Trespass

Trespassing by FWS wolf biologists was about to become a big issue, eventually resulting in charges being filed against Mike Jimenez, court battles over the issue, and the charges eventually being dropped.[1]

Randy Kruger, a soft-spoken cattleman with the Larsen Ranch Company, described an incident that took place at the ranch on the afternoon of February 14, 2004. The ranch is located twenty-six miles southwest of Meeteetse, an agricultural community located to the east of YNP.

"I was driving up the road and I looked down in some bushes and here were these two men," Kruger said. "Here they were with these wolves laid out, tranquilized, and no truck."

Kruger was describing four wolves — two blacks and two grays — laid out in a row, tranquilized (Figure 34). "I was shocked and amazed. I thought it was a really strange sight. The men were hiding, they were trying to stay out of sight of the road." Kruger stopped to see what was going on, knowing that the men were hiding in the bushes in the ranch's calving pasture — on deeded land for which they did not have permission to be present.

The men introduced themselves as Mike Jimenez of FWS and Wes Livingston, of Cody, who worked for the aviation company Hawkins and Powers of Greybull.

"They were really acting guilty, it seems to me," Kruger said, noting that Jimenez said they were capturing and putting radio collars on the wolves.

"It seemed odd that they would move the wolves into one spot beside the road and under two powerlines. They said the helicopter had gone to get fuel," Kruger said, and that is why the men were on foot with no transportation. "It seemed very odd to me."

Figure 34. When driving into his ranch near Meeteetse one day, Randy Kruger discovered two men and four tranquilized wolves on what was private property. (Photo courtesy Randy Kruger)

"[The wolves] were good-sized and in really good condition. They looked like well-fed animals," Kruger said. Since he often carried a camera and had one that day, he took photographs of the two men with the wolves — and of their location.

"I didn't tell them to get off or anything," Kruger said. "I didn't really know I could do anything with government people . . . I did explain that they were in our calving pasture. I was ignorant of the law [but] I've learned since then."

According to Kruger, Jimenez said that he and Livingston had "just moved them in there from the surrounding area," but Kruger did not believe this. He also was told that the men had worked two more wolves — one had gotten away and the other one had been collared.

Kruger, however, believed that the only logical explanation for having four tranquilized wolves lined up alongside a road with no vehicle in sight and two men hiding in the bushes is that the men had transported the wolves in from another area. "That's what I think. I can't prove that. What I can prove is that they were in our calving pasture."

The ranch was due to begin calving 350 cows in that pasture beginning March 20. Between the Larsen outfit and a few of their neighbors, there would be about 1,000 head of cows in the area to give birth.

Once the wolves had recovered from being tranquillized, they "went up through our cows and stirred them up."

The cows were in a pasture about three miles away. The next morning when Kruger and his wife entered the pasture to break open the water holes, "the cows acted completely different than they have been."

A few days later, one of the neighbors drove by and reported having seen the cows chase four wolves through the pasture. The wolves were not seen again, Kruger said, and FWS soon reported that the pack in question had landed back near Dubois, an appreciably long distance from the Meeteetse country.

Kruger said Jimenez called both Kruger and ranch co-owner Ralph Larsen to apologize for the trespassing incident, but Kruger and Larsen decided to press the matter. "I told him it was a matter of principle," Kruger said. "We're going to do whatever we can to represent ourselves, to protest this."

Kruger met with Park County Commissioners and the county attorney to see about having trespassing charges filed against the men. Both trespassing and littering charges were filed against both men.[2]

Park County Commissioner Tim Morrison lives in the Meeteetse region and knows the Krugers and Larsens well. "My reaction is the utmost feelings for Randy and his family and the ranch because of the stress involved in this," Morrison said. "I know him personally. He's a good and quiet man. It was very sad to see the look on his face, to see him taken through that."

Morrison was not buying the explanations that are being offered either. "It's my thought that the wolves were brought in," Morrison said. "I've got so many unanswered questions."

Morrison, agitated at what he viewed as "subjugation of the constitutional rights of a citizen of this country . . . by the acts of a federal government doing the bidding of an international law," was not idle in his reaction to Kruger's story.

Among other actions, the Park County Commission requested a congressional inquiry into the matter.[3] Morrison said the federal government in this case appears to have "gone too far." He questioned, "If they can do it here, where else is it happening?"

FWS said little about the incident, although Ed Bangs did write that: "A landowner near Meeteetse, Wyo., apparently is claiming that the FWS trespassed on his land during the routine helicopter capture and radio-collaring on the Washakie pack on Valentine's Day. False rumors quickly spread that wolves were being 'reintroduced' onto private land. This incident is being looked into and if trespass truly did occur it was completely unintentional, the Service is deeply sorry and offers its apologies, and we will accept full responsibility. We do not knowingly go onto private property without permission."[4]

Officials with USDJ took over the case for Jimenez's defense, and were successful at getting a change of venue into federal court, which later dismissed the charges.[5]

Meanwhile, state officials had filed a lawsuit in federal court over the FWS rejection of the Wyoming wolf plan. Park County officials soon joined the case.

The state's complaint asserted that the USDI exceeded its own authority and ignored the weight of science when it rejected Wyoming's wolf management plan in January. Both Governor David Freudenthal and Attorney General Pat Crank said they had been reluctant to pursue litigation, but that little choice remained.

"I had frankly hoped it wouldn't come to this," Freudenthal said in a release. "I had hoped that the Department of the Interior would abide by the Endangered Species Act and make its decisions according to science, but the department has amply demonstrated that is not the case."[6]

When FWS rejected Wyoming's wolf management plan, the State of Wyoming claimed, it did so based on political considerations, fear of lawsuits by environmental organizations, and speculation regarding future actions by Idaho and Montana to adopt plans similar to

Wyoming's.[7] The state maintained that USDI had acted arbitrarily and capriciously when it put a legal-risk analysis above science in rejecting Wyoming's wolf management plan and that it usurped Wyoming's rights under the 10th Amendment of the US Constitution, which guarantees state sovereignty. In its complaint, the state argued:

"In developing its wolf reintroduction program, the FWS recognized that the reintroduced wolves would come into contact with livestock production and other human activities. From the outset of the program, the federal government assured ranchers that the FWS would control the wolves in order to limit the harm to landowners. In its environmental impact statement, FWS explained that the 'overriding goal of the wolf control program' is to minimize wolf depredation on livestock. FWS recognized that a responsive program to address conflicts between wolves and domestic livestock reduces the degree of livestock depredation by wolves.

"Despite the formal declaration of a policy of preventing and responding to wolf depredation, the federal government has repeatedly neglected to fulfill its commitment to Wyoming residents. Wolves have killed a very large number of livestock in many parts of the state to the detriment of Wyoming residents and directly to the detriment of the state. Wolf predation of livestock causes income loss for Wyoming residents, which then results in a loss of expenditure within the Wyoming economy and a corresponding loss of sales tax income for Wyoming.

"Because ranches in Wyoming can be very large, and livestock often is scattered over a vast area, ranchers frequently do not find carcasses from wolf kills, if at all, until well after evidence of the cause of death is available. Ranchers are therefore unable to demonstrate, to the degree demanded by FWS, that wolves killed the animals at issue. As a consequence, FWS statistics grossly understate the number of cattle and sheep wolves have killed."

The state's complaint alleged harm to Wyoming's wildlife as well. It stated:

"Wolf predation has caused a decrease in elk and moose herds in Wyoming. Calf-cow ratios and populations for both elk and moose in

Wyoming have declined significantly where wolves have become established. Cow-calf ratios in elk herds not in close proximity to substantial wolf populations have maintained pre-wolf reintroduction levels, while cow-calf ratios in elk herds near Yellowstone National Park have decreased by up to 26 percent since the reintroduction of the gray wolf to Wyoming."

The reduction in wildlife herds meant a reduction in revenue to WGF. The complaint said:

"The elimination or significant reduction in the sources of revenue, which is the direct result of the FWS's unlawful refusal to approve the Wyoming plan, causes an irreparable harm to Wyoming's sovereignty. Wyoming's ability to exercise its authority as a sovereign state in managing Wyoming's wildlife, both game and non-game species, is eroded by the unlawful withholding of agency action by the FWS.

"By unlawfully withholding agency action, the FWS is not only compelling Wyoming to forego revenue that could be used by Wyoming to manage game and non-game species, but also is compelling Wyoming to use other resources to address negative wolf impacts. These two results, caused by the FWS's unlawful withholding of agency action, cause an immediate and irreparable harm to Wyoming's sovereignty."

FWS repeatedly acknowledged that the reason for rejecting the Wyoming wolf plan was more political than biological, according to the state complaint. Ed Bangs was quoted as stating that, while his agency "is mandated to focus on science and biology, public attitudes and comments will influence subsequent litigation." This fear of litigation was a driving force in rejecting the wolf plan, according to the complaint.

FWS Director Steve Williams told state officials that his agency would approve the Wyoming plan only if three changes were made: eliminate the "predatory animal" status and classify the gray wolf as a "trophy game animal" only; amend the law to unambiguously commit to managing for at least fifteen wolf packs in Wyoming; and Wyoming's definition of the term "pack" must be consistent with the definitions in the Idaho and Montana state plans, and, if the pack size must be established by law, the state law must define pack size as at least six wolves traveling together in the winter.

The Wyoming complaint noted that under the Administrative Procedures Act, "a reviewing court shall compel agency action unlawfully withheld or unreasonably delayed." Wyoming argued that the FWS rejection of the Wyoming wolf plan is unlawful. Rather than complying with the ESA mandate to use the "best scientific and commercial data" in making decisions, FWS "disregarded the best scientific and commercial data available regarding the Wyoming Plan and rejected the Wyoming Plan based upon political considerations, fear of litigation by environmental groups, and speculation regarding Montana and Idaho adopting plans similar to the Wyoming Plan."

The state argued that FWS would not propose a rule to delist the gray wolf until Wyoming changed its statutes and the Wyoming plan, even though the gray wolf population in the northern Rocky Mountain region satisfies all of the legal requirements for delisting under the ESA, and the Wyoming plan satisfies the "adequate existing regulatory mechanism" requirement for delisting. According to the complaint:

"Unless Wyoming capitulates to the Defendants' unlawful and unconstitutional political demands, Wyoming's wildlife resources will continue to be harmed, Wyoming's economy will continue to be harmed, and Wyoming's sovereignty will be compromised.

"FWS has offered Wyoming a choice between two coercive alternatives: either the gray wolf will remain 'protected' under the ESA and Wyoming will thereby lose its authority to manage the species in a way that limits harmful impacts on livestock and wild game and permits control of the wolf population consistent with Wyoming's management of other species; or Wyoming succumbs to FWS's mandate that the Legislature enact a statute of FWS's choosing."

Chapter 30

Compounding Problems

In January, 2005, WGF asked FWS to remove or relocate wolves from the Daniel pack in western Wyoming. This pack had been chasing large numbers of elk from winter feedgrounds onto private lands and, in some cases, highways.[1]

In a letter to Mike Jimenez, WGF Director Terry Cleveland pointed out that FWS had the authority to remove wolves that are negatively impacting ungulate populations. But because wolves are protected under the federal ESA, state officials had no authority to manage them.

WGF was prompted to write the letter after several weeks of having wolves chasing elk from feedgrounds and onto private property, causing property damage and leading to increased commingling of elk and livestock and the danger of disease transmission. On two occasions, wolves chased elk onto highway right-of-ways, creating public safety concerns.

"Having large numbers of elk displaced from feedgrounds onto private property creates poor public relations with local livestock producers, increases damage problems and greatly increases the potential for brucellosis transmission from elk to cattle," said Cleveland. "It also costs the Game and Fish Department thousands of dollars in administrative expenses each time elk must be returned to established feedgrounds after being displaced by wolves."

During December, 2004, WGF personnel dealt with six separate situations involving the displacement of more than 3,400 elk from established feedgrounds. Wolf interactions with elk on feedgrounds were occurring daily.

A month after receiving WGF's letter, FWS responded. The letter did not offer much in terms of a solution to the problems.[2] FWS wrote:

"We are not prepared to routinely relocate wolves found on or near the numerous elk feeding grounds in the state, but we understand that the Wyoming Game and Fish Department views this instance as a one-time short-term solution. Wyoming's elk feeding grounds have a history of disease issues that predate the reintroduction of wolves. Wolves have occurred on at least eight other elk feeding grounds in addition to the five you mentioned.

"[Until a long-term solution is found for the conflicts,] we suggest radio-collaring and re-releasing a wolf or two on the Daniel site, so that the pack can be better monitored."

Focusing on the part of the WGF letter suggesting the pack be "relocated" rather than removed, FWS wrote that to comply with WGF's request it would need far more information, including information on how it would address disease transmission from elk to cattle, the potential for success, and "we ask that you also identify the potential release sites you are considering, as most available wolf habitat is fully occupied by resident packs."

The short letter, signed by FWS Regional Director Ralph Morgenweck, said once FWS received more detailed information, "we then propose to discuss your request as well as any long-term solutions to the feeding ground problems."

The relationship between Wyoming and FWS had been tenuous since FWS rejected Wyoming's wolf management plan and state officials had sued the agency over the rejection. The case was pending in the federal court system. Meanwhile, it did not appear from the FWS letter that the federal agency was eager to help Wyoming resolve its conflicts with wolves without a "long-term" solution. What FWS sought were changes to the Wyoming wolf plan that would rid the plan of its "predator" status for wolves in portions of the state.

Late March, 2005, brought major snowstorms to northern Sublette County, but also brought some unwelcome visitors to Gene and Stella Taylor's ranch near Merna.[3] A pack of wolves entered the Taylors' cattle herd under the cover of darkness, resulting in the deaths of two cows. One of the cows had its hindquarters consumed, but was still alive, so had to be put down. Both of the cows were due to give birth, as calving in the herd was already underway, so their deaths doubled the losses for the ranch.

Stella Taylor said she believed the wolves had entered the herd early in the morning, before daybreak. The downed cows, attacked not far from the ranch house, were discovered during the early morning check. The rest of the herd had milled together and stayed in one big bunch. When finished at the Taylor Ranch, the wolves moved on to the Bar W Bar Ranch where they killed a yearling cow, according to ranch manager Merrill Dana.

FWS and USDA Wildlife Services confirmed the kills, all of which occurred on private land. FWS issued shoot-on-site permits to three ranches and authorized Wildlife Services to kill the entire wolf pack.

Mike Jimenez said that a few days later, Wildlife Services flew the area of the last confirmed kill, spotted a pack of five wolves and was able to shoot and kill all five.

Jimenez noted that although these members of the Daniel pack had been in the news because of WGF's concerns with the pack harassing elk on elk feedgrounds, control actions were undertaken based solely on the pack's livestock depredations.

FWS reported that "Five wolves were removed from the pack last year during a series of control actions on a still ongoing chronic pattern of livestock depredations, 13 confirmed depredations last year."

Jimenez added that since 2000, the Daniel pack had been confirmed as being involved in killing at least twenty-one head of livestock.

The conflict between state officials and FWS did not improve anytime soon because, by April of 2005, a new conflict developed. FWS included an acknowledgement in its weekly wolf update that a pair of wolves was expected to begin denning in the middle of a domestic sheep lambing ground northeast of Farson.[4]

The FWS update reported that a Wildlife Services field specialist had seen a pair of wolves feeding on a moose calf kill the week before. The female was very pregnant and expecting to den any day. The area is in the middle of a sheep lambing area and the local producers were contacted about the situation.

Jimenez said that Wildlife Services had been authorized to trap and radio-collar the wolves on site so that the pair could be monitored. "It's not in the mountains, it's on the flatlands," Jimenez said. "And there's a lot of sheep . . . It's a routine deal. Wolves show up and we go into gear . . . We try to monitor."

However, FWS had no plans to move the animals, despite their presence amid a lambing ground. "We don't move things proactively," Jimenez said. The wolves had not yet caused a problem with the domestic sheep and noted that area livestock producers had been alerted to the situation. But two of the three domestic sheep producers who used the region as a lambing ground said they had not been notified. Dick Thoman and Pete Arambel confirmed that their bands of domestic sheep, just a few short weeks away from lambing, were due on the lambing grounds the next week.

Wyoming Governor David Freudenthal joined the fray of those outraged by the lack of action by FWS.[5] Freudenthal sent a letter requesting that FWS remove the pair of wolves from the lambing ground, but FWS did not comply with the request.

Freudenthal's letter to USDI referred to the presence of the wolves as "the latest predicament," noting that FWS had halted its efforts to capture and collar the animals. FWS reported that recent snowfall hindered capture efforts, so trapping was stopped.

"While I am very skeptical of the excuse for suspending the capture and collaring of the wolves, I believe that a better and more reasoned approach would recognize the inevitability that the wolves will become 'problem' wolves and will ultimately have to be removed," Freudenthal wrote:

"In my view, it would be in the best interest of the wolves, the Service, producers and livestock to capture and not only collar, but relocate the wolves prior to their establishing a den.

"To me, this is akin to small children playing at a railroad crossing. Peril is a certainty in the absence of active supervision. This is a chance for the Service to be responsible and proactively manage wolves in a way that, in the end, will preclude fatal take of wolves and livestock depredation."

Freudenthal referred to the FWS removal of five wolves in the Daniel pack earlier in the year when the animals repeatedly killed livestock, but added:

"Wolf management is not relegated to such isolated and single decisions; rather it is an active and daily responsibility.

"As a result, in the absence of state-sanctioned wolf management, the people of the state of Wyoming must recurrently turn to the US Fish and Wildlife Service for day-to-day management of the species, including conflict mitigation. Thus, my correspondence."

FWS, in its weekly wolf report, expressed dismay at the interest in the Farson wolf situation, noting: "For some reason this fairly routine situation for us has received considerable media attention, some misinformed rhetoric, and even requests that these 'suspected' potentially problem wolves be 'preemptively' removed."[6]

FWS pledged to closely monitor the situation, adding, "If there are wolf depredations on legally present livestock in that area, we will deal with those situations as they develop — just as we always have — including lethal removal of wolves if ultimately necessary."

Within a few days, one of the sheep producers in the area heard a wolf howl and two wolves were reportedly seen chasing sheep on the lambing ground. Wolves attacked and wounded one of the guardian dogs used to protect the sheep, but FWS was not able to capture any of the wolves. The wolves began preying on the pregnant sheep. FWS noted it would prefer to capture, collar and release sheep-killing wolves in the Farson area, but agreed that two wolves could be "lethally removed" by federal animal damage control officials, if possible.

FWS reported that, in response to the depredation, Wildlife Services "began trapping to radio-collar and release a wolf on site so we could determine if they might have a den and how many wolves there may be," FWS reported.[7]

The wolves returned to a nearby band of sheep the next night and five more ewes were killed. FWS reported that Wildlife Services "was still requested to collar and release any trapped wolf on site, but in addition they should lethally remove two wolves by shooting, if possible."

After a few weeks, federal animal damage control personnel finally killed the female wolf and four of her six pups.[8] The adult male wolf seen in the area earlier was not found. Neither were her other two pups.

In April, 2005, a federal court judge dismissed the lawsuit challenging FWS's rejection of Wyoming's wolf management plan.[9]

Each claim made in the case was denied, with US District Court Judge Alan Johnson noting that the court lacked jurisdiction because the January, 2004, letter from FWS rejecting the wolf plan did not constitute final agency action to be reviewed under the Administrative Procedures Act. The court noted: "Wyoming is under no mandate to regulate gray wolves. The letter sent to Wyoming critiquing the Wyoming plan does not carry the force of law with it — Wyoming is free to ignore it. But such an action is not without consequences. If Wyoming chooses to ignore the letter and the critiques contained therein, the state simply will find itself perpetually pre-empted from regulating the gray wolf."

Johnson noted that state officials had argued that any delay in the delisting of the gray wolf would infringe upon Wyoming's sovereignty by preventing Wyoming from assuming management authority over the gray wolves in state. Johnson called this argument "problematic," noting:

"The most obvious deficiency is that Wyoming's purported sovereignty in this area has been unmistakably pre-empted by Congress. Therefore, Wyoming's claim to sovereignty as to threatened or endangered species lacks legal foundation.

"Moreover, if there was some type of injury to Wyoming's sovereignty, it occurred on the date that the wolves traversed onto Wyoming land not upon receipt of the letter in question. Thus, the injury complained of flows not from the FWS's letter, but rather from the initial decision to release wolves back into the ecosystem — a valid exercise of Congress' power under the Commerce Clause."

In addition, the court declined to review the plaintiffs' claims regarding any ESA violations, "because they have failed to establish that the Federal Defendants have a mandatory duty to delist the gray wolf, or lack discretion as to management of the wolf depredations . . . Neither the Plaintiffs nor the Plaintiff-Intervenors have succeeded on the merits of any of their claims in this litigation."

The lawsuit also had challenged the FWS failure to control wolf depredations. FWS argued that it has no mandatory duty to control gray wolf depredations, to which the federal court agreed. Judge Johnson wrote:

"The Plaintiff-Intervenors have failed to demonstrate that the Federal Defendants have a mandatory duty to control wolf depredations. The court has examined the Plaintiff-Intervenors' reply brief very carefully and it is unable to find a reference to any regulation or statute that would create a non-discretionary duty requiring FWS to control depredations. In fact a review of the relevant regulations clearly demonstrates that the Federal Defendants are not mandated to control wolf depredations.

"Frankly put, the Plaintiff-Intervenors have not demonstrated that the Federal Defendants are under a discrete non-ministerial duty to control the depredations. The only arguably mandatory actions that FWS must take are related to chronic problem wolves.

"That is not to say that the Federal Defendants do not have the authority to control wolf depredations. However, the authority granted to the Federal Defendants is discretionary in nature. The regulations clearly demonstrate a legislative choice to create discretion on how to deal with the gray wolf depredation and human-wolf conflicts.

"By their very nature the gray wolf preys on other animals for survival, and at times the gray wolf preys on livestock. This result is fully contemplated by the regulations, namely that there will be depredations. How these depredations are mitigated, however, is left to the expertise and sound discretion of the FWS.

"[In conclusion,] The court is at a loss to explain the actions of the State of Wyoming. The statutory mechanisms, namely the petition process, are in place for the state to create a reviewable record. This action, if it had been taken, would have forced the Federal Defendants to make choices under hard deadlines set by Congress. It would have also triggered the 'best science available' mandate, and much of the Federal Defendants' arguments presented here would have melted away, allowing this court to reach the merits of many of Wyoming's claims. The statutory requirements are not mere bureaucratic hoops to jump through, but rather are the stated will of Congress, and the people, and as such should be adhered to with great care.

"This case touches the heart of federalism. The complaints filed here are not cognizable under the limited jurisdiction of this court. This does not mean that the court is not sympathetic to the claims being made, however, the arguments brought to this court are more appropriately laid at the feet of the Wyoming Congressional delegation. This court is not in the position to step into the shoes of the Secretary of the Interior and begin administrating the Endangered Species Act. Nor is this Court in a position to micromanage the Fish and Wildlife Service's authority to manage the gray wolf population."

Chapter 31

Higher Court

The biological requirements for wolf recovery in Idaho, Montana, and Wyoming were met in December, 2002. To take wolves off the endangered species list, however, each of the three states needed to have a federally approved wolf management plan in place. FWS had approved the Idaho and Montana plans in 2003, but asked Wyoming to make adjustments to its plan and associated state laws.

Officials of the State of Wyoming and attorneys for the Wyoming Wolf Coalition filed briefs in the Tenth Circuit Court of Appeals in June, 2005, appealing the federal court decision upholding FWS's rejection of Wyoming's wolf management plan.

The State of Wyoming's brief focused on correspondence and statements made by FWS that Wyoming must make three changes to its state laws in order for federal officials to be satisfied. If Wyoming failed to do so, the delisting of wolves in a three-state area would be put on hold.[1] State officials alleged that FWS "acted arbitrarily and capriciously" in rejecting the Wyoming plan and stated in the state's brief:

"No reasonable person could read these statements and believe that the federal defendants will ever change their position regarding the Wyoming plan as written or about proceeding with delisting if Wyoming does not make the demanded changes.

"In reviewing the Wyoming plan, they disregarded the best scientific data available and instead relied upon concerns regarding possible litigation by conservation groups and concerns about the public perception of the term 'predator' as the reason for rejecting the Wyoming plan.

"The federal defendants violated the Tenth Amendment as applied to Wyoming by using the 'adequate regulatory mechanisms' required by the Endangered Species Act as an excuse to force the Wyoming

Legislature to enact wolf management guidelines that promote a federal political agenda unrelated to the legal requirements of the ESA."

The state's brief also keyed on the district court's ruling that federal regulations "clearly demonstrate that the federal defendants are not mandated to control wolf depredations. While conceding that the federal defendants arguably have a mandatory duty to control chronic problem wolves, the district court characterized the federal defendants' legal obligation to control wolf depredations as discretionary in nature." The state argued that federal regulations impose a mandatory duty on FWS "to remove all chronic wolves from the wild."

The Wyoming Wool Growers Association and its supporting organizations that made up the Wyoming Wolf Coalition also filed their appellant brief in the court. This brief raised the same issues as were in the state's appeal, but emphasized FWS's failure to properly manage and control wolves in Wyoming; to address the killing of livestock, domestic animals, and wildlife; and to prepare a supplemental environmental impact statement to analyze protection and propagation of wolves outside the YNP area.[2]

While the litigation continued, FWS turned over most responsibility for Montana's recovered, but still federally protected, wolf population to the state to allow it to carry out much of its approved wolf management plan. Idaho would soon follow.

Under the agreement, Montana would conduct population monitoring, research, and public outreach, in addition to determining when non-lethal and lethal wolf-control actions are appropriate to reduce conflicts with livestock. Because wolves in northern Montana were classified as "endangered" and wolves in southern Montana were managed under a less restrictive "experimental, non-essential" classification, Montana still had to follow federal guidelines related to lethal control. The state's plan was based on a benchmark of fifteen breeding pairs of wolves in Montana.

Until Wyoming had an approved plan, however, the gray wolf would remain listed in the region. "The hoped for proposal to delist gray wolves in the northern Rocky Mountains is delayed indefinitely because Wyoming has not made the requested adjustments," FWS reported.[3]

Chapter 32

Canine Aggression

By July, 2005, FWS reported two accounts of wolves behaving aggressively toward members of the public.[1]

On June 20, a man who had camped on private land near New Meadows, Idaho, encountered what he suspected to be wolves. The man reportedly had seen two gray and two black adult wolves and a smaller wolf the week before. FWS reported that the man said he was cutting firewood with a chainsaw and his dog was by him when a wolf "appeared out of nowhere and went for his dog." The man "grabbed the dog away and was bitten on the wrist."

The man had fired his pistol at the wolf, but reportedly was unsure if he hit it. This incident apparently was first reported as an assault by another dog, FWS stated. The man had been treated at a hospital for scrapes and a small puncture wound and then released.

A wolf biologist investigated the scene three days later, but did not see any wolf sign. The local sheriff, however, said he had received a report of five wolves, one of them small, in the same area.

"At this point in time, nothing else has turned up, and it appears doubtful it could have been wild wolves," FWS reported.

The second incident occurred near Jackson, Wyoming. FWS reported that on July 3, a Jackson man, his girlfriend, and their dog were walking on the Flat Creek Trail near Jackson and entered the territory of a wolf den site claimed by the Flat Creek pack, which consisted of three adult wolves and six pups.

One newspaper account noted that one of the adult wolves, a male facing the trio, "was baring his teeth, chomping and snarling with his ears back, as though he were about to attack."[2] Even once the female wolf retreated with the pups, the male wolf continued to harass the couple. The man was able to keep a tight grip on his dog's collar, but the wolf was very aggressive and followed the couple back for more than a mile, chasing them from the area.

FWS commented on the incident by stating:

"It was reportedly a frightening experience for the couple, who knew nothing about wild wolf behavior. When wolves attempt to protect their pups, especially if a dog is involved, they bark, howl and run around close-by, but do not bite or attack people. They will kill trespassing dogs that are perceived as a threat to their pups, if given a chance.

"Reportedly, the male wolf was barking, howling, and closely followed the people for nearly a mile . . . until he had 'escorted' the people and dog a safe distance from the pups."

Ed Bangs commented, "Don't we all wish for a Dad like that." Bangs added that the man involved in the harrowing encounter contacted the media. "The media story apparently attracted both the 'normal' and polarized extreme camps, the antis [wolves attack people, feds are liars, etc.] and pros [close sites around dens, prohibit dogs while hiking, etc.], responded strongly enough that the reporter is doing another story on the huge emotional response . . . and so on it goes," Bangs wrote in his weekly report.

In a second interview about the incident, Bangs was reported as stating that someday, wolves may attack someone. The article quoted him as saying: "I think someday they will, sure. I think at some point in North America, a wolf will get in some weird situation and kill somebody. Whether that happens in my lifetime or not, I don't know. It hasn't happened in 400 years."[3]

In November, 2005, the FWS reported that the Royal Canadian Mounted Police in Saskatchewan "reported the possible first human death attributed to wolves in North America in more than a century."[4] The mounties said wolves likely killed a twenty-two-year-old Ontario man in northern Saskatchewan. FWS offered more on the event:

"This incident is being investigated further but at this point it appears several wolves were involved. This is the same area where a lone wolf attacked a man this past winter. He managed to grab and hold that wolf until help arrived from the mining camp. A few wolves were shot after that incident. At that time the wolves were fairly habituated to people because they were feeding at a mining camp's garbage site. After last year's incident, the company was working with Canadian wildlife officials to secure the garbage dump and reduce the potential for conflicts. However, the wolves are still in regular close contact to the camp and are still highly habituated to people."

Chapter 33

Pandora's Box

Although FWS refused to initiate a proposal to delist wolves in the northern Rockies until the Wyoming wolf management plan was approved, state officials grew tired of waiting for FWS action. In July, 2005, the Wyoming Game and Fish Commission voted unanimously to petition FWS to remove gray wolves from the list of federally protected species. The commissioners' signatures joined that of Wyoming Governor David Freudenthal in requesting the action.[1] The complaint stated: "The Northern Rocky Mountain population of gray wolf has exceeded the Service's numerical and distributional goals for recovery since December of 2000 and no longer requires the protections afforded by its listed status under the Endangered Species Act of 1973. Wolves in this population are unacceptably impacting the state's big game populations, and are increasingly involved in livestock depredations and other conflicts. Costs of monitoring and managing Northern Rocky Mountain wolves are currently high and will escalate as additional wolves disperse from the main recovery area into less suitable and unsuitable areas."

The petition summarized the wolf's impact on big game animals, noting that in the original analysis of wolf predation impacts on big game herds in the region, FWS made several assumptions, including basing its projections upon a recovered wolf population that would consist of ten packs comprising approximately one hundred wolves. State officials questioned why FWS based its projections "upon such a minimal recovered wolf population, especially given that the current recovery goal is now 15 packs for Wyoming alone." The state noted that the Greater Yellowstone Area wolf population "has exceeded 100 wolves since 1998. When both the numerical and distributional recovery goals were met in 2000, 177 wolves inhabited the Greater

Yellowstone Area. By fall, 2004 the wolf population in the Greater Yellowstone Area was a minimum of 30 packs and 324 wolves, far exceeding the original basis of the Service's projections."

The state's petition noted that the Northern Yellowstone elk herd had declined by more than fifty percent since wolves were introduced in 1995.

The economic benefit of wolf presence had been minimal. The petition stated:

"There is little evidence visitation increased when wolves were introduced. Whatever minor increase may have happened in 1995, when wolves were a novelty, was clearly not sustained. Petitioners submit there appears to be little or no offsetting economic gain from the presence of wolves . . .

"Many persons hold a perception that the Greater Yellowstone Area constitutes much of the last, intact habitat that remains in the contiguous United States. A person whose frame of reference is the Eastern Seaboard or the West Coast or most other places in the US understandably might adopt such a viewpoint. However, ecologically speaking, Yellowstone and Grand Teton are the 'Central Park' of the American West. Both are surrounded by highly altered landscapes and neither is a self-contained ecosystem. Most wildlife that inhabit the parks in the late spring and summer months, migrate to lower elevations outside park jurisdictions during fall and winter. The milder climates and topography that once made these lower elevations suitable winter habitat for wildlife were also highly attractive for human settlement, so the native winter ranges were settled, developed, fragmented, and converted to various land uses. Traditional migration corridors were blocked by growth of towns and cities such as Jackson, Wyoming. Even within the parks, natural ecosystem processes have been altered by decades of park policy, most notably fire suppression, which caused ecological stagnation, forest litter buildup, and decadent, unproductive plant communities. Those policies led to the Yellowstone fires of 1988, which were an unnaturally severe event due to excess fuel loading. Liberalized burn policies and progressive management may eventually restore fire ecology to the parks, though not to the surrounding national forests. However, it will take many decades to undo the impacts caused by a century of prior management policy. This describes the setting into which wolves were released — a highly altered ecosystem.

"[Simply replacing a top predator] did nothing to repair the much more substantial ecological issues and problems that continue to challenge management of all natural resources throughout the Greater Yellowstone Area. Indeed, wolf introduction has exacerbated many aspects of our efforts to manage natural resources within this permanently altered landscape."

In addition, wolf-related conflicts, including livestock depredations, escalated as the wolf population grew and dispersed into less suitable habitat, the petition stated. In 2004, wolves killed 128 cattle, 270 sheep, nine dogs and five "other" livestock in the Yellowstone region. Eighty-five wolves were killed in control actions. The numbers of wolf depredations and wolf-control actions increased exponentially since wolves were first introduced into YNP in 1995.

"Although control actions likely alleviated some depredation on a temporary basis, the overall trend has been increasing consistently," the petition stated, while only a fraction of kills are actually discovered and confirmed.

The state's petition once again raised the issue of subspecies and Nowak's work. It noted:

"In 1994, L. D. Mech raised the issue in a white paper in which he stated, 'A major problem in conducting a reassessment at present is the EIS being prepared for a possible reintroduction of the wolf into Yellowstone. Such a reintroduction was predicated on the basis of the need for three populations of *C. l. irremotus*. That subspecies is not recognized by the new classification; rather the former *irremotus* range now covers both *nubilus* and *occidentalis* range, with Yellowstone, Idaho, and southern Montana in the *nubilus* range, the same as most other northern US wolves. What effect a reassessment of wolf legal status might have on the legal basis of the possible reintroduction into Yellowstone is unknown. However, it would seem that even the reclassification might provide new grounds for legal challenges.'

"This 'Pandora's box' as Dr. Steve Fritts called it, began a lengthy sequence of internal agency meetings and discussions within the FWS regarding a possible revision of the Northern Rocky Mountain Recovery Plan and the development of a 'National Wolf Recovery Strategy.' Dr. Fritts also stated in his memo, 'The source of wolves might become an issue. It would be better for Yellowstone to let the whole thing lie dormant until the final EIS has been signed.'

"[FWS has not] rigorously explored the biological question and the legality under the ESA of 'recovering' a taxon or type by expanding the historic range of a less similar type, when more closely related founder stock still remains available (i.e., the Minnesota/Wisconsin wolves)."

The state argued that FWS's actions had "reflected an eagerness to move the wolf introduction program forward without resolving taxonomic issues."

This was ironic. Ten years after the first Canadian wolves were released in YNP, Wyoming was finally arguing that the wrong subspecies had been reintroduced.

Epilogue

In the summer of 2007, a small, fixed-wing airplane flew over the Prospect Mountains northeast of Farson, Wyoming, searching for a wolf pack that everyone knows is there, but that FWS cannot document. The Prospects are a small range west of the Wind Rivers, but they hold an elusive wolf pack that emerges onto the desert lowlands several times a year, leaving dead calves, ewes, and lambs in its wake. From time to time, federal control agents manage to kill a wolf or two from the pack, and sometimes even manage to take out what seems to be the entire pack, but somehow, the wolves return to strike again.

Yet these wolves, each reincarnation of which is called the Prospect pack, are not part of the official wolf population of Wyoming. They are not included in the count toward wolf recovery. Neither are any other wolf packs in Sublette County, despite the fact that more wolves are killed in control actions in this, my home county, than in any other.

That is because the only time that wildlife officials ever find them to count them is when they are responding to a livestock depredation problem. When they kill the wolves, the packs then officially cease to exist, even though they officially never existed in the first place. The wolves always return. In 2006, twenty-three wolves were killed in control actions in Sublette County. There were only forty-four killed in control actions in the entire state of Wyoming that year.

The wolf population in the tri-state region around Yellowstone continues to increase. Recovery goals of the reintroduction program were first achieved in 2002, now more than five years ago. YNP's wolf population has saturated the park, bringing with it social strife and disease as the new challenges facing the booming population.

With the original recovery goal of thirty breeding pairs and more than three hundred wolves well distributed among Idaho, Montana, and Wyoming for at least three consecutive years, the Northern Rocky Mountain wolf population has exceeded that goal every year since 2002. The 2007 count exceeded eighty-nine breeding pairs and 1,243 wolves in Idaho, Montana, and Wyoming. There were thirty-seven documented wolf packs residing predominantly in Wyoming, according to FWS. Fourteen of these packs, including ten breeding pairs, were present in YNP, while an additional twenty-three packs, including fifteen breeding pairs, were present outside the national parks.

In 2007, FWS allowed for more aggressive wolf control as a way of dealing with problem wolves. Throughout the years, wolf packs have preyed on livestock. In 2007, FWS instructed USDA Wildlife Services to remove entire packs as soon as one started to commit livestock depredations.

"We went after them right off the bat," Mike Jimenez said. Instead of killing one or two wolves from a pack, the majority of the pack members were killed. That seemed to have made a big difference in terms of damage. In 2006, forty-five wolves were killed in control actions. In 2007, about fifty-five wolves were killed in control actions. While confirmed cattle kills due to wolves in 2006 totaled about 120, that number dropped by half — to less than sixty — in 2007. While not all kills are found or can be confirmed, it appeared that in 2007 there was less damage to livestock from wolves in Wyoming than in previous years due to aggressive control actions early in the season.

The states of Idaho and Montana had assumed responsibility for managing the wolf population in their states in 2005 and 2006, respectively, under agreements with FWS. Wyoming reached agreement with FWS late in 2007, a situation that led to the Yellowstone wolf population being removed from the list of protected species early in 2008.

With the new plan, Wyoming committed to maintaining at least fifteen breeding pairs of wolves statewide, including at least seven breeding pairs to be maintained outside the national parks. The state must assure that Wyoming's wolf population never drops below ten breeding pairs and one hundred wolves.

With delisting, wolves in northwestern Wyoming are managed by state officials as a trophy game species. That means that the WGF will manage wolves as a huntable species, respond to livestock conflicts involving wolves, and provide for compensation in areas where wolves are designated as trophy game.

Throughout the remainder of the state, however, wolves will be considered predators and WGF will not manage nuisance activities in those areas, nor will it compensate livestock producers for livestock that are killed by wolves where they are designated as predatory animals. That includes most of Sublette County. Those having conflicts with wolves in these areas are simply on their own and local predator management boards will feel the pressure to provide wolf control for those in need.

Regardless of the state's intentions, environmental groups once again sued, and in July, 2008, were successful at temporarily regaining federal protection for wolves in the northern Rockies, so the issue may be argued for years to come. While humans continue howling in court and in the press, the wolves will continue on their own path. Whether it is the native subspecies of wolf, the Canadian transplants, or a cross between, we know that humans have little control over these intelligent beasts.

This entire experience in fighting for the native wolves was a good one, despite what Jim and I view as a bad outcome for the native wolves. We had a great deal of personal growth during that time, as our knowledge and experience of politics, the legal system, many realms of science, and human social behavior grew by leaps and bounds. We gained a great deal in that sense.

We also know that environmental groups and their governmental counterparts will pay for this mess for years to come. One result has been the creation of a ground swell of animosity toward wildlife management among many that live in the West. There were new organizations created solely from the backlash against the wolf program.

But more importantly, the standard for protection of unique ecological units has been lowered to the ground. This will be hard to overcome once the environmental groups finally pick the life form they actually wish to protect, since the current standard is that anything less than a species is entirely "discretionary" when it comes to deserving or qualifying for protection.

In a 1987 paper in *Social Studies of Science* entitled "Paradigms and ferrets,"[1] Tim Clark and Ron Westrum questioned the adequacy of traditional wildlife management approaches when applied to endangered species, using the black-footed ferret as a case study. They used the term "ecology of applied ignorance" to describe the influence of expectation on perception, which is based on four concepts: what is expected is what is looked for; what is looked for is what is seen; what is unexpected is unobserved; and what is unexpected is unreported.

Clark and Westrum provided specific examples of how each of these concepts have led to faulty "scientific reality," which, given time and additional observation, were corrected. These expectations are a powerful force, with powerful social effects. Since survival of an organization is a natural goal for its members, Clark and Westrum assert, "It is only human for an organization's scientists to be more favorable to facts and theories which present it [the organization] in a positive light." In addition, an organization's stance on an issue can become an anchoring point for future opinion. Success in science leads to recognition, which leads to power, as evidenced by control of access to research sites and funding, gatekeeping of publications, and even the ability to determine what is to be considered "scientifically competent."

"In time what was merely a consensus begins to appear as objective fact. Critiques of the established view are received with surprise, incomprehension and ridicule," according to Clark and Westrum. "As the establishment becomes larger and more dominant, it can present its critics as misguided, badly informed or even dishonest."

Thus, the scientific establishment represents a concentration of both opinion and power, and if unopposed and not subject to criticism, can become too self-centered and close-minded to actually accomplish its objectives, such as preserving endangered species.

The quest for taxonomic truth in wildlife seems to have been abandoned, as wildlife management has turned to pursuit of homogenized species. Cases abound as wildlife managers move animals around without regard to maintaining the taxonomic integrity of ecological forms, affecting everything from numerous fish species and orangutans to pronghorn antelope and bighorn sheep.

The determination of what constitutes a species, subspecies, and a distinct population is a critical factor in future implementation of the ESA. The words of the act are powerful, including the provision calling for conservation of threatened and endangered species, including "any subspecies of fish or wildlife or plants, and any distinct population segment of any species." Taxonomic units lower than subspecies are to be protected, according to the law, including those "distinct population segments," which should be reason to rejoice. But it is not.

Those who were, and are, determined to have the reintroduction of wolves into Yellowstone, at any price, have helped to create a collusion of sorts between government and environmentalists to sacrifice taxonomic units below the species level. Today, FWS is busy delisting large carnivore populations that it designates "distinct population segments" — not because of any real ecological distinction, but because of the distinctions of jurisdictional lines, including state boundaries. The legacy left by the wolf reintroduction program includes harm to the conservation of biological diversity far into the future.

Notes

Chapter 1

[1] Hadly, E. 1990. "Late Holocene Mammalian Fauna of Lamar Cave and its Implications for Ecosystem Dynamics in Yellowstone National Park, Wyoming." Master's thesis, Northern Arizona University, Flagstaff: 117.

[2] Northwest Territories, Wildlife Division. Wolves: Reproduction. July 25, 2005. *www.nwtwildlife.com/NWTwildlife/wolf/reproduction.htm*.

[3] Cannon, K. 1992. "A review of archeological and paleontological evidence for the prehistoric presence of wolf and related prey species in the northern and central Rockies physiographic provinces." Pp. 1-175–1-265 in J. D. Varley and W. G. Brewster, editors, *Wolves for Yellowstone? A Report to the United States Congress, Volume IV: Research and Analysis*. Yellowstone National Park, Wyoming: National Park Service.

[4] Goldman, E. A. 1937. "The wolves of North America." *Journal of Mammalogy* 18 (1: February): 37–45.

[5] Young, S. P., and E. A. Goldman. 1944. *The Wolves of North America*. Washington, DC: American Wildlife Institute.

[6] Nowak, R. M. 2003. "Wolf evolution and taxonomy." Pp. 239–258 in L. D. Mech and L. Boitani, editors, *Wolves: Behavior, Ecology, and Conservation*. Chicago, Illinois: University of Chicago Press.

[7] Young and Goldman, 424–425, 445–446.

[8] Nowak, R. M. 1983. "A perspective on the taxonomy of wolves in North America." Pp. 10–19 in L. N. Carbyn, editor, *Wolves in Canada and Alaska: Their Status, Biology, and Management*. Canadian Wildlife Service, Report Series 45; Nowak, R. M. 1995. "Another look at wolf taxonomy." Pp. 375–397 in L. N. Carbyn, S. H. Fritts, and D. R. Seip, editors, *Ecology and Conservation of Wolves in a Changing World: Proceedings of the Second North American Symposium on Wolves*. Canadian Circumpolar Institute, University of Alberta, Occasional Publication 35.

Chapter 2

[1] Irving, W. 1895. "The adventures of Captain Bonneville." Pp. 129–131 in W. Irving, *Irving's Works*, New York, New York: A. L. Burt: 130.

[2] Ibid., 131; DeVoto, B. 1947. *Across the Wide Missouri*. Boston, Massachusetts: Houghton Mifflin Company; Coues, E., editor, 1893. *Forty Years a Fur Trader on the Upper Missouri: The Personal Narrative of Charles Larpenteur 1833–1872*. New York,

New York: Francis P. Harper; Roop, L. 1971. "The last days of the buffalo wolf." *Wyoming Wildlife* 35 (2: February): 33–37.

[3] Chittenden, H. M. 1954. *The American Fur Trade of the Far West*. Stanford, California: Academic Reprints: 829.

[4] Ibid., 830.

[5] Russell, O. 1965. *Osborne Russell's Journal of a Trapper*. Edited by A. L. Haines. Lincoln, Nebraska: University of Nebraska Press: 110.

[6] Porter, C., and Mae Reed Porter. 1950. *Ruxton of the Rockies*. Edited by LeRoy R. Hafen. Norman, Oklahoma: University of Oklahoma Press.

[7] Allen, D. A. 1979. *The Wolves of Minong; Their Vital Role in a Wild Community*. Boston, Massachusetts: Houghton Mifflin Company: 402–403.

[8] Russell, 35.

[9] Ibid., 129.

[10] Chittenden, 830.

[11] Russell, 46.

[12] Schullery, P., and L. Whittlesey. 1992. "The documentary record of wolves and related wildlife species in the Yellowstone National Park area prior to 1882." Pp. 1-3–1-173 in J. D. Varley and W. G. Brewster, editors, *Wolves for Yellowstone? A Report to the United States Congress, Volume IV: Research and Analysis*. Yellowstone National Park, Wyoming: National Park Service.

[13] Porter and Porter, 204–205.

[14] Ibid., 261.

[15] Raynolds, W. F. 1868. "The report of Brevet General W. F. Raynolds on the exploration of the Yellowstone and the country drained by that river." 40th Congress, 1st Session, Senate Executive Document 77. Washington, DC: US Government Printing Office.

[16] Grinnell, G. B. 1897. "Wolves and wolf nature." Pp. 152–202 in G. B. Grinnell and T. Roosevelt, editors, *Trail and Camp-fire*. New York, New York: Forest and Stream Publishing Company.

[17] Young and Goldman, 125–126.

[18] Ibid.

[19] Schullery and Whittlesey, 1-3–1-173.

[20] Ibid., 1–48.

[21] Evert, T. 1871. "Thirty-seven days of peril." *Scribner's Monthly* 3 (1: November): 1–17.

[22] Divine, R. A., T. H. Breen, G. M. Fredrickson, and R. H. Williams. 1984. *America Past and Present, Volume II*. Glenview, Illinois: Scott Foresman and Company: 495.

[23] Chittenden, 829.

[24] Young and Goldman, 216–217.

[25] Norris, P. W. 1881. Annual Report of the Superintendent of the Yellowstone National Park to Secretary of the Interior for the Year 1880. Washington, DC: US Government Printing Office: 42.

[26] Yellowstone National Park wolf sighting records.

[27] Young and Goldman, 378.

Chapter 3

[1] Curnow, E. 1969. "The History of the Eradication of the Wolf in Montana." Master's thesis, University of Montana, Missoula.

[2] Curnow; Bailey, V. 1907. *Wolves in Relation to Stock, Game and the National Forest Reserves.* USDA Forest Service Bulletin 72; *Forest and Stream,* February 25, 1899:145.

[3] Platts, D. B. 1989. *Wolf Times in the Jackson Hole Country: A Chronicle.* Wilson, Wyoming: Privately published by author: 7.

[4] *Pinedale Roundup*, May 24, 1905.

[5] *Pinedale Roundup*, February 7, 1906.

[6] Ibid.

[7] *Pinedale Roundup,* February 14, 1906

[8] *Pinedale Roundup,* April 4, 1906.

[9] *Pinedale Roundup*, April 11, 1906.

[10] Bailey, 1907.

[11] Hebard, G. R. 1911. *The Government of Wyoming, the History, Constitution and Administration of Affairs.* Fourth edition. San Francisco, California: Whitaker and Ray-Wiggins Company.

[12] *Pinedale Roundup*, April 25, 1912.

[13] Curnow.

[14] *Pinedale Roundup,* April 25, 1912.

[15] *Jackson Hole Courier*, May 28, 1914.

[16] *Pinedale Roundup*, January 8, 1914; *Jackson Hole Courier*, February 25, 1914, and July 10, 1914.

[17] Bailey, V. 1930. *Animal Life of Yellowstone National Park.* Baltimore, Maryland: Charles C. Thomas.

[18] *Jackson Hole Courier*, March 25, 1915, April 1, 1915, and April 8, 1915.

[19] *Jackson Hole Courier*, April 22, 1915, May 13, 1915, and May 20, 1915.

[20] *Jackson Hole Courier*, April 10, 1916, and April 13, 1916.

[21] *Jackson Hole Courier*, March 22, 1917.

[22] *Wyoming State Journal*, November 24, 1993.

[23] Yellowstone National Park files; *Jackson Hole Courier,* April 19, 1917, and January 10, 1918.

[24] *Livingston Enterprise*, July 13, 1922.

[25] Yellowstone National Park files; *Jackson Hole Courier,* January 11, 1923.

[26] *Jackson Hole Courier*, May 6, 1926.

[27] Day, A. M., and A. P. Nelson. 1928. *Wild Life Conservation and Control in Wyoming.* US Biological Survey: 4.

[28] Ibid., 1, 3.

[29] Brewster, W., and S. H. Fritts. 1992. "Taxonomy, genetics, and status of the gray wolf, *Canis lupus*, in western North America: A review." Pp. 3-33–3-94 in J. D. Varley

and W. G. Brewster, editors, *Wolves for Yellowstone? A Report to the United States Congress, Volume IV: Research and Analysis.* Yellowstone National Park, Wyoming: National Park Service.

[30] Personal communication, April 3, 1995, John R. Gunson, wildlife biologist with the Alberta Fish and Wildlife Service, Edmonton, Alberta, Canada.

[31] Personal communication, April 3, 1995, Sean Sharp, large carnivore specialist, British Columbia Ministry of Wildlife, Wildlife Branch, Victoria, British Columbia.

[32] Kaminski, T., and J. Hansen. 1984. "The Wolves of Central Idaho." Unpublished report. Montana Cooperative Wildlife Research Unit, Missoula, Montana.

[33] Kaminski, T., and A. Boss. 1981. "Gray Wolf: History, Present Status and Management Recommendations." Unpublished report. Boise National Forest, Idaho.

[34] Young and Goldman.

[35] Kaminski and Hansen, 46.

[36] Cornia, C. 1972. "The History of Woodruff 1870–1970." Mesa Regional Family History Center, Mesa, Arizona.

[37] Personal communication, April 7, 1988, Jay Sundberg.

[38] Roop.

[39] *Pinedale Roundup*, March 14, 1929.

[40] Young and Goldman, 54–55.

[41] Baldes, D., and D. Skates. 1993. "*Yellowstone Science* interview: Leo Cottenoir." *Yellowstone Science* 1 (4: Summer): 10–12 ; *Wyoming State Journal*, November 24, 1993; Personal communication, March 3, 1995, Leo Cottenoir.

[42] Young and Goldman, 285.

Chapter 4

[1] All wolf observation reports for Yellowstone are from (1) Yellowstone National Park Animal Observation File 1915–1953 (contains references to forty wolf observations); (2) Yellowstone National Park wolf reports dating from 1930–1971, indexed by Glen Cole (contains references to approximately 232 wolf observations); (3) Yellowstone National Park wolf reports dating from 1926–1991 (contains references to 493 wolf observations). All of these reports were obtained by the author on September 19, 1991.

[2] *Jackson Hole Courier,* July 25, 1946.

[3] Thomas, E. M. 1954. *Wyoming Fur Bearers: Their Life Histories and Importance.* Wyoming Game and Fish Department Bulletin 7.

[4] Baldes and Skates; *Wyoming State Journal*, November 24, 1993; Personal communication, March 3, 1995, Leo Cottenoir.

[5] Wilson, C. A. 1985. *Bloody Tracks on the Mountain Where the Wild Winds Blow.* Rapid City, South Dakota: Fenske Printing, Inc.; Personal communication, April 4, 1995, Chuck Faulkner.

[6] Personal communication, September 5, 1995, Snook and Evelyn Moore.

[7] Ibid.

[8] *Smoke Signals*, October 21, 1953.

[9] Ibid.

[10] *Jackson Hole Guide*, October 23, 1969.

[11] Memo, April 11, 1969, G. F. Cole, supervisory research biologist to Yellowstone superintendent.

[12] Cole, G. F. April 1969. Research note: gray wolf.

[13] Chase, A. 1986. *Playing God in Yellowstone: The Destruction of America's First National Park.* Boston, Massachusetts: Atlantic Monthly Press; Weaver, J. L. 1978. *The Wolves of Yellowstone.* National Park Service, Natural Resource Report 14.

[14] Schullery, P. 1980. *The Bears of Yellowstone.* Yellowstone National Park, Wyoming: Yellowstone Library and Museum Association: 77.

[15] *Jackson Hole Guide*, August 16, 1989.

[16] Letter dated January 7, 1976 from A. Starker Leopold to Dr. Durward L. Allen.

[17] Letter dated January 15, 1976 from Durward L. Allen to A. Starker Leopold.

[18] Letters, October 13, 1988, and July 30, 1991, Ronald Nowak, with reference to a conversation between Nowak and Leopold in 1976.

[19] Schullery, 82–86.

[20] Personal communication, May 6, 1991, Glen Cole.

[21] Memo, October 29, 1971, from Clifford E. Ruhr to Acting Chief, Office of Endangered Species, re: first interagency meeting for the management of the Northern Rocky Mountain Wolf, Yellowstone National Park.

[22] Allen, D. 1970. "Some philosophical considerations about wolf management." Pp. 45–49 in S. E. Jorgensen, C. E. Faulkner, and L. D. Mech, editors, *Proceedings of a Symposium on Wolf Management in Selected Areas of North America.* USDI, Region 3 Bureau of Sport Fisheries and Wildlife, Twin Cities, Minnesota.

Chapter 5

[1] Weaver.

[2] Cole, G. F. 1971. Research Note No. 4, Yellowstone National Park, Wyoming.

[3] Mech, L. D. 1971. "Where the wolves are and how they stand." *Natural History* 80 (4):26–29.

[4] Memo, October 30, 1974, from J. C. Antweiler, USDI Geological Survey, Denver, Colorado, to James A. Lawrence, District Ranger, Buffalo District, Bridger-Teton National Forest, Moran, Wyoming.

[5] Wolf observation report file, Worland District Office, Bureau of Land Management, Worland, Wyoming, obtained December 2, 1991.

[6] Vining, W. 1975. Final report on wolf survey as per memorandum of understanding by and between Wyoming Game and Fish Department, USDA Forest Service, USDI Bureau of Sport Fisheries and Wildlife, and Wes Vining. Unpublished manuscript.

[7] Lemke, T. 1978. Final report on 1978 wolf survey. Unpublished report. WY-019-PH8-000092, Bureau of Land Management, Worland, Wyoming.

[8] Memo, October 30, 1974, from James Hoover, Animal Damage Control, Billings, Montana to state supervisor, US Fish and Wildlife Service, Billings, re: Wolf investigations-Ruby Reservoir; Memo, June 25, 1975, from State Supervisor, ADC,

Billings, to Northern Rocky Mountain Wolf Recovery Team, re: Wolf sighting-Gravelly Range-June 20, 1975.

[9] Memo, n.d., from G. Gruell, Bridger-Teton National Forest, entitled "Wolf sighting on Slate Creek."

[10] Endangered Species Act. United States Code, Title 16, 1532 (16).

[11] Threatened Wildlife of the United States. Resource Publication 114, March 1973. US Bureau of Sport Fisheries and Wildlife, Washington, DC: US Government Printing Office: 235.

[12] *Federal Register,* 38 (106: June 4, 1973): 14678.

[13] *Federal Register,* 42 (111: June 9, 1977): 29527.

[14] *Federal Register,* 43 (47: March 9, 1978): 9610.

[15] Weaver, J. L. 1976. The wolves of Yellowstone: 1975 Survey. Unpublished report. Yellowstone National Park, Wyoming.

[16] Weaver, 1976.

[17] Ibid., 22.

[18] Ibid., 21.

[19] *Casper Star-Tribune,* May 27, 1988.

[20] Flath, D. 1979. "The Nature and Extent of Reported Wolf Activity in Montana." Paper presented at the joint meeting of Montana chapters of the Soil Conservation Society of America, the American Fisheries Society, the Society of American Foresters, and the Wildlife Society. Missoula, Montana.

[21] Day, G. L. 1981. "The Status and Distribution of Wolves in the Northern Rocky Mountains of the United States." Master's thesis, University of Montana, Missoula.

[22] Computer printout, Beaverhead National Forest Wolf Observation Inventory, January 6, 1992.

[23] Ream, R. R., and U. I. Matson. 1982. "Wolf status in the Northern Rockies." Pp 362–381 in F. H. Harrington and P. C. Pacquet, editors, *Wolves of the World: Perspectives of Behavior, Ecology and Conservation.* Park Ridge, New Jersey: Noyes Publications.

[24] Minutes of wolf recovery team meeting for March 4, 1986, by Bart W. O'Gara, Leader, Northern Rocky Mountain Wolf Recovery Team.

[25] Meagher. M. 1986. Summary of possible wolf observations 1977–1986. Unpublished report, Yellowstone National Park.

[26] Biological evaluation for the Rocky Mountain Gray Wolf, Minnie-Holden Timber Sale, 1986. Jackson, Wyoming: USDA Bridger-Teton National Forest; Wolf observation reports, Bridger-Teton National Forest, November 18, 1991.

[27] Memo, December 7, 1982, from Jim Straley, Wyoming Game and Fish Department, to Dale Strickland; Memo, January 21, 1987, from Duke Early, Wyoming Game and Fish Department, to Tom Toman. These documents were obtained by the author on February 27, 1992.

[28] *Casper Star-Tribune*, August 6, 1989.

[29] *Jackson Hole Guide*, February 15, 1989.

[30] Memo, June 28, 1998, from Dan Palmisciano, Montana Department of Fish, Wildlife and Parks, to Dick Johnson, with enclosures.

[31] Letter, October 23, 1992, from Steven H. Fritts, US Fish and Wildlife Service, to Steven R. Fain, US Fish and Wildlife Service forensics lab.

[32] Letter, June 11, 1988, from Ronald Nowak, Staff Zoologist, US Fish and Wildlife Service Office of Scientific Authority, to Dan Palmisciano, Montana Fish, Wildlife and Parks.

Chapter 6

[1] US Fish and Wildlife Service. 1987. Northern Rocky Mountain Wolf Recovery Plan. US Fish and Wildlife Service, Denver, Colorado: 4.

[2] 16 United States Code 1539 (j)(1).

[3] US House of Representatives. Report No. 567. 97th Congress, 2d Session, at 33 (1982).

[4] US Fish and Wildlife Service, Northern Rocky Mountain Wolf Recovery Plan, 59.

[5] *Casper Star-Tribune*, October 20, 1986, November 8, 1987, and November 9, 1987.

[6] *Billings Gazette*, April 10, 1987.

[7] *Casper Star-Tribune,* November 8, 1987.

[8] Ibid.

[9] *Casper Star-Tribune*, June 2, 1988 and July 25, 1988.

[10] The results were provided in *Wolves for Yellowstone? Volumes I and II,* published May, 1990.

[11] The results were provided in Varley and Brewster, editors, *Wolves for Yellowstone? Volumes III and IV*, published in July, 1992.

[12] *Casper Star-Tribune*, July 15, 1988.

[13] *Salt Lake Tribune*, February 25, 1988.

[14] Testimony on September 19, 1990, by Hank Fischer on S. 2674, the Northern Rocky Mountain Gray Wolf Restoration Act of 1990, before the Committee on Energy and Natural Resources, US Senate.

[15] Testimony on September 19, 1990, by Senator Malcolm Wallop on S. 2674, the Northern Rocky Mountain Gray Wolf Restoration Act of 1990, before the Committee on Energy and Natural Resources, US Senate.

[16] Testimony on September 19, 1990, by Thomas Geary on S. 2674, the Northern Rocky Mountain Gray Wolf Restoration Act of 1990, before the Committee on Energy and Natural Resources, US Senate.

[17] Testimony on September 19, 1990, by Representative Craig Thomas on S. 2674, the Northern Rocky Mountain Gray Wolf Restoration Act of 1990, before the Committee on Energy and Natural Resources, US Senate.

[18] Testimony on September 19, 1990, by Senator Alan Simpson on S. 2674, the Northern Rocky Mountain Gray Wolf Restoration Act of 1990, before the Committee on Energy and Natural Resources, US Senate.

[19] *Casper Star-Tribune,* October 24, 1989.

[20] Warren E. Leary, "Interior secretary questions law on endangered species," *New York Times*, May 12, 1990: 8.

[21] *Casper Star-Tribune*, January 7, 1991.

[22] Minutes of Wolf Management Committee Meeting, February 6, 1991 Cheyenne, Wyoming; Minutes of Wolf Management Committee Meeting, March 6–7, 1991, Boise, Idaho.

[23] *Wyoming State Journal,* March 21, 1991.

[24] Minutes, Wolf Management Committee, February 6, 1991

[25] Minutes, Wolf Management Committee, March 6–7, 1991.

[26] Ibid.

[27] *Casper Star-Tribune*, May 9, 1991.

[28] *Wolf Action*, June 1991-Issue 11.

[29] *Casper Star-Tribune,* February 7, 1991.

[30] *Casper Star-Tribune,* May 9, 1991.

[31] *Casper Star-Tribune,* August 17, 1991.

[32] Personal communication, September 9, 1991, US Fish and Wildlife Service Director John Turner.

[33] *Wolf Action*, September 1991-Issue 12.

[34] *Wolf Action*, December 1991-Issue 13.

[35] *Wyoming Landowner Newsletter*, 9 (1: Winter, 1994).

[36] *Casper Star-Tribune*, January 5, 1991.

Chapter 7

[1] Memo, February 5, 1992, from Daniel Reinhart, Yellowstone National Park, to Wayne Brewster, Yellowstone National Park.

[2] Letter to author, March 3, 1992, Norm Bishop, Yellowstone National Park.

[3] Letter to author, September 20, 1991, John L. Spinks Jr., US Fish and Wildlife Service.

[4] US District Court for Wyoming, Order, May 22, 1992. James R. and Cat D. Urbigkit v. Manuel Lujan, Jr., and John Turner, No. 91-CV-1053-B.

[5] Wolf observation reports, approximately 170 reports dating from 1990 through 1992, obtained from US Fish and Wildlife Service, Cheyenne, Wyoming, 1994.

[6] Status of Gray Wolf Environmental Impact Statement, Month of February 1992.

[7] *Federal Register,* 57 (65: April 3, 1992): 11505–11506.

[8] Letter, May 1, 1992, from Alan Simpson, Malcolm Wallop, Steve Symms, Larry Craig, Conrad Burns, Ron Marlene, and Craig Thomas to Manuel Lujan, Jr.

[9] *Wolf Action Alert*, May 1, 1992 — letter from Congressmen.

[10] *Wolf Action,* June 1991 - Issue 11.

[11] Ibid.

[12] Status of Gray Wolf Environmental Impact Statement, Week of August 17, 1992.

[13] *Casper Star-Tribune*, January 7, 1991.

[14] *Wolf Action Alert,* July 15, 1992 — memo from Brian Peck, wolf specialist.

[15] *Wolf Action*, July 1992 - Issue 15.

[16] Status of Gray Wolf Environmental Impact Statement, Week of April 6, 1992.

[17] Status of Gray Wolf Environmental Impact Statement, Week of May 4, 1992.

[18] Status of Gray Wolf Environmental Impact Statement, Week of June 8, 1992.

[19] Status of Gray Wolf Environmental Impact Statement, Week of July 20, 1992.

[20] Status of Gray Wolf Environmental Impact Statement, Week of July 27, 1992.

[21] Status of Gray Wolf Environmental Impact Statement, Week of August 10, 1992.

[22] Status of Gray Wolf Environmental Impact Statement, Week of August 3, 1992.

[23] US Department of the Interior, Fish and Wildlife Service, 1994. Final Environmental Impact Statement on the Reintroduction of Gray Wolves to Yellowstone National Park and Central Idaho.

[24] Approximately 167 wolf observation reports obtained from National Park Service August 22, 1994.

[25] Yellowstone National Park Rare Animal Observation Form.

[26] Wyoming Game and Fish Department. 1992. "Wyoming wolf?" *Wyoming Wildlife*, Vol. LVI, 11 (November): 12–17.

[27] *Casper Star-Tribune,* August 15, 1992, and August 18, 1992.

[28] *Casper Star-Tribune*, August 15, 1992.

[29] Status of Gray Wolf Environmental Impact Statement, Week of August 10, 1992.

[30] Issue statement, August 17, 1992, from Northern Rocky Mountain Wolf Recovery Coordinator Steven Fritts and Gray Wolf Environmental Impact Statement Project Leader Ed Bangs to US Fish and Wildlife Service Regional Director.

Chapter 8

[1] *Jackson Hole Guide*, December 9, 1992.

[2] All information regarding Jerry Kysar's killing of a wolf in the Teton Wilderness, which included the National Park Service investigative file and reports for case number 924407, was obtained by the author in September, 1993, from the US Fish and Wildlife Service Law Enforcement Division, Washington, DC, via the Freedom of Information Act and from Jerry Kysar's guest editorial in the *Jackson Hole Guide*, December 9, 1992.

[3] Report on wolf being shot near Yellowstone National Park, September 30, 1992 and survey of area to search for other wolves by Steven Fritts, October 12, 1992; Issue statement, October 19, 1992, by Northern Rocky Mountain Wolf Recovery Coordinator, "Re: Shooting of a canid that appeared to be a wolf near Yellowstone National Park on September 30, and the significance of the event."

[4] Yellowstone National Park rare sighting form Report No. 92-64 by Michael Keator, with attached sheets by Keator and Mary Taber.

[5] *Jackson Hole Guide,* October 7, 1992.

[6] *Jackson Hole Guide,* November 18, 1992.

[7] Status of Gray Wolf Environmental Impact Statement, Week of November 9, 1992.

[8] Status of Gray Wolf Environmental Impact Statement, Week of October 13, 1992.

[9] *Riverton Ranger,* April 6, 1993.

[10] *Riverton Ranger*, December 11, 1992.

[11] Issue statement, October 19, 1992, from Northern Rocky Mountain Wolf Recovery Coordinator to Regional Director.

[12] *Casper Star-Tribune,* November 15, 1992; *Riverton Ranger,* November 3, 1992.

[13] *Casper Star-Tribune,* October 7, 1992.

[14] *Riverton Ranger,* October 9, 1992.

[15] *Riverton Ranger,* December 11, 1992.

[16] *Jackson Hole Guide,* October 14, 1992.

[17] *Casper Star-Tribune,* October 25, 1992.

[18] *Jackson Hole News,* November 25, 1992.

[19] Ibid.

[20] *Jackson Hole Guide,* December 23, 1992.

[21] George Gruell, guest editorial in the *Jackson Hole Guide,* "Officials should pay heed to wolf sightings," December 30, 1992.

[22] *Casper Star-Tribune* guest editorial by Jeannine R. Stallings, undated, from US Fish and Wildlife Service Law Enforcement Division in Washington, DC. Obtained through the Freedom of Information Act in September 1993.

[23] *Casper Star-Tribune,* June 4, 1993.

[24] Ibid.

[25] *Casper Star-Tribune,* June 28, 1993.

Chapter 9

[1] Approximately 167 wolf observation reports obtained from National Park Service, August 22, 1994; Nine wolf observation reports, all for 1993, obtained from National Park Service, September 6, 1994.

[2] US Fish and Wildlife Service, July 31, 1991. Montana Wolf Monitoring Program. Unpublished report, Helena, Montana.

[3] US Fish and Wildlife Service, January, 1993. "Establishing a gray wolf monitoring and information and education program for Northwestern Wyoming." Unpublished report, Helena, Montana.

[4] James R. and Cat D. Urbigkit vs. Manuel Lujan, Jr. and John Turner, Civil Action No. 91CV1053B, US District Court for Wyoming, 1991.

[5] Notes from meeting in Cody, October 19, 1990 by Steven Fritts, US Fish and Wildlife Service.

[6] Memo, December 18, 1985, from Robert L. Riddle, Bridger-Teton National Forest District Ranger, to Forest Supervisor. "Re: draft wolf recovery plan."

[7] Letter, August 18, 1985, from Forrest Hammond, Wyoming Game and Fish Department, to Bart O'Gara, Wolf Recovery Team.

[8] Steven Fritts as quoted in the *Casper Star-Tribune,* December 30, 1990.

[9] Bangs's Labrador retriever remark was printed in the *Riverton Ranger,* October 9, 1992, while his Bigfoot remark was printed in the June 27, 1994, edition of the *Casper Star-Tribune*.

[10] Personal communication, August 13, 1991, Galen Buterbaugh.

[11] Wolf sighting form dated November 9, 1984, by Jeff Denton, Bureau of Land Management, Worland District.

[12] Memo, December 16, 1991, from Larry Roop, Wyoming Game and Fish Department, to Jim Yorgason.

[13] Memo, March 18, 1987, from Tina Crump Lanier, Bridger-Teton National Forest wildlife biologist, to Kemmerer District Ranger — "Re: wolf search by helicopter and snowmachine, March 1987."

[14] *Casper Star-Tribune,* May 16, 1990.

[15] *Casper Star-Tribune,* October 16, 1990.

[16] *Casper Star-Tribune,* December 30, 1990.

[17] McWhirter, Doug. "Report of findings, DuNoir wolf reconnaissance 8/1/91–8/4/91." Wyoming Game and Fish Department.

[18] *Casper Star-Tribune*, September 9, 1991.

[19] US Fish and Wildlife Service, Lakewood, Colorado, News Release 94-15 — "Survey reveals no sign of wolves."

[20] US Fish and Wildlife Service, January, 1994, Wyoming Wolf Surveys, obtained July 25, 1994, from US Fish and Wildlife Service, Helena, Montana.

[21] Issue statement, August 17, 1992, from Northern Rocky Mountain Wolf Recovery Coordinator and Gray Wolf Project Leader to US Fish and Wildlife Service Regional Director.

[22] Issue statement, October 19, 1992, from Northern Rocky Mountain Wolf Recovery Coordinator to US Fish and Wildlife Service Regional Director.

[23] *Jackson Hole News*, November 18, 1992.

Chapter 10

[1] *Casper Star-Tribune*, February 5, 1993, and February 10, 1993.

[2] Status of Gray Wolf Environmental Impact Statement, Week of February 8, 1993.

[3] Press release, March 18, 1993, US Fish and Wildlife Service Region 6 — "Re: Forensics lab confirms animal killed near Yellowstone National Park is gray wolf."

[4] *Billings Gazette*, March 17, 1993.

[5] *Billings Gazette*, March 19, 1993.

[6] *Casper Star-Tribune,* March 19, 1993.

[7] *Casper Star-Tribune,* March 23, 1993.

[8] *Casper Star-Tribune,* March 19, 1993.

[9] Yellowstone National Park rare animal sighting information, Report 93-22.

[10] *Casper Star-Tribune*, February 19, 1994.

[11] *Casper Star-Tribune*, October 10, 1993.

[12] *Casper Star-Tribune*, May 10, 1992.

[13] Status of Gray Wolf Environmental Impact Statement, Week of May 31, 1993.

[14] *Casper Star-Tribune*, April 3, 1994.

[15] Memo, undated, from Betsy Buffington and Liz Howell — "Re: Plea for help in upcoming wolf hearings."

[16] *Riverton Ranger*, July 9, 1993.

[17] *Casper Star-Tribune*, July 2, 1993.

[18] *Riverton Ranger*, July 6, 1993.

[19] US Department of the Interior, Fish and Wildlife Service, 1993. Draft Environmental Impact Statement on the Reintroduction of Gray Wolves to Yellowstone National Park and Central Idaho ("DEIS"): 1-3.

[20] Ibid., 1-20.

[21] Ibid.

[22] DEIS 3-7 through 3-10.

[23] DEIS 3-10 and 6-20.

[24] Bath, A. J. 1987. Statewide survey of the Wyoming general public attitude toward wolf reintroduction in Yellowstone National Park. A report submitted to the US National Park Service.

[25] Bath, A. J. 1992. "Identification and documentation of public attitudes toward wolf reintroduction in Yellowstone National Park." Pp 2-3–2-30 in J. D. Varley and W. G. Brewster, editors, *Wolves for Yellowstone? A Report to the United States Congress, Volume IV: Research and Analysis.* Yellowstone National Park, Wyoming: National Park Service.

[26] DEIS 1-25.

[27] 50 CFR, Chapter 1, Section 17.4.

[28] DEIS 1-25.

[29] Letter, September 22, 1993, from Ronald M. Nowak to Ed Bangs.

[30] Nowak, 1995.

[31] News release, July 13, 1993, from US Senator Malcolm Wallop.

[32] *Casper Star-Tribune*, July 2, 1993.

[33] *Rocket Miner*, July 2, 1993.

[34] *Rocket Miner*, May 5, 1994.

[35] *Casper Star-Tribune*, May 5, 1994.

[36] Personal communication, February 27, 1992, Francis "Pete" Petera.

[37] Cat Urbigkit v. USDI, United States District Court for the District of Wyoming, No. 93-CV-0232-J.

[38] Alan Johnson, May 31, 1994, order granting plaintiff's cross-motion for summary judgment: 3.

[39] Ibid., 13.

[40] *Riverton Ranger*, July 7, 1993.

[41] *Casper Star-Tribune*, April 25, 1996.

[42] *Jackson Hole Guide,* November 9, 1994.

[43] US Department of the Interior, Fish and Wildlife Service. 1994. Final environmental impact statement on the reintroduction of gray wolves to Yellowstone National Park and Central Idaho: I-21.

[44] Kay, C. 1993. "Wolves in the West." *Petersen's Hunting*, 21 (8: August): 34–37, 103.

[45] Gray Wolf Environmental Impact Statement Project Report, Month of August, 1993, by Project Leader Ed Bangs to US Fish and Wildlife Service Regional Director.

[46] Status of Gray Wolf Environmental Impact Statement, Week of July 19, 1993, by Project Leader Ed Bangs to US Fish and Wildlife Service Regional Director.

[47] Status of Gray Wolf Environmental Impact Statement, Week of August 2, 1993, by Project Leader Ed Bangs to US Fish and Wildlife Service Regional Director.

[48] Letter, July 27, 1993, from Ed Bangs to Editor, *Petersen's Hunting*.

[49] Letter, July 27, 1993, from Ed Bangs to Environmental Impact Statement team member/ reviewer.

[50] Status of Gray Wolf Environmental Impact Statement. Week of November 22, 1993.

[51] Letter, December 8, 1993, from Troy R. Mader — "Dear Friend."

[52] Letter, September 23, 1993, from Carolyn Paseneaux, Wyoming Wool Growers Association, to Senator Alan Simpson.

[53] Letter, September 1, 1993, from Robert Taylor to US Fish and Wildlife Service Deputy Director Richard N. Smith.

[54] Letter, October 20, 1993, from Randy Simmons to Richard N. Smith.

[55] Letter, November 9, 1993, from John L. Spinks to Senator Alan Simpson.

[56] Letter, November 18, 1992, from Steven H. Fritts, Northern Rocky Mountain Wolf Recovery Coordinator — "Dear Wolf Biologist."

[57] Letter, December 7, 1992, from Mark Boyce, Professor of Zoology and Physiology, University of Wyoming, to Steven Fritts.

[58] Letter, undated, from Diane Boyd in response to Steven Fritts's letter.

[59] Letter, December 15, 1992, from Dan Pletscher, University of Montana, to Steven Fritts.

[60] Letter, Todd Fuller, University of Massachusetts at Amherst, November 29, 1992.

[61] Letter, Mike Phillips, FWS Red Wolf Recovery Program, response dated December 11, 1992.

[62] Letter, Michael E. Nelson — FWS Wildlife Research Biologist. December 2, 1992 response to Fritts.

Chapter 11

[1] Endangered Species Act. United States Code, Title 16 §1531–1544.

[2] *Federal Register*, 38 (106: June 4, 1973): Appendix D to part 17.

[3] *Federal Register*, 42 (111: June 9, 1977): 29527–29531.

[4] *Federal Register*, 43 (47: March 9, 1978): 9607–9615.

[5] *Federal Register*, 59 (224:November 22, 1994): Section 17.84, (iii), 60266.

[6] Ley, W. 1968. *Dawn of Zoology*. Englewood Cliffs, New Jersey: Prentice-Hall, Inc.

[7] Wayne, R. K., N. Lehman, and T. K. Fuller. 1995. "Conservation genetics of the gray wolf." Pp 399–407 in L. N. Carbyn, S. H. Fritts, and D. R. Seip. *Ecology and Conservation of Wolves in a Changing World*. Canadian Circumpolar Institute, University of Alberta, Occasional Publication 35.

[8] Dowling, T. E., B. D. DeMarais, and W. L. Minckley. 1992. "Use of genetic characters in conservation biology." *Conservation Biology* 6 (1): 7–8.

[9] Cronin, M. A. 1993. "Mitochondrial DNA in wildlife taxonomy and conservation biology: cautionary notes." *Wildlife Society Bulletin* 21:339–348.

[10] Young and Goldman.

[11] Nowak, 1983.

[12] Letter, September 22, 1993, from Ronald Nowak to Ed Bangs.

[13] Letter, June 14, 1988, from Ronald Nowak to Dan Palmisciano.

[14] Letter, October 29, 1992, from Ronald Nowak to Steven R. Fain.

[15] Declaration of Edward E. Bangs, March 18, 1997.

[16] *Casper Star-Tribune*, October 10, 1998.

[17] *Riverton Ranger*, June 12, 1997.

[18] Letter, National Fish and Wildlife Forensics Laboratory Director Ken Goddard to Dave Mullen, Law Enforcement Region 1, December 4, 1992.

[19] Memo, December 7, 1992, from Steven R. Fain to Terry Groz.

[20] Serology examination report, April 5, 1993, by Steven R. Fain, Senior Forensic Scientist.

[21] Draft serology report, February 25, 1993, by Steven R. Fain.

[22] Theberge, J. B. 1983. "Considerations in wolf management related to genetic variability and adaptive change." Pp. 86–89 in L. N. Carbyn, editor, *Wolves in Canada and Alaska: Their Status, Biology and Management*. Canadian Wildlife Service, Report Series 45.

[23] Shields, W. M. 1983. "Genetic considerations in the management of the wolf and other large vertebrates: An alternative view." Pp. 90–92 in L. N. Carbyn, editor, *Wolves in Canada and Alaska: Their Status, Biology and Management*. Canadian Wildlife Service, Report Series 45.

[24] US Fish and Wildlife Service. 1982. Mexican Wolf Recovery Plan. Mexican Wolf Recovery Team.

[25] Bailey, 1907: 8, 22.

[26] Zimen, E. 1981. "Italian wolves." *Natural History*, 99 (2: February): 67–81.

[27] Flath.

[28] Mech, L. D. 1970. *The Wolf: The Ecology and Behavior of an Endangered Species*. Minneapolis, Minnesota: University of Minnesota Press: 9.

[29] Brewster, W. G., and S. H. Fritts. 1994. "Taxonomy and genetics of the gray wolf in western North America: a review." Unpublished.

[30] Varley and Brewster, Volume IV: 3–81.

[31] Letter, March 2, 1995, from Ronald Nowak to the author.

Chapter 12

[1] Letter, August 24, 1994, from Ray Demarchi, British Columbia Environment Wildlife Management Manager, to Ed Bangs.

[2] Letter, October 17, 1994, from John Talbott, Wyoming Game and Fish Department, to Ed Bangs.

[3] *Jackson Hole Guide*, November 30, 1994.

[4] *Jackson Hole Guide*, January 18, 1995.

[5] Ibid.

[6] *Casper Star-Tribune*, January 15, 1995.

[7] Letter, January 16, 1995, from Wyoming Governor Jim Geringer to Interior Secretary Bruce Babbitt.

[8] *Casper Star-Tribune*, January 31, 1995.

[9] *Jackson Hole Guide*, February 1, 1995; *Casper Star-Tribune*, January 31, 1995, and March 10, 1995; Personal communications from Gene Hussey and Brett Barsalou.

[10] Affidavit of Reid Jackson dated February 5, 1995.

[11] Affidavit of Al Boss dated March 8, 1995.

[12] Affidavit of George Gruell dated February 7, 1995.

[13] Order Denying Plaintiffs' Motion for Preliminary Injunction, March 19, 1995.

[14] Personal communication, February 6, 1995, Senator Alan K. Simpson.

[15] *Casper Star-Tribune*, March 21, 1995.

[16] Letter, March 20, 1995, Wyoming Governor Jim Geringer to Interior Secretary Bruce Babbitt.

[17] *Riverton Ranger*, March 22, 1995.

[18] Press release, April 18, 1995, US Fish and Wildlife Service — "Missing Montana 'pet' wolf found dead in El Paso; Fish and Wildlife Service investigating case."

[19] *Casper Star-Tribune*, April 29, 1995.

[20] *Casper Star-Tribune*, January 16, 1996.

[21] Ibid.

[22] *Casper Star-Tribune*, January 20, 1996.

[23] *Casper Star-Tribune*, January 18, 1996, and January 19, 1996.

[24] *Casper Star-Tribune*, January 22, 1996.

[25] *Casper Star-Tribune*, January 27, 1996.

[26] *Casper Star-Tribune*, January 28, 1996.

[27] *Casper Star-Tribune*, January 25, 1996.

[28] Dave Hunter, personal communication, July 10, 1996.

[29] *Cody Enterprise*, January 31, 1996.

[30] Defendant-Intervenors' Reply Brief, January 27, 1996: 6.

[31] Ibid., 1.

[32] Ibid., 14.

[33] Ibid., 27.

[34] Stipulated dismissal without prejudice of Plaintiff Sierra Club, March 1, 1996.

Chapter 13

[1] All quotes from trial from transcript of oral argument on administrative appeals hearing, proceedings volumes I and II, US District Court for the District of Wyoming, February 8 and 9, 1996, Civil Case numbers 94 CV 0286D, 95CV 0027D, 95CV 1015D Wyoming Farm Bureau Federation, et al., v. Bruce Babbitt, et al.

[2] *Casper Star-Tribune*, February 13, 1996.

[3] *Casper Star-Tribune*, February 1, 1996.

[4] *Jackson Hole Guide*, February 28, 1996.

[5] Ibid.

[6] *Casper Star-Tribune*, January 25, 1996.

[7] *Casper Star-Tribune,* July 5, 1996.

[8] *Casper Star-Tribune*, July 25, 1996.

Chapter 14

[1] *Casper Star-Tribune*, September 4, 1996 and September 10, 1996. Ten of the thirteen captive wolves were naturally occurring wolves from near Augusta, Montana, located in the northwestern part of the state, outside the Yellowstone recovery area. US Fish and Wildlife Service moved the livestock-killing wolves to Yellowstone National Park — an action neither discussed nor authorized in the FEIS or the experimental population rules published in the *Federal Register*.

[2] *Riverton Ranger,* December 9, 1996.

[3] *Riverton Ranger,* December 13, 1996.

[4] *Riverton Ranger,* January 14, 1997.

[5] *Casper Star-Tribune,* March 5, 1997; *Riverton Ranger,* March 6, 1997.

[6] *Riverton Ranger,* April 2, 1997.

[7] *Riverton Ranger*, March 6, 1997.

[8] Ibid.

[9] *Riverton Ranger*, March 17, 1997.

[10] Personal communication, February 23, 1997, Wyoming Game and Fish Department Warden Dennis Almquist; *Pinedale Roundup*, February 27, 1997.

[11] Personal communication, February 24, 1997, FWS Special Agent Roy Brown.

[12] *Riverton Ranger,* February 25, 1997; *Pinedale Roundup*, February 27, 1997.

[13] Personal communication, February 24, 1997, FWS Ed Bangs.

[14] *Riverton Ranger*, February 25, 1997.

[15] *Riverton Ranger*, March 6, 1997.

[16] Letter, undated, from Joel E. Bousman to Editor, *Casper Star-Tribune,* in response to February 24, 1997, article.

[17] Letter, March 29, 1997, from Bill Mayo to Ed Bangs.

[18] Memo, undated, marked "Restricted: Big Sandy Wolf," obtained via Freedom of Information Act with request dated September 29, 1997. The material was received with letter dated October 21, 1997, from US Fish and Wildlife Service, Denver, Colorado.

[19] United States District Court for the District of Wyoming: Wyoming Farm Bureau Federation, et al. (Lead Case Civil No. 95-CV-10015D), National Audubon Society, et al. (Consolidated Civil No. 95-CV-027D), and James R. and Cat D. Urbigkit (Consolidated Civil No. 95-CV-286D) v. Bruce Babbitt, et al. *See* Urbigkits' Second Motion to Show Cause, Memorandum in Support of Urbigkits' Second Motion to Show Cause, and Federal Defendants' Response to Urbigkits' Second Motion to Show Cause.

[20] *Federal Register,* 59 (224: November 22, 1994): 60281 at (iii).

[21] Federal Defendants' Response to Urbigkits' Second Motion to Show Cause at 4.

[22] *Riverton Ranger*, March 26, 1997.

[23] Letter, April 18, 1997, from US Attorney David D. Freudenthal to James and Cat Urbigkit.

[24] US Fish and Wildlife Service National Fish and Wildlife Forensics Laboratory Serology Examination Report, Lab Case No. 97-000199, dated April 18, 1997.

[25] *Federal Register*, 59 (224: November 22, 1994): Section 17.84, (iii), 60266.

[26] Ibid.

[27] Federal Defendants Response to Urbigkits' Second Motion to Show Cause.

[28] Letter, June 9, 1997, from US Attorney John Schneider to US Fish and Wildlife Service Deputy Assistant Regional Director Law Enforcement.

[29] Memo, September 9, 1997, US Fish and Wildlife Service.

Chapter 15

[1] FEIS at 1–21.

[2] Ibid., 6–90.

[3] Ibid.

[4] Ibid.

[5] Ibid.

[6] FEIS at 6–93.

Chapter 16

[1] US District Court for Wyoming, Order Nunc Pro Tunc.

[2] *Casper Star-Tribune,* January 10, 1998.

[3] *Casper Star-Tribune,* February 4, 1998.

[4] *Greater Yellowstone Report,* Winter 1998.

[5] *Casper Star-Tribune,* January 13, 1998.

[6] *Casper Star-Tribune,* December 19, 1997.

[7] *Casper Star-Tribune,* March 3, 1998.

[8] Letter, January 7, 1998, to Editor, *Jackson Hole Guide.*

[9] Brief of Plaintiffs/Appellees. Wyoming Farm Bureau Federation, et al., July 29, 1998. Wyoming Farm Bureau Federation, et al., v. Bruce Babbitt, et al. In the United States Court of Appeals for the Tenth Circuit.

[10] Ibid., 34.

[11] Ibid., 36.

[12] Federal Register 59 (224): 60252-60281, 50 CFR Part 17, November 22, 1994.

[13] Brief of Federal Appellants. Wyoming Farm Bureau Federation, et al., v. Bruce Babbitt, et al. In the United States Court of Appeals for the Tenth Circuit.

[14] Reply and Answering Brief of Federal Appellants/Cross-Appellees. November 12, 1998. Wyoming Farm Bureau Federation, et al., v. Bruce Babbitt, et al. In the United States Court of Appeals for the Tenth Circuit: 32.

Chapter 17

[1] Brief of Amici Curiae. Environmental Defense Fund, World Wildlife Fund, Wildlife Conservation Society, Izaak Walton League of America, Idaho Conservation League, Wolf Recovery Foundation and Center for Marine Conservation. Wyoming Farm Bureau Federation, et al., v. Bruce Babbitt, et al. In the United States Court of Appeals for the Tenth Circuit.

[2] Ibid., 3.

[3] Ibid.

[4] Ibid., 5.

[5] Ibid.

[6] Ibid.

[7] Brief For Amicus Curiae. National Parks and Conservation Association in Support of Appellant Department of the Interior. May 12, 1998. Wyoming Farm Bureau Federation, et al., v. Bruce Babbitt, et al. In the United States Court of Appeals for the Tenth Circuit.

[8] Ibid., 1.

[9] Ibid., 14.

[10] Ibid.

[11] Ibid.

[12] Ibid., 16.

[13] Ibid.

[14] Ibid., 17.

[15] Amicus Curiae Brief in Support of Plaintiffs-Appellees. James Hill, May 11, 1998, Wyoming Farm Bureau Federation, et al., v. Bruce Babbitt, et al. In the United States Court of Appeals for the Tenth Circuit: 3.

[16] Ibid., 3.

[17] Ibid., 4.

[18] Ibid., 2.

[19] Motion to Dismiss and Re-align, August 21, 1998.

[20] Plaintiffs/Appellees Wyoming Farm Bureau Federation, et al.'s Opposition to National Audubon Society's Motion to Dismiss and Realign, August 31, 1998.

[21] Audubon Reply to Farm Bureaus' Opposition to Motion to Dismiss and Realign, September 25, 1998.

[22] Audubon Council of Wyoming annual meeting, Trail Lake, Dubois, Wyoming. August 22, 1992.

[23] Plaintiff/Appellees Wyoming Farm Bureau Federation, et al.'s Brief in Response to Plaintiffs/Appellants Predator Project, et al.'s Opening Brief. December 24, 1998, at 1. Wyoming Farm Bureau Federation, et al., v. Bruce Babbitt, et al. In the United States Court of Appeals for the Tenth Circuit: 3.

[24] Brief for Plaintiffs-Appellants/Appellees Predator Project, Sinapu, Gray Wolf Committee, August 21, 1998, Wyoming Farm Bureau Federation, et al., v. Bruce Babbitt, et al. In the United States Court of Appeals for the Tenth Circuit:19.

[25] Ibid., 19.

[26] Reply brief for Plaintiffs-Appellants/Appellees Predator Project, Sinapu, Gray Wolf Committee, January 11, 1999. Wyoming Farm Bureau Federation, et al., v. Bruce Babbitt, et al. In the United States Court of Appeals for the Tenth Circuit: 17.

[27] Ibid., 19.

[28] Brief for Intervenor-Defendants-Appellants National Wildlife Federation, Defenders of Wildlife, et al., June 22, 1998. Wyoming Farm Bureau Federation, et al., v. Bruce Babbitt, et al. In the United States Court of Appeals for the Tenth Circuit.

[29] *Casper Star-Tribune,* July 21, 1986; *Pronghorn*, August, 1986.

[30] Brief for Intervenor-Defendants-Appellants National Wildlife Federation, Defenders of Wildlife, et al., June 22, 1998. Wyoming Farm Bureau Federation, et al., v. Bruce Babbitt, et al. In the United States Court of Appeals for the Tenth Circuit: 7–8.

[31] Ibid., 9.

[32] Ibid., 12.

[33] Ibid., 17.

[34] Ibid., 18.

[35] Ibid., 20.

[36] Ibid., 21.

[37] Ibid.

[38] Ibid.

[39] Ibid., 23.

[40] Ibid.

[41] Ibid., 29.

[42] Ibid., 35.

[43] Ibid., 42.

[44] Ibid.

[45] Ibid., 44.

[46] Ibid., 47–48.

[47] Brief of Amicus Curiae Applicant Nez Perce Tribe, June 22, 1998. Wyoming Farm Bureau Federation, et al., v. Bruce Babbitt, et al. In the United States Court of Appeals for the Tenth Circuit.

[48] Ibid.

[49] Ibid., 1.

[50] Ibid., 8.

[51] Brief For Plaintiffs-Appellants/Appellees Predator Project, Sinapu, Gray Wolf Committee, August 21, 1998. Wyoming Farm Bureau Federation, et al., v. Bruce Babbitt, et al. In the United States Court of Appeals for the Tenth Circuit.

[52] Brief of Amicus Curiae, Friends of Animals, Inc., September 10, 1998. Wyoming Farm Bureau Federation, et al., v. Bruce Babbitt, et al. In the United States Court of Appeals for the Tenth Circuit.

Chapter 18

[1] Urbigkits' Emergency Motion For An Injunction Pending A Decision On Appeal To Prevent Further Killing Of Naturally Occurring Wolves Of Unknown Origin, October 19, 1998. Filed In The United States Court Of Appeals For The Tenth Circuit, Nos. 97-8127, 98-8000, 98-8007, 98-8008, 98-8009, 98-8011.

[2] *Pinedale Roundup,* September 3, 1998.

[3] *Pinedale Roundup,* October 15, 1998.

[4] Urbigkit, Jim, and Cat Urbigkit. Evidence suggesting gray wolf occurrence in the Commissary Ridge area of Wyoming. Unpublished.

[5] Affidavit of Reid Jackson, Exhibit 13; Affidavit of George Gruell, Exhibit 14; Affidavit of Al Boss.

[6] ADC investigative report.

[7] Opposition of the Intervenor-Defendant-Appellants/Cross-Appellees to the Urbigkits' Emergency Motion for an Injunction Pending Appeal, October 28, 1998. Wyoming Farm Bureau Federation, et al., v. Bruce Babbitt, et al. In the United States Court of Appeals for the Tenth Circuit.

[8] Bangs, E., S. H. Fritts, J. Fontaine, D. W. Smith, K. M. Murphy, C. M. Mack, and C. C. Niemeyer. 1998. Status of Gray Wolf Restoration in Montana, Idaho, and Wyoming. *Wildlife Society Bulletin* 26 (4: Winter): 785–798.

[9] *Powell Tribune,* December 15, 1998.

[10] *Cody Enterprise*, January 4, 1999.
[11] *Pinedale Roundup*, February 4, 1999.
[12] Yellowstone Wolf Hotline, April 1999.

Chapter 19

[1] *Casper Star-Tribune*, July 30, 1999.

Chapter 20

[1] *Riverton Ranger*, July 2, 1999.
[2] *Pinedale Roundup*, October 5, 2000.

Chapter 21

[1] Personal interviews 2000 and 2004; *Sublette Examiner,* November 26, 2003.

Chapter 22

[1] *Sublette Examiner,* January 9, 2003.

Chapter 23

[1] *Sublette Examiner,* January 16, 2003.
[2] Ibid.
[3] Ibid.
[4] *Sublette Examiner*, September 18, 2003.
[5] *Sublette Examiner,* September 25, 2003.
[6] Ibid.
[7] *Sublette Examiner,* January 8, 2004.
[8] FWS press release June 24, 2004.

Chapter 25

[1] *Sublette Examiner*, February 6, 2003.

Chapter 26

[1] *Sublette Examiner*, January 30, 2003.
[2] *Sublette Examiner,* January 9, 2003.
[3] *Sublette Examiner,* February 20, 2003.
[4] *Sublette Examiner*, December 24, 2003.
[5] *Sublette Examiner,* January 29, 2004.

Chapter 27

[1] *Sublette Examiner,* January 22, 2004.

Chapter 28

[1] *Sublette Examiner,* October 2, 2003.

Chapter 29

[1] *Sublette Examiner,* March 4, 2004.
[2] Press release, April 16, 2004, Park County and Prosecuting Attorney Bryan Skoric.

[3] Letter, Park County Board of Commission undated 2004 request for Congressional investigation to US Senator Mike Enzi.

[4] Gray Wolf Recovery Status Report, Week of February 21–27, 2004.

[5] Gray Wolf Recovery Status Report, Week of April 10–23, 2004.

[6] Press release, April 22, 2004, Wyoming Governor Dave Freudenthal — "State files wolf complaint in district court."

[7] Complaint, Civil Action No. 04CV0123J, State of Wyoming v. USDI Gale Norton and Steven Williams. Filed April 22, 2004, US District Court for Wyoming.

Chapter 30

[1] Press release, January 4, 2005, Wyoming Game and Fish Department; *Sublette Examiner,* January 6, 2005.

[2] Letter, February 8, 2005, Ralph Morgenweck, US Fish and Wildlife Service.

[3] *Sublette Examiner,* March 30, 2005.

[4] *Sublette Examiner,* April 28, 2005.

[5] *Casper Star-Tribune,* May 11, 2005.

[6] Status of Gray Wolf Recovery, weeks of April 29 to May 13, 2005. US Fish and Wildlife Service Gray Wolf Recovery Coordinator.

[7] Status of Gray Wolf Recovery, Week of June 3 to June 10, 2005. US Fish and Wildlife Service Gray Wolf Recovery Coordinator.

[8] Status of Gray Wolf Recovery, Week of June 24 to July 1, 2005. US Fish and Wildlife Service Gray Wolf Recovery Coordinator.

[9] Memorandum Opinion and Order dated March 18, 2005 by US District Judge Alan B. Johnson.

Chapter 31

[1] State of Wyoming Appeal Opening Brief filed June 20, 2005, Tenth Circuit Court of Appeals.

[2] Wyoming Wolf Coalition Appeal Opening Brief filed June 20, 2005, Tenth Circuit Court of Appeals.

[3] Status of Gray Wolf Recovery, Week of June 17–24, 2005. US Fish and Wildlife Service Gray Wolf Recovery Coordinator.

Chapter 32

[1] Status of Gray Wolf Recovery, Week of July 1–8, 2005. US Fish and Wildlife Service Gray Wolf Recovery Coordinator.

[2] *Casper Star-Tribune,* July 5, 2005.

[3] *Casper Star-Tribune,* July 10, 2005.

[4] Status of Gray Wolf Recovery, Week of November 11–18, 2005. US Fish and Wildlife Service Gray Wolf Recovery Coordinator.

Chapter 33

[1] Press release, July 13, 2005, Wyoming Game and Fish Commission — "Wolf delisting petition approved at July meeting" and "Wyoming Wolf Delisting Petition: Petition to revise the listed status of the gray wolf (*Canis lupus*) by establishing the Northern

Rocky Mountain Distinct Population Segment and to concurrently remove the gray wolf in the Northern Rocky Mountain Distinct Population Segment from the list of endangered and threatened species." Office of the Governor, State of Wyoming, and the Wyoming Game and Fish Commission.

Epilogue

[1] Clark, T., and R. Westrum. 1987. "Paradigms and ferrets." *Social Studies of Science* 17 (1: February): 3–33.

References Cited

Unpublished Wolf Occurrence Reports

The majority of the wolf occurrence reports referred to in this book was obtained by the author via Freedom of Information Act (FOIA) requests to natural resource agencies, as identified below. The date(s) upon which the report(s) were provided are given for each agency.

Beaverhead National Forest, Dillon, Montana, February 7, 1992.

Bridger-Teton National Forest, Jackson, Wyoming, November 18, 1991.

Bureau of Land Management, Worland, Wyoming: December 2, 1991; January 24, 1992; March 4, 1992.

Caribou National Forest, Pocatello, Idaho, February 19, 1992.

Gallatin National Forest, Bozeman, Montana, February 18, 1992.

Grand Teton National Park, Moose, Wyoming, March 19, 1993.

Shoshone National Forest, Cody, Wyoming, September 17, 1991 and October 23, 1991.

Targhee National Forest, Saint Anthony, Idaho, January 27, 1992.

US Fish and Wildlife Service, Denver, Colorado, and Washington, DC, September 16, 1993.

US Fish and Wildlife Service, Cheyenne, Wyoming, February 16, 1993.

US Fish and Wildlife Service, Helena, Montana, July 25, 1994.

US Fish and Wildlife Service, Mountain-Prairie Region, Denver, Colorado, October 21, 1991.

Yellowstone National Park, Mammoth, Wyoming: September 19, 1991; March 3, 1992; August 22, 1994; September 6, 1994.

Additional wolf occurrence reports were obtained by the author via a Wyoming Public Records Act request to the Wyoming Game and Fish Department, Cheyenne, Wyoming, February 27, 1992.

Unpublished US Fish and Wildlife Service Reports

Gray Wolf EIS Project Report, monthly reports by Project Leader Ed Bangs to the Regional Director, Region 6, US Fish and Wildlife Service.

"Status of Gray Wolf EIS." Weekly reports by FWS Project Leader Ed Bangs.

"Status of Gray Wolf Recovery." Weekly reports by US Fish and Wildlife Service Gray Wolf Recovery Coordinator, Helena, Montana.

Website URLs

Northwest Territories, Wildlife Division. Wolves: reproduction. July 25, 2005. *www.nwtwildlife.com/NWTwildlife/wolf/reproduction.htm.*

Newspapers

Billings Gazette (Billings, Montana): April 10, 1987; March 17, 1993; March 19, 1993.

Casper Star-Tribune (Casper, Wyoming): July 21, 1986; October 20, 1986; November 8, 1987; November 9, 1987; May 27, 1988; June 2, 1988; July 15, 1988; July 25, 1988; August 6, 1989; October 24, 1989; May 16, 1990; October 16, 1990; December 30, 1990; January 5, 1991; January 7, 1991; February 7, 1991; May 9, 1991; August 17, 1991; September 9, 1991; May 10, 1992; August 15, 1992; August 18, 1992; October 7, 1992; October 25, 1992; November 15, 1992; February 5, 1993; February 10, 1993; March 19, 1993; March 23, 1993; June 4, 1993; June 28, 1993; July 2, 1993; October 10, 1993; February 19, 1994; April 3, 1994; May 5, 1994; July 27, 1994; January 15, 1995; January 31, 1995; March 10, 1995; March 21, 1995; April 29, 1995; January 16, 1996; January 18, 1996; January 19, 1996; January 20, 1996; January 22, 1996; January 25, 1996; January 27, 1996; January 28, 1996; February 1, 1996; February 13, 1996; April 25, 1996; July 5, 1996; July 25, 1996; September 4, 1996; September 10, 1996; February 24, 1997; March 5, 1997; December 19, 1997; January 10, 1998; January 13, 1998; February 4, 1998; March 3, 1998; October 10, 1998; July 30, 1999; May 11, 2005; July 5, 2005; July 10, 2005.

Cody Enterprise (Cody, Wyoming): January 31, 1996; January 4, 1999.

Jackson Hole Courier (Jackson, Wyoming): February 25, 1914; May 28, 1914; July 10, 1914; March 25, 1915; April 1, 1915; April 8, 1915; April 22, 1915; May 13, 1915; May 20, 1915; April 10, 1916; April 17, 1916; March 22, 1917; April 19, 1917; January 10, 1918; January 11, 1923; May 6, 1926; July 25, 1946.

Jackson Hole Guide (Jackson, Wyoming): October 23, 1969; February 15, 1989; August 16, 1989; October 7, 1992; October 14, 1992; November 18, 1992; December 9, 1992; December 23, 1992; December 30, 1992; November 9, 1994; November 30, 1994; January 18, 1995; February 1, 1995; February 28, 1996; January 7, 1998.

Jackson Hole News (Jackson, Wyoming): November 18, 1992; November 25, 1992.

Livingston Enterprise (Livingston, Montana): July 13, 1922.

New York Times (New York, New York): May 12, 1980.

Pinedale Roundup (Pinedale, Wyoming): May 24, 1905; February 7, 1906; February 14, 1906; April 4, 1906; April 11, 1906; April 25, 1906; January 8, 1914; March 14, 1929; February 27, 1997; September 3, 1998; October 15, 1998; February 4, 1999; October 5, 2000.

Powell Tribune (Powell, Wyoming): December 15, 1998.

Riverton Ranger (Riverton, Wyoming): October 9, 1992; November 3, 1992; December 11, 1992; April 6, 1993; July 6, 1993; July 7, 1993; July 9, 1993; March 22, 1995; December 9, 1996; December 13, 1996; January 14, 1997; February 25, 1997; March 6, 1997; March 17, 1997; March 26, 1997; April 2, 1997; June 12, 1997; July 2, 1999.

Rocket-Miner (Rock Springs, Wyoming): July 2, 1993; May 5, 1994.

Salt Lake Tribune (Salt Lake City, Utah): February 25, 1988.

Smoke Signals (Pinedale, Wyoming): October 21, 1953.

Sublette Examiner (Pinedale, Wyoming): January 9, 2003; January 16, 2003; January 30, 2003; February 6, 2003; February 20, 2003; September 18, 2003; September 25, 2003; October 2, 2003; November 26, 2003; December 24, 2003; January 8, 2004; January 22, 2004; January 29, 2004; March 4, 2004; January 6, 2005; March 30, 2005; April 28, 2005.

Wyoming State Journal (Lander, Wyoming): March 21, 1991; November 24, 1993.

Newsletters

Greater Yellowstone Report, Greater Yellowstone Coalition, Winter 1998.

Pronghorn, Wyoming Wildlife Federation, August 1986.

Wolf Action, Defenders of Wildlife: June 1991 - Issue 11; September 1991 - Issue 12; December 1991 - Issue 13; July 1992 - Issue 15.

Periodicals

Baldes, D., and D. Skates. 1993. "Yellowstone science interview: Leo Cottenoir." *Yellowstone Science* 1 (4: Summer): 10–12.

Bangs, E., S. H. Fritts, J. Fontaine, D. W. Smith, K. M. Murphy, C. M. Mack, and C. C. Niemeyer. 1998. "Status of gray wolf restoration in Montana, Idaho, and Wyoming." *Wildlife Society Bulletin*, 26 (4: Winter): 785–798.

Clark, T., and R. Westrum. 1987. "Paradigms and ferrets." *Social Studies of Science* 17 (1: February): 3–33.

Cronin, M. A. 1993. "Mitochondrial DNA in wildlife taxonomy and conservation biology: Cautionary notes." *Wildlife Society Bulletin* 21: 339–348.

Dowling, T. E., B. D. DeMarais, and W. L. Minckley. 1992. "Use of genetic characters in conservation biology." *Conservation Biology* 6 (1): 7–8.

Evert, T. 1871. "Thirty-seven days of peril." *Scribner's Monthly* 3 (November): 1–17.

Goldman, E. A. 1937. "The wolves of North America." *Journal of Mammalogy* 18 (1: February): 37–45.

Kay, C. 1993. "Wolves in the West." *Petersen's Hunting* 21 (8: August). 34–37, 103.

Mech, L. D. 1971. "Where the wolves are and how they stand." *Natural History* 80 (4): 26–29.

Roop, L. 1971. "The last days of the buffalo wolf." *Wyoming Wildlife* 35 (2: February): 33–37.

Wyoming Game and Fish Department. 1992. "Wyoming wolf?" *Wyoming Wildlife*. 56 (11: November): 12–17.

Zimen, E. 1981. "Italian wolves." *Natural History* 99 (2: February): 67–81.

Unpublished Manuscripts

Allen, D. 1970. "Some philosophical considerations about wolf management." Pp. 45–49 in S. E. Jorgensen, C. E. Faulkner, and L. D. Mech, editors, *Proceedings of a Symposium on Wolf Management in Selected Areas of North America*. USDI, Region 3 Bureau of Sport Fisheries and Wildlife, Twin Cities, Minnesota.

Bath, A. J. 1987. Statewide survey of the Wyoming General Public Attitude Towards Wolf Reintroduction in Yellowstone National Park. A report submitted to the US National Park Service.

Cornia, C. 1972. "The History of Woodruff 1870–1970." Mesa Regional Family History Center, Mesa, Arizona.

Curnow, E. 1969. "The History of the Eradication of the Wolf in Montana." Master's thesis, University of Montana, Missoula.

Day, G. L. 1981. "The Status and Distribution of Wolves in the Northern Rocky Mountains of the United States." Master's thesis, University of Montana, Missoula.

Flath, D. 1979. "The Nature and Extent of Reported Wolf Activity in Montana." Paper presented at the joint meeting of Montana chapters of the Soil Conservation Society of America, the American Fisheries Society, the Society of American Foresters, and the Wildlife Society, Missoula, Montana.

Hadly, E. 1990. "Late Holocene Mammalian Fauna of Lamar Cave and its Implications for Ecosystem Dynamics in Yellowstone National Park, Wyoming." Master's thesis, Northern Arizona University, Flagstaff.

Kaminski, T., and A. Boss. 1981. "Gray Wolf: History, Present Status and Management Recommendations." Boise National Forest, Idaho.

Kaminski, T., and J. Hansen. 1984. "The Wolves of Central Idaho." Montana Cooperative Wildlife Research Unit, Missoula, Montana.

Weaver, J. L. 1976. The Wolves of Yellowstone: 1975 Survey. Yellowstone National Park, Wyoming.

Government Documents

Bailey, V. 1907. *Wolves in Relation to Stock, Game and the National Forest Reserves*. USDA, Forest Service Bulletin 72.

Bath, A. J. 1992. "Identification and documentation of public attitudes toward wolf reintroduction in Yellowstone National Park." Pp 2-3–2-30 in J. D. Varley and W. G. Brewster, editors, *Wolves for Yellowstone? A Report to the United States Congress, Volume IV: Research and Analysis*. Yellowstone National Park, Wyoming: National Park Service.

Brewster, W., and S. H. Fritts. 1992. "Taxonomy, genetics, and status of the gray wolf, *Canis lupus*, in western North America: A review." Pp. 3-33–3-94 in J. D. Varley and W. G. Brewster, editors, *Wolves for Yellowstone? A Report to the United States Congress, Volume IV: Research and Analysis*. Yellowstone National Park, Wyoming: National Park Service.

Cannon, K. 1992. "A review of archeological and paleontological evidence for the prehistoric presence of wolf and related prey species in the northern and central Rockies physiographic provinces." Pp. 1-175–1-265 in J. D. Varley and W. G. Brewster, editors, *Wolves for Yellowstone? A Report to the United States Congress, Volume IV: Research and Analysis*. Yellowstone National Park, Wyoming: National Park Service.

Day, A. M., and A. P. Nelson. 1928. *Wild Life Conservation and Control in Wyoming*. US Biological Survey.

Federal Register: June 4, 1973, 38 (106): Appendix D to part 17; June 9, 1977, 42 (111): 29527–29531; March 9, 1978, 43 (47): 9607–9615; November 22, 1994, 59 (224): Section 17.84, (iii), 60266.

Lemke, T. 1978. Final Report on 1978 wolf survey. WY-019-PH8-000092, Bureau of Land Management, Worland, Wyoming.

Norris, P. W. 1881. Annual Report of the Superintendent of the Yellowstone National Park to Secretary of the Interior for the year 1880. Washington, DC: US Government Printing Office.

Raynolds, W. F. 1868. "The report of Brevet General W. F. Raynolds on the exploration of the Yellowstone and the country drained by that river." 40th Congress, 1st Session, Sen. Ex. Doc. 77. Washington, DC: US Government Printing Office.

Schullery, P., and L. Whittlesey. 1992. "The documentary record of wolves and related wildlife species in the Yellowstone National Park area prior to 1882." Pp. 1-3-1-173 in J. D. Varley and W. G. Brewster, editors, *Wolves for Yellowstone? A Report to the United States Congress, Volume IV: Research and Analysis.* Yellowstone National Park, Wyoming: National Park Service.

Thomas, E. M. 1954. *Wyoming Fur Bearers: Their Life Histories and Importance.* Wyoming Game and Fish Department Bulletin 7.

Threatened Wildlife of the United States. Resource Publication 114, March 1973. US Bureau of Sport Fisheries and Wildlife, Washington, DC.: US Government Printing Office.

US Department of Agriculture, Bridger-Teton National Forest. 1986. "Biological evaluation for the Rocky Mountain Gray Wolf, Minnie-Holden Timber Sale." USDA Bridger Teton National Forest, Jackson, Wyoming.

US Department of the Interior, Fish and Wildlife Service. 1993. Draft Environmental Impact Statement on the Reintroduction of Gray Wolves to Yellowstone National Park and Central Idaho.

US Department of the Interior, Fish and Wildlife Service. 1994. Final Environmental Impact Statement on the Reintroduction of Gray Wolves to Yellowstone National Park and Central Idaho.

US Department of the Interior, National Park Service. 1990–1992. *Wolves for Yellowstone? A Report to the United States Congress.* 4 volumes. Yellowstone National Park, Wyoming: National Park Service.

US Fish and Wildlife Service, 1982. Mexican Wolf Recovery Plan. US Fish and Wildlife Service, Washington, DC.

US Fish and Wildlife Service. 1987. Northern Rocky Mountain Wolf Recovery Plan. US Fish and Wildlife Service, Denver, Colorado.

US Fish and Wildlife Service. 1991. Montana Wolf Monitoring Program. Unpublished document, US Fish and Wildlife Service. Helena, Montana.

US Fish and Wildlife Service. 1993. "Establishing a Gray Wolf Monitoring and Information and Education program for Northwestern Wyoming." Unpublished document, US Fish and Wildlife Service, Helena, Montana.

US House of Representatives. 1982. 97th Congress, 2d Session, Report No. 567.

Vining, W. 1975. Final Report on Wolf Survey as per memorandum of understanding by and between Wyoming Game and Fish Department, USDA Forest Service, USDI Bureau of Sport Fisheries and Wildlife, and Wes Vining. Unpublished manuscript, Shoshone National Forest: Cody, Wyoming.

Weaver, J. L. 1978. *The Wolves of Yellowstone.* National Park Service, Natural Resource Report 14.

Wyoming Landowner Newsletter. 1994. Wyoming Game and Fish Department: Cheyenne, Wyoming. 9 (1:Winter).

Books

Allen, D. A. 1979. *The Wolves of Minong; Their Vital Role in a Wild Community.* Boston, Massachusetts: Houghton Mifflin Company.

Bailey, V. 1930. *Animal Life of Yellowstone National Park.* Baltimore, Maryland: Charles C. Thomas.

Chase, A. 1986. *Playing God in Yellowstone: The Destruction of America's First National Park.* Boston, Massachusetts: Atlantic Monthly Press.

Chittenden, H. M. 1954. *The American Fur Trade of the Far West.* Stanford, California: Academic Reprints.

Coues, E., editor. 1893. *Forty Years a Fur Trader on the Upper Missouri: The Personal Narrative of Charles Larpenteur 1833–1872.* New York, New York: Francis P. Harper.

DeVoto, B. 1947. *Across the Wide Missouri.* Boston, Massachusetts: Houghton Mifflin Company.

Divine, R. A., T. H. Breen, G. M. Fredrickson, and R. H. Williams. 1984. *America Past and Present.* Volume II. Glenview, Illinois: Scott Foresman and Company.

Grinnell, G. B. 1897. "Wolves and wolf nature." Pp. 152–202 in G. B. Grinnell and T. Roosevelt, editors, *Trail and Camp-Fire.* New York, New York: Forest and Stream Publishing Company.

Hebard, G. R. 1911. *The Government of Wyoming, The History, Constitution and Administration of Affairs.* Fourth edition. San Francisco, California: Whitaker and Ray-Wiggins Company.

Irving, W. 1895. *Irving's Works.* New York, New York: A. L. Burt.

Ley, W. 1968. *Dawn of Zoology.* Englewood Cliffs, New Jersey: Prentice-Hall, Inc.

Mech, L. D. 1970. *The Wolf: The Ecology and Behavior of an Endangered Species.* Minneapolis, Minnesota: University of Minnesota Press.

Nowak, R. M. 1983. "A perspective on the taxonomy of wolves in North America." Pp. 10–19 in L. N. Carbyn, editor, *Wolves in Canada and Alaska: Their Status, Biology, and Management.* Edmonton, Alberta: Canadian Wildlife Service.

Nowak, R. M. 1995. "Another look at wolf taxonomy." Pp. 375–397 in L. N. Carbyn, S. H. Fritts, and D. R. Seip, editors, *Ecology and Conservation of Wolves in a Changing World: Proceedings of the Second North American Symposium on Wolves.* Canadian Circumpolar Institute, University of Alberta, Occasional Publication 35.

Nowak, R. M. 2003. "Wolf evolution and taxonomy." Pp. 239–258 in L. D. Mech and L. Boitani, editors, *Wolves: Behavior, Ecology, and Conservation.* Chicago, Illinois: University of Chicago Press.

Platts, D. B. 1989. *Wolf Times in the Jackson Hole Country: A Chronicle.* Wilson, Wyoming: Privately published by author.

Porter, C., and M. R. Porter. 1950. *Ruxton of the Rockies.* Edited by L. R. Hafen. Norman, Oklahoma: University of Oklahoma Press.

Russell, O. 1965. *Osborne Russell's Journal of a Trapper.* Edited by A. L. Haines. Lincoln, Nebraska: University of Nebraska Press.

Ream, R. R., and U. I. Matson. 1982. "Wolf status in the Northern Rockies." Pp 362–381 in F. H. Harrington and P. C. Pacquet, editors, *Wolves of the World: Perspectives of Behavior, Ecology and Conservation.* Park Ridge, New Jersey: Noyes Publications.

Schullery, P. 1980. *The Bears of Yellowstone.* Yellowstone National Park, Wyoming: Yellowstone Library and Museum Association.

Shields, W. M. 1983. "Genetic considerations in the management of the wolf and other large vertebrates: An alternative view." Pp. 90–92 in L. N. Carbyn, editor, *Wolves in Canada and Alaska: Their Status, Biology and Management.* Canadian Wildlife Service, Report Series 45.

Theberge, J. B. 1983. "Considerations in wolf management related to genetic variability and adaptive change." Pp. 86–89 in L. N. Carbyn, editor, *Wolves in Canada and Alaska: Their Status, Biology and Management.* Canadian Wildlife Service, Report Series 45.

Wayne, R. K., N. Lehman, and T. K. Fuller. 1995. "Conservation genetics of the gray wolf." Pp 399–407 in L. N. Carbyn, S. H. Fritts, and D. R. Seip. *Ecology and Conservation of Wolves in a Changing World.* Canadian Circumpolar Institute, University of Alberta, Occasional Publication 35.

Wilson, C. A. 1985. *Bloody Tracks on the Mountain Where the Wild Winds Blow.* Rapid City, South Dakota: Fenske Printing, Inc.

Young, S. P., and E. A. Goldman. 1944. *The Wolves of North America.* Washington, DC: American Wildlife Institute.

Index